W9-BLG-796

AN INTRODUCTION TO THE UNITARIAN AND UNIVERSALIST TRADITIONS

How is a free faith expressed, organized, and governed? How are diverse spiritualities and theologies made compatible? What might a religion based in reason and democracy offer today's world? This book will help the reader to understand the contemporary liberal religion of Unitarian Universalism in a historical and global context. Andrea Greenwood and Mark W. Harris challenge the view that the Unitarianism of New England is indigenous and the point from which the religion spread. Relationships between Polish radicals and the English Dissenters existed, and the English radicals profoundly influenced the Unitarianism of the nascent United States. Greenwood and Harris also explore the US identity as Unitarian Universalist since a 1961 merger, and its current relationship to international congregations, particularly in the context of twentieth-century expansion into Asia.

ANDREA GREENWOOD holds degrees from Hampshire College, Brown University, and Meadville Lombard, and is a member of the Unitarian Universalist Ministers Association, having served congregations in Atlanta, Georgia, and Watertown, Massachusetts. She has been active in disability advocacy work in the broader community, and brought her interest in special needs into subsequent work as a director of religious education.

MARK W. HARRIS is an ordained Unitarian Universalist minister, currently serving as Minister at the First Parish of Watertown, and has previously served as the Director of Information at the Unitarian Universalist Association. He is also adjunct professor at Andover Newton Theological School. He is the author of the *Historical Dictionary of Unitarian Universalism* (2004) and *Elite: Uncovering Classism in Unitarian Universalist History* (2010).

AN INTRODUCTION TO THE UNITARIAN AND UNIVERSALIST TRADITIONS

ANDREA GREENWOOD

Independent Scholar

MARK W. HARRIS

Minister at the First Parish of Watertown (Massachusetts)
Adjunct Professor at the Andover Newton Theological School

CAMBRIDGE
UNIVERSITY PRESS

10/3/12
Lan
$29.99

CAMBRIDGE UNIVERSITY PRESS
Cambridge, New York, Melbourne, Madrid, Cape Town,
Singapore, São Paulo, Delhi, Tokyo, Mexico City

Cambridge University Press
The Edinburgh Building, Cambridge CB2 8RU, UK

Published in the United States of America by Cambridge University Press, New York

www.cambridge.org
Information on this title: www.cambridge.org/9780521707718

© Cambridge University Press 2011

This publication is in copyright. Subject to statutory exception
and to the provisions of relevant collective licensing agreements,
no reproduction of any part may take place without the written
permission of Cambridge University Press.

First published 2011

Printed in the United Kingdom at the University Press, Cambridge

A catalogue record for this publication is available from the British Library

Library of Congress Cataloging in Publication data
Greenwood, Andrea, 1961–
An introduction to the Unitarian and Universalist traditions /
Andrea Greenwood, Mark W. Harris.
p.   cm. – (Introduction to religion)
Includes bibliographical references and index.
ISBN 978-0-521-88148-7 (hardback) – ISBN 978-0-521-70771-8 (pbk.)
1. Unitarian Universalist Association – Doctrines.
I. Harris, Mark W.   II. Title.
BX9841.3.G74   2011
230'.9132 – dc23   2011017497

ISBN 978-0-521-88148-7 Hardback
ISBN 978-0-521-70771-8 Paperback

Cambridge University Press has no responsibility for the persistence or
accuracy of URLs for external or third-party internet websites referred to
in this publication, and does not guarantee that any content on such
websites is, or will remain, accurate or appropriate.

*This book is dedicated to Sandy and Bruce Kirkman,
founding members of the Unitarian Universalists of
Transylvania County in Brevard, NC.*

Contents

Acknowledgements

Without the support and flexibility of our congregation, the First Parish of Watertown, Massachusetts, this book could never have been written. We are grateful to them for their encouragement, and appreciate their role as home church to our sons Levi, Dana, and Asher. We love the history of our congregation, and admire the way members minister to one another. How lucky that we ended up among this group! We also wish to recognize the other congregations which have nurtured us along the way: The Unitarian Universalist Congregation of Reading, Massachusetts, where Andrea grew up and was ordained; Third Unitarian in Chicago, where she worked as a student; Community Church of New York, her internship site; and Northwest Unitarian Universalist Congregation in Atlanta, her first settled ministry. Mark was ordained by and served St. Paul's Universalist Church in Palmer, Massachusetts; a congregation which supported him and his son, Joel, for some important years. He is also indebted to the First Parish of Milton, Massachusetts. Three British congregations have been wonderful homes to us, two of which remain open: Rosslyn Hill Chapel in London, and Underbank Chapel in Sheffield, where Mark had his first ministry after his student time at the Davis, California church. With an infant, a toddler and a four-year-old, we were able to return to Sheffield for a few months in 1999. It was a formative experience in ways we are still discovering! Lastly, we acknowledge the First Universalist Church of Rockland, Maine, where we are fortunate enough to spend some time each summer, and which was Andrea's grandmother's community.

A note on names

Certain figures in Unitarian history have become known through anglicized forms of their names. Texts produced in the twentieth-century United States virtually all use "Michael Servetus" and "Francis David" rather than the Spanish "Miguel" or Hungarian "Ferencz." Moodelliar Vellazha is almost always referred to as "Robert Williams." This book generally uses birth names, but does interchange those names with their English counterparts at times. The index uses birth names, and cross-references where necessary. Japanese names are indexed the way they are traditionally written, with family name first and no comma.

CHAPTER I

Introduction

Flaming Chalice, symbol of Unitarian Universalism in most of the world. (A serpent and dove symbolize Transylvanian Unitarianism, representing wisdom and peace.)

Once there were three men who were in the same book club, and also of different faiths. Michael, George, and Francis – or Miguel, Giorgio, and Ferencz – had very different backgrounds, spoke different languages, practiced different professions. Like us, they lived in an era when technology completely changed how information spread. For us it is the digital age and globalization; for them, half a millennium ago, it was the printing press, and the establishment of trans-Atlantic trade routes. Their book club was centered permanently on one book – the Bible; but because of the printing press, that Book could be studied outside of monasteries and in several languages. People began to read the words themselves. The atmosphere for discussion grew much larger. It was everywhere. It was not necessary to actually attend religious services to be heavily involved in the dialogue. Miguel Servetus, who trained as a lawyer and also worked as a cartographer, noticed that there was no trinity in the Bible, and he wrote about this, advocating for unitarian understandings of God. His books were banned.

Originally from Aragon, Servetus had moved throughout Germany, Italy, and France, but when his religious ideas created trouble, he went to Geneva, where the Protestant reformation was under way. This could have worked out for him. Some of the reformers were open to discussions of Unitarianism. But Servetus also decided that he could not believe in predestination, so he offended Calvin, too. Servetus' story ended in the same manner as that of many other independent thinkers in the sixteenth century: at the stake, in flames.

Giorgio Biandrata landed in Geneva, too – fleeing Italy because he had read the Bible carefully and could not find any evidence of a trinity there. He decided to leave the Catholic Church. Although most copies of Miguel Servetus' book had been destroyed, Biandrata managed to have one. A doctor, he traveled in high circles, eventually becoming the court physician in Poland, and then in Transylvania. There he was able to find a sympathetic ear. He lent his copy of Servetus' book to a Hungarian Protestant minister, Francis Dávid, and then persuaded King John Sigismund to have Dávid appointed court preacher. Dávid read the book, talked with the doctor, and converted Sigismund, and both Unitarianism and freedom of conscience were born.

So we have a lawyer, a doctor, a minister, and a king. One was born in Spain, one in Italy, another in Transylvania, and the fourth in Hungary. The German invention of moveable type made it possible for them to share ideas, although not all of them met face to face. Nevertheless, a new community was created, centered on a faith that made use of reason, conscience, and democracy. They were dedicated to exploring truth, and some of them left their homes in order to speak honestly. Yet they believed that love taught us more about religion than truth did. They wanted to live in a way that promoted both clean consciences and good will. They noticed differences among their neighbors, and wanted to get along with all of them – to practice the Golden Rule. Servetus' book said, "Faith is with respect to God, love is with respect to God **and** to our neighbor . . . Loving is more difficult than believing. Love bears all difficulties, endures all things, and renders easy all things, including poverty and death . . . Because love is more lasting; love is a natural symbol of the future kingdom . . . Faith begins; love completes. Most wicked people believed in Christ, but no wicked person loved Christ . . . There is nothing that makes us more like God than love because God is love . . . Loving, not believing, is a property of divine nature."[1]

[1] Miguel Servetus, *Christianismi Restitutio* (1532), trans. Christopher Hoffman and Marian Hiller (Lewiston, NY: The Edwin Mellen Press, 2008). From "Treatise on Faith and Justice in Christ's

For centuries, Unitarianism has existed as a creedless faith because of this belief that growth is godly; that beliefs limit and love expands. Unitarian Universalism is currently present in twenty-nine countries. Historically, Unitarianism had a global presence and Unitarian Universalism existed only in the US and Canada, as the result of a 1961 merger between the American Unitarian Association and the Universalist Church of America. Universalism as an organized denomination was a uniquely American faith, although its theology of salvation for all was preached by Protestants elsewhere. Unitarianism, on the other hand, as the opening story illustrates, has a long history dating back to the Italian humanist movement of the fifteenth century, and resulting in organized Unitarian churches in Poland, Transylvania, Great Britain, and British colonies.

Since the creation of the International Council of Unitarians and Universalists (ICUU) in 1995, it is more common for congregations outside of North America to use the name "Unitarian Universalist." Expatriates formed some of these congregations, while others began as quasi-missions, and some grew from local leadership. What is indigenous and what is grafted on can be a matter of perspective, and influence flows in more than one direction. There are congregations in Japan and Indonesia, across Europe and South America. Cuba is home to twelve Unitarian Universalist congregations. Currently, Africa is the site of most growth. This international use of the names "Unitarian" and "Universalist" is a radical departure for liberal religionists, who have long struggled with whether or not to claim a sectarian identity. The International Association for Religious Freedom (IARF) was founded in 1900, at the seventy-fifth anniversary of both the American and British Unitarian Associations, as the "International Council of Unitarians and Other Liberal Religious Thinkers," but by the second meeting the word "Unitarian" had disappeared. Freedom soon took its place.

The existence of the ICUU does not mean there is one global religion. The expression of the faith varies from region to region, according to history, native practices, and outside leadership. Unitarianism as practiced in Kolozsvár, where the Unitarian Church is almost 500 years old and very much a result of the Reformation, looks very different from that practiced in the Khasi Hills, where Unitarianism dates to the late nineteenth century and represents an encounter among the British Raj, Scottish missionaries,

Kingdom," p. 313. Miguel Servetus, *Christianismi Restitutio, De Charitate*, Book 3 (Vienne, France, 1553), pp. 350–351, translated from the Latin for the authors by Peter Hughes. (Note: Servetus is quoting from 1 Cor. 13:7 and 1 John 4:8.)

Unitarian reformers, and a native population creatively preserving their own faith. Neither of these look like what one might experience in Berkeley, which has a tradition of lay leadership and ministers as consultants, or Toronto, which is minister led but incorporates testimony from members on a regular basis. British Unitarian practice differs from American, and in the US there are some congregations that use prayer books and others that would not utter the word "prayer." The range and diversity of the worship experiences offered in churches under the umbrella of Unitarian Universalism can cause confusion. The ICUU, while fostering the growth of different expressions to this faith globally, also builds connections that help demonstrate how these diverse practices are part of the same faith. The technological revolution is a major factor in establishing supportive networks, sharing resources, and participating in relationships that continue the theological journey of growth through encounter and new definitions of who one's neighbors might be. Indeed, a large proportion of the ICUU's mission is accomplished via the internet. Worship and educational materials are made available, as are leadership papers for those unable to attend live symposia.

Unitarianism is an ethical, not creedal, religion. Ethics generally derive from a revealed religion, in which a supernatural force breaks into human activity and shows the correct way; for example, Moses receiving the tablets on Mount Sinai, or Mohammed hearing Allah's word and writing it down for the faithful. Unitarian Universalism is based on Christian ethics, which express an ideal of shared justice. But Unitarian Universalism is not formally Christian. Traditional Christians believe that the life and death of Jesus revealed God to humanity: Jesus was the supernatural event interrupting human affairs and pointing out a new way. Unitarians elevate Jesus' teachings instead, believing that working towards the one beloved community he promoted is the true purpose of religious practice. Thus, for Unitarians, ethical religion does not require a belief in the supernatural. The moral order of the universe is not a reflection of God's character; it is a natural order revealed over time, and one in which we participate. Universalists focused more on God's love than Jesus, and believed that salvation for anyone meant salvation for all. But there is a paradox in Unitarian Universalism: A Christian vision of unity is embedded in the faith, and the purpose of the ethical religion promoted is the creation of one beloved community; yet radical religious individualism invites diverse practices from myriad traditions.

This inconsistency is managed by focusing on ethical behavior and personal fulfillment rather than the theological source of a moral code, making it quite possible to be a Buddhist Unitarian, a Taoist Unitarian, or a Hindu Unitarian, or any other kind of Unitarian. Modifying the word "Unitarian" with another faith tradition signifies an individual's embrace of a devotional practice as part of a religious life that values the Unitarian Universalist vision of a beloved community, in which all are free to develop faith using the disciplines of all world religions. One might follow the eightfold path, which is meant to help people achieve enlightenment as Gautama did; study tai chi to control the flow of energy, in order to relate well to others and to one's own best self; or practice vegetarianism and yoga, which are rooted in a belief in reciprocity. Hindu belief in reincarnation is part of a worldview in which all living beings are part of one another, and so learning to take the perspective of others is what keeps creation whole. This theological pluralism can confound, keeping depth, shared language, and practice out of reach; and it can enliven, by demonstrating the possibilities of true faith to cross borders. The challenge of Unitarian Universalism is to hold its paradoxical elements in creative tension, in a sustaining, complex, and rich manner; to let the contradictions augment faith rather than divide it with rigid, politicized definitions.

Some of the disciplines pursued by people within Unitarian Universalism are a response to the lack of visible structure to the faith. The free Christian tradition and its continuing evolution means that there are no specific prayers associated with Unitarian Universalism, or beads to count, or rituals to enact. There are not many rules or boundaries that can make people feel contained; reassured that they are acting as proper members. Some embrace the freedom as openness, and others as an opportunity to create meaningful practices of their own, often borrowed from religions that have a more physical component. The religion is broad enough to hold both responses comfortably.

This breadth is a legacy of a very strong tradition of literacy. The early Unitarians' certainty that they were apostles of the true faith, correctly understood, was born of reading; and the Universalist belief in salvation for all derived from Bible study. Today, noting the importance of reading Scripture seems an illiberal statement, and a contradiction. Many Unitarian Universalists do not use the Bible at all, and some congregations have biblically based services about as frequently as they have lectures on astrophysics. Isn't it conservatives who are centered on the Bible? But it was a radical and inherently political religion that would dare take the text out of the hands of the priestly class and make it available to all. The religious dissenters wanted a culture in which everyone could read so that those in power would not be able to claim God's word as a method of control. They wanted to live according to an understanding of God acquired first hand, and believed texts would help them to do so. Reading was inherently tied to reason and a distrust of authority, which led to vernacular translations of the Bible. Making the text available in the languages people spoke transformed the Bible into a living thing, an object with which people had real relationships. The Dissenters were people of the Book, and went where biblical study led. This eventually was to archeology, higher criticism, evolution, comparative religions, and a general respect for the written word as a repository of human wisdom.

It also led to a religious tradition that is largely verbal, not ritualistic. This is not a rebellion against the pageantry of worship so much as it is a begging for meaning and authenticity among people who are skeptical of power. The physical enactment of Unitarian Universalism has always been through social justice work. Far from being elitist, this tradition of literacy represents a deep commitment to social equality and the empowerment of the laboring classes. The democratization of the Bible is what caused royal leaders to fuse heresy with treason.

The population with the largest concentration of Unitarians can be found in Transylvania, an area of Romania that was once an independent kingdom. About 20 percent of the 1.4 million people in Transylvania are linguistic-ethnic Hungarians, whose presence on this land in the Carpathian Mountains goes back for over a thousand years. In the sixteenth century, Hungary was conquered and divided in three parts: one ruled by the Habsburg empire, another by the Ottomans, and the third, "the land beyond the forest," was ruled by nobility. With Christians to one side and Muslims to the other, Transylvania became home to the only Unitarian king in history thus far.[2] John Sigismund was the king converted to Unitarianism by Francis Dávid, the court preacher from the opening story. Under his leadership, religious tolerance was practiced and reason was valued more than force. Large numbers of the Transylvanian population became Unitarian, and have remained so, in spite of persecutions which grew over the centuries, and have only recently ceased. After World War I, the native Hungarian language was expunged, and the Unitarians' lands were taken and redistributed. Programs to force assimilation were put in place. Yet Unitarians remain. Five percent of the general population of

[2] Czechoslovakia's first president, Tomas Masaryk (1850–1937), in office from 1918 to 1935, was extremely sympathetic to Unitarianism, and spoke at the 1906 International Conference on Religious Freedom. His wife, Charlotte Garrigue, was a committed Unitarian who had grown up in the Brooklyn, NY congregation. The US has had four Unitarian presidents: John Adams, John Quincy Adams, Millard Fillmore, and William Howard Taft.

Transylvania is Unitarian; a full quarter of the linguistic-ethnic Hungarians living there are members of this faith.

The Unitarianism of Transylvania is Christian. Jesus is a great teacher, not part of a trinitarian God-head, but the faith is a Protestant one, with a catechism. The 125 churches (70,000 members) are organized into six districts, and governed with a system of bishops. Freedom here means freedom to embrace their identity and heritage. Children are nurtured in this faith. Since the fall of Ceauşescu's regime in 1989, restrictions against Unitarian ministers have been lessened, and many churches in Transylvania are partnered with congregations across the globe, especially in the US. A pastoral letter dated June 29, 2010 and sent by Bishop Ferenc Balint-Benczédi in the wake of a tragedy in the Transylvanian Unitarian community, articulated this religion as a lived faith in an all-too-real world. A minister who had served three different churches over the past decade suffered a breakdown, and murdered his two young children in the church before killing himself, leaving behind a terminally ill spouse and extended family. The bishop expressed some shock that the Unitarian faith had been able to sustain members through the severe trials of the past, only to find themselves lost at this moment. Balint-Benczédi was also concerned about a revival of hatred towards and misunderstanding of Unitarianism in the wake of this event. He made clear the reliance on one God and the human conscience, promoting action in service to life. "Let us remember that our forebears made difficult but sustaining sacrifices for this precious faith, in order that they may pass it on to us. Let us remember the pure and simple faith . . . that has always compelled us to love God and serve people. Over four and a half centuries, our church has enriched humanity with immeasurable values. Let us ensure that this legacy lives on . . . May God give us spiritual strength so we can stand firm beside those in need. With our godly lives, let us prove that we are brothers and sisters, children of God."

Whether Unitarian Universalism is Christian or not is answered partially by location, and partially by individualism. In Transylvania, it is definitely Christian. In Great Britain and in Ireland, it is generally Christian. In the US and Canada, the faith is technically and formally not Christian. The Unitarian Universalist Association was never admitted to the National Council of the Churches of Christ, because the faith does not require a confession of Christianity as a means to salvation, and in fact promotes other religions as equally valid. There are many Unitarian Universalists who believe broadly in theism, a God beyond all the other gods, uniting them. Some are natural theists: that broad God is expressed in the laws of nature. And there are many Unitarian Universalists who believe in no god at all, but put their faith in people and the known universe. Nevertheless, there are Unitarian Universalists in the US who do consider themselves Christian, and there are some congregations that are explicitly Christian in their worship. These are a distinct minority, and tend to be congregations that date back to the early days of the movement in the US. More than a third of the current congregations in the US and Canada were started after World War II, many of them without clergy, at least for some time. The practice of Unitarian Universalism is open, and incorporates diverse traditions and resources. The roots of Unitarian Universalism are decidedly Christian, and the forms remain vaguely Protestant. Services tend to be on Sunday mornings. There are readings, hymns, and spoken reflections. The religion of Jesus is respected; the exclusivity of institutional Christianity is not. The story of Jonah, in which a faithful Jew must use his knowledge of God to assist the people of Nineveh, represents a message Unitarian Universalists embrace: God would not be God if only one group of people were blessed. Yet it remains a challenge to be simultaneously a particular faith and a universal one.

Unitarian Universalists believe strongly in freedom. It is perceived as the natural condition of life, and a necessity for growth. As a free faith, Unitarianism meant that people were not compelled to attend services in the way they had been coerced to attend Catholic, Anglican, or Calvinist ones. The distrust of external authority and questioning stance of Unitarianism is related to a belief in freedom that must be protected. The services themselves also expressed a theological freedom, in which conscience was valued over conformity. This form of freedom to use the heart and mind as guides in the embrace of a meaningful truth was intended to prevent empty religion, or hypocrisy. It was an embodiment of Luther's complaint that "forced worship stinks in God's nostrils." Real religion – real worship – was contingent upon the soul or spirit of the worshiper being truly present, involved, and caring. But assuming a freely chosen faith as infinitely more powerful and motivating than anything inherited creates a tension over the generations. How is the institution to provide children with a religious identity if that identity must be freely chosen? Unlike most traditional religions, Unitarian Universalism does not raise its own next generation. Growth is contingent upon people finding the faith and choosing it as their own. Other minority religions keep their children in protective cells and inculcate loyalty to the faith. Unitarian Universalists have, in recent years, been more interested in explicitly teaching their children to remain in the fold. This is a test of both a culture that resists evangelizing and a conception of freedom that has limited the religion by its very openness, but it may also be a corrective. Ten percent of the Unitarian Universalist population was brought up in the faith. Evidence does not support the self-defeating notion that everyone will eventually choose this faith on her or his own.

Professional leadership has been increasingly valued in the last generation, as people have come to realize that embracing individualism without supporting institutions to defend individuals and combat ideologues allows humanitarian crises to develop. In the late twentieth century, authority grew more centralized. Still, Unitarian Universalism struggles with professionalism in religion, which can sometimes be perceived as antithetical to congregationalism and democratic practice. An average Unitarian Universalist congregation in the US has 156 adult members, but the median number is smaller. There are some very large churches, but for the most part this is a small group practice of direct participation.

Unitarianism has been understood as a natural religion, in which people living on different continents and at different times have independently come to discover truth through the process of reason. This is clearly most prominent in a Christian context, because biblical study revealed conflicts with church doctrine and practice, and led to a reliance on reason and conscience for guidance. Unitarians deny the trinity as both unreasonable and non-biblical. They are also against infant baptism, since it denies the child the opportunity to decide to participate. But this process of applying reason to faith is not limited to Christianity. The Unitarians of northeast India practice a faith that evolved from a tribal system of ancestor worship. The Japanese never applied reason to Christianity: instead they adopted Unitarianism because the lack of supernatural beliefs complemented their Shinto and Buddhist backgrounds. The use of reason is what ties humanists to this faith as well. The material world, and action taken within it, is understood as the source of all meaning.

Long-term Unitarians associate the principles of freedom and reason with a third religious value: tolerance. Since the emergence of the faith in Eastern Europe, religious tolerance has been upheld as a central tenet. This does not sound particularly revolutionary in the twenty-first century, and in today's globalized economy and ecology. But religious tolerance as a precept of faith takes on enormous significance in the context of the persecution and exclusion that Unitarians suffered. This is not political correctness, but a radical belief that everyone counts, and the people who insisted on this form of tolerance were punished for it. In many ways, Unitarians were harbingers of modernity; a group of people who responded to their exposure to differences with openness, curiosity, and respect rather than cruelty and prohibitions. The use of reason demanded that all people be treated equally, and that all faiths be treated as valid. Since 1945, when Earl Morse Wilbur (1866–1956) published his magnum opus, the two-volume *History of Unitarianism*, "Freedom, reason, and tolerance," has been the triumvirate. Wilbur's history is also the source of the notion that Unitarianism evolved independently on separate continents. This volume does not support that notion. Global interchange has a longer history than our memories. This volume also challenges the interpretation that Unitarianism developed from Puritan congregations in Massachusetts, and spread west. That is one strand, complementing another, more liberal, strand of Unitarianism transplanted from Great Britain.

Wilbur's was an academic examination of what Unitarianism meant. Institutionally, his principles were not formally present in mission statements, Principles and Purposes, or covenants. These statements differ from continent to continent. The General Assembly of British Unitarian and Free Christian Churches revised its statement of purpose in 2001, for the first time since 1928, saying that they exist "to promote free and inquiring religion through the worship of God and celebration of humanity, and respect for all creation and the upholding of the liberal Christian tradition." Since 1985, the US and Canada have had seven principles; the ICUU affirms five. These five are: liberty of conscience in matters of faith; the inherent worth and dignity of every person; justice and compassion in human relations; responsible stewardship of the earth's living system; and a commitment to democratic principles. Some of the language is exactly the same as that of the principles adopted by the Unitarian Universalist Association (UUA); but some is not. The UUA principles include a goal of world community, which does not appear in the international group.

The question of what it means to be a Unitarian Universalist plagues the US part of the movement, and raises questions about how the legitimacy of a faith is determined. Is it achieved through longevity? Unitarianism has roots in the Radical Reformation, but if length of existence becomes a criterion for a valid religion, Unitarians can go back further, to 325 CE and the Council of Nicaea. This is when the first creed was established, and legally recognized a father/son relationship between God and Jesus. Unitarians can claim to have maintained the original, pre-Council faith; and to practice the religion *of* Jesus, rather than the one *about* him. Establishing a line of succession in which the Unitarian idea is passed down from one thinker to the next may not be completely true, and may even run counter to the notion that the religion develops naturally, but it achieves a narrative that shows Unitarianism moving through time. As a religion that was formed only reluctantly, with the name being assigned by those outside, tracing the faith backwards was a way to redeem it.

If the legitimacy of a faith is determined by its connection to history, and important events or great achievements, then the great scientists, writers, and promoters of social justice can be listed. Unitarian Universalists have been disproportionately influential in a number of arenas, and it is far simpler to list the people than explain what ties them all together. We eat off Wedgwood china, decorate our nurseries with Beatrix Potter illustrations, read Louisa May Alcott to the children, and vindicate women's rights along with Mary Wollstonecraft. We once called each other on an invention of Alexander Graham Bell's; now we use the World Wide Web, courtesy of Tim Berners-Lee. We can list the Members of Parliament, early ordinations of women into the ministry, or the pioneering of integrated schools. This list could go on, and easily become counterproductive, as it begins to sound like a faith in achievement and status, rather than in the conditions that allow an individual to flourish. For in the end, that is what Unitarian Universalists believe in: establishing beneficial conditions for all. This means supportive, open, and accepting communities; a tradition of reason and literacy; and constant change.

Religion is generally understood as a source of stability. It represents tradition and timelessness, even as it hints at a better life; of progress toward some heavenly ideal. Unitarian Universalism can be difficult to describe to people accustomed to defining faith by the unchanging rituals and professions, or by the gods worshipped and saints prayed to. In 2003, then UUA president William Sinkford advised readers of the *UU World* magazine to refine their "elevator speeches" so that they might explain this faith in the time they rode from the sixth floor to the lobby. Church newsletters, blogs, and YouTube videos are awash with the results. The feeling persists that if the identity could be simply claimed and communicated, this is a faith that would attract people. If the general population understood that this religion is affirming, democratic, does not require a suspension of natural law, and promotes justice, the pews, folding chairs, and aisles would all be full to bursting. Never mind that very few people of any religion can actually explain their faith. If they are not members of a marginal, somewhat alternative group, they do not need to. There is common understanding. This is not true of Unitarian Universalism.

Officially, there are about a quarter million certified Unitarian Universalists in the world: 160,000 in the UUA (which includes the Unitarian Universalist Church of the Philippines); 70,000 in Romania and Hungary;

10,000 in India; 5,000 in Great Britain and Ireland; 5,000 in Canada; and numbers under 500 in many other places across Europe, Asia, South America, and Africa. The ICUU reports twice as many, a half million Unitarian Universalists, in the world. This may be right. In 2001, a survey of religious affiliation in the US reported over 600,000 Unitarian Universalists in that country alone, and a 2007 Pew Forum survey counted 340,000. More people identify with this religion than are formally committed to it. Officially, there are about the same number of people living in Plymouth, England, from whence the first group of Puritans departed in 1620, as there are Unitarian Universalists in the entire world.

This is a minority religion. It can sometimes be depicted as a minority religion with status, or privilege, but it remains a faith with a tiny following. The recitation of famous people can be a defense against the religion's smallness; advertising quality, not quantity, and masking the deeper hope that the number of adherents will grow; that others will resonate with the desire to leave the world a better place, and be inspired by the community of thoughtful, caring, interesting people. To some degree, Unitarian Universalists are mystified as to their failure to thrive. Believing intensely in individual rights and social justice, Unitarian Universalists are supportive of diversity and want desperately to promote freedom for all. Integrity matters profoundly to the kind of people who become Unitarian Universalists; perhaps is even the largest source of comfort. Right action soothes, even if it fails to completely heal the world.

While Unitarian Universalism is grounded in compassion, to some people, this religion seems intellectual, or self-referential. It is clearly centered on a human ability to act, and to derive comfort from one's own behavior, rather than being provided relief by a ritual or something outside of human agency. The belief in human equality and democracy at the center of the faith can lead to false assumptions about the world, in which people do not have equal measures of power, money, health, or strength. While Unitarian Universalists know this, and are motivated to act for social justice because of it, a strong reliance on reason can lead to an expectation that principles have more power than they do. There is a level of suffering and a component of tragedy in life that Unitarian Universalists do not accept. In some ways, this is a beautiful part of the faith: the belief in justice is so strong, adherents are continually surprised by a world that is not fair, and are moved to work to repair the wrong. These are people who go to church because they are desperate to make sense of the world, and willing to take responsibility for improving life for all on the planet. In other ways, it is a weakness; and represents the degree to which members have lived with privilege. Social justice projects can arise from a notion of those who act, and those who are acted upon, rather than grow from a reciprocal web of connections among human beings who will all suffer the same fate. Ethical eating programs are currently supported in many congregations, without much acknowledgement of how much money it takes to feed a family in this way.

In the last several decades, there has been tremendous renewal of interest in spirituality, which seems to be an attempt to rectify a perception of "headiness" and removal from ordinary lives. The language used in worship has been a topic of interest, with Sinkford promoting a "language of reverence," and an end to the habitual defining of the faith as one of opposition to the values of Christian fundamentalists. Music programs have grown more diverse, and reached beyond traditional hymns and folk music. In recent years, clergy have increasingly used their titles, and been called "Reverend Sue" or "Reverend Mark." Spiritual practice, such as Buddhist meditation, formal prayer, yoga, or breath work, is actively encouraged; and ritual has been increasingly incorporated into both religious education programs and church services in the form of candle lighting, bell ringing, and silence. Occasionally, these changes can have a flavor of marketing to them, an attempt to appeal to people looking for something not quite incorporated into Unitarian Universalist practice. The eclecticism can overwhelm coherence, and seem patronizing. But for the most part, what is conveyed is a community of very sincere searchers, willing to learn from diverse sources; wanting to be accepted and to accept others. It is a religion based on the admonition to love one's neighbor as one's self.

The accretion and erosion of a religious identity is complex and happens over centuries, even as it is a profoundly personal experience. Unitarianism and Universalism both had a clan-like identity, in which the persecuted members married one another, creating a common ancestry as well as a shared social and cultural life. Yet the religion is comprised overwhelmingly of converts; of people who are not physical descendants of those tribes, but are the spiritual inheritors of the same belief in compassion and integrity. There is a common dream of a good life, for all people. A separate denomination had never been the goal. The ambition was a world made fair, and all her people one. But as with Adam and Eve, leaving the Garden of Eden is what lets the story begin, and the word spread, and the work begin anew.

CHAPTER 2

Beginnings

Map of Eastern Europe

EUROPE
AT THE END OF THE
SIXTEENTH CENTURY CE

Unitarianism and Universalism are both ways of thinking about God and the meaning of life that have always had a presence in the history of Christianity, and which were both condemned as heresies. They date to the years closely following the birth of the Christian Church, but it was a millennium and a half before they took organized institutional form. There were always those Christians who preferred a more human Jesus because having a relationship with him was more important than worshipping him. They were engaged with this world, and wanted to play a key role in their own salvation rather than focusing primarily on the next world and the afterlife.[1] This became especially true after the Reformation when Unitarianism became institutionalized and belief in the invisible world became more and more suspect.

Although there was a variety of beliefs about the identity of Jesus among the early Christians, Unitarian beginnings are often traced to the rejection of the ideas of Arius at the Council of Nicaea in 325 CE. Arius (256–336), a priest from Alexandria, claimed that Jesus was not God, but instead was a created being who was subordinate to the Father, not co-eternal. Arius' renown was founded upon his penchant for writing his theology as poetry, and then chanting it to his congregation, creating the first hymns. Arius said that Jesus never claimed divinity but stressed that "the Father is greater than I." He believed that Jesus exercised human freedom to embrace righteousness, and that his moral perfection led God to adopt him as his son, granting him divine status.[2] The bishops at Nicaea, led by Athanasius, were concerned about maintaining control of the church, and countered with their own textual evidence that Jesus and God were one. In condemning Arius' teaching, they bolstered their beliefs with the "Nicene Creed," which identified Jesus as being of the same substance (*homoousios*) as God the Father.

Later, the Arian heresy was suppressed again at the Council at Constantinople in 381 CE, when the Nicene Creed was reaffirmed. After this, Arianism disappeared among the Romans, but persisted among the Visigoths and other tribal invaders. It was firmly rooted in what later became the Eastern Orthodox Church, perhaps contributing to the split with the Latin West. In trying to solve the problem of worshipping one God, and yet have a divine savior, the Arians believed they needed an intermediary figure who could bring heaven and earth together. The popularity of Arianism in the East may have also meant that the insistent monotheism of

---

[1] Richard E. Rubenstein, *When Jesus Became God* (New York: Harcourt, Inc., 1999), pp. 146, 179.
[2] Rowan Williams, *Arius: Heresy and Tradition* (Grand Rapids, MI and Cambridge, UK: Eerdmans Publishing Co., revised 2001), pp. 114–115.

Islam with its human, rather than divine, Jesus facilitated conversions that were less likely to happen in the more trinitarian West.

Although it was more than two centuries later when Universalism was condemned as heresy in 553 CE, at Constantinople at the Fifth Ecumenical Council, its public expression predated Arianism. Credit for this heresy is often bestowed upon the church father Origen (185–254), who is sometimes remembered for his willingness to follow his father into Christian martyrdom, but was prevented from doing so by a quick-witted mother, who hid all of his clothes so that the naked boy could not leave the house. In his *De Principiis*, Origen posited that God would restore all creatures to the equal state in which they had been created. Origen's fundamental belief in God's goodness convinced him that God was guiding creation towards an ultimate reunion with God.[3] Emperor Justinian condemned Origenism in 542/3 CE, and ten years later the Council assented to an official ecclesiastical condemnation of Origenism. Centuries passed before these heretical ideas emerged in movements, which found institutional form.

A few years prior to the advent of the Protestant Reformation in the sixteenth century, a group of Catholics were trying to reform the church. This disparate group, some of whom remained within the Catholic fold, while others fled to more tolerant places in Europe when the sword of the Inquisition fell, was known collectively as Humanists. They called for a revival of interest in Classical literature and learning in general. Among the most famous was Erasmus of Rotterdam (1466–1536), whose negative experiences of monastic life led him to affirm the ethical manifestations of Christianity over dogmatic traditions, rituals and ceremonies. Wanting to submit all things to the "judgment of reason," Erasmus even questioned the authority of the church when he stated that "Pope, abbot are terms meaning love, not power."[4] He thought that the Bible was a guide for living, which should be studied in the original texts. Working on a Latin translation of the New Testament, he discovered that the verse usually quoted to prove the veracity of the Trinity (1 John 5:7) was a later addition to the text, and not part of the Greek manuscript. The new, improved edition of the Bible left Erasmus open to the charge of heresy, and he was even called an Arian by the Englishman Edward Lee.[5] Yet Erasmus refused to reject the authority of the church, and so when the anti-Trinitarian,

---

[3] Joseph Wilson Trigg, *Origen: The Bible and Philosophy in the Third-Century Church* (Atlanta, GA: John Knox Press, 1983), p. 115.

[4] Desiderius Erasmus, *The Handbook of the Militant Christian*, in *The Essential Erasmus*, ed. John P. Dolan (New York: The New American Library, 1964), pp. 46–47, 74.

[5] Roland H. Bainton, *Erasmus of Christendom* (New York: Crossroad, 1982), p. 136.

Michael Servetus, tried to send him a copy of his book *On the Errors of the Trinity*, Erasmus rebuffed him.[6] Nevertheless, Erasmus' emphasis on original scriptural texts, the question of the Trinity, and a purer form of Christianity were ideas that had already found favor with Servetus.

Michael Servetus (1511–1553) was born in Spain, where belief in the Trinity was already regarded with suspicion. This was due to the large number of Marranos (Jews who had converted to Christianity), who resided in the Iberian Peninsula, as well as the Moorish heritage. Servetus spent much of his life avoiding the religious authorities. Before he reached the age of twenty, his biblical studies resulted in a belief that the Trinity was non-scriptural. Then when he attended the coronation of Charles V, and witnessed the papal pomp, he called the Pope a "harlot."[7] The publication of his heretical works led to the adoption of more than one alias and a life on the run.

Servetus' first published work against the Trinity, *On the Errors of the Trinity* (1531), endowed Christ with two distinct natures. According to Servetus, Jesus was both fully divine and fully human; the union of the eternal Word with the mortal man. The reformer, who had developed an unusually deep understanding of both Judaism and Islam, believed that monotheistic Jews and Muslims might want to consider conversion to Christianity, but the three persons in the Trinity prevented them from doing so.[8] He felt the "persons" in the Trinity were merely different modes of God's action. Servetus believed the Trinity was a doctrine, which tended to divide the three great monotheistic religions – Judaism, Islam, and Christianity – from one another.

Servetus lived in Lyon, France working as an editor and cartographer, and later practiced medicine in nearby Vienne. He made important discoveries about the circulation of the blood, and continued to write about theology. An authority on the Qur'an, Servetus used his knowledge of the holy book to attack Trinitarianism in *The Restoration of Christianity*. He says the Muslims rightly "censure us!" Mohammed teaches that the three Gods are "children of Beelzebub," and that the Trinitarians "worship them in place of God."[9] When the *Restoration* was published in 1553, its blasphemous

---

[6] Roland H. Bainton, *Hunted Heretic: The Life and Death of Michael Servetus, 1511–1553* (Boston, MA: Beacon Press, 1953), pp. 30–31, 35, 58.

[7] Earl Morse Wilbur, *A History of Unitarianism, Socinianism and its Antecedents* (Boston, MA: Beacon Press, 1945), p. 55.

[8] Wilbur, *History of Unitarianism*, p. 54.

[9] Peter Hughes, "Servetus and the Qur'an," *The Journal of Unitarian Universalist History*, Volume XXX (2005), p. 61.

content led to his quick demise. His heresies included the rejection of original sin, an idea that would find favor when he was read in Poland.

Servetus had sent Calvin a manuscript of the *Restoration* in 1546, initiating a debate that did not end well. Calvin wrote that Servetus had addressed him with an "arrogant spirit." Then in 1547, Calvin wrote that if Servetus came to visit, he "would not let him leave alive."[10] By this time Calvin considered Servetus a "mad dog, barking and biting, without sense or reason," who considered the Trinity, "nothing but a fable." Servetus in turn accused Calvin of devising a God who was a Cerberus with three heads. In an uneasy alliance with the Catholics, Calvin sent them a copy of the *Restoration*. In April, Servetus was interrogated by the Inquisition in France, escaped, and then was condemned in absentia. Finally, Servetus foolishly appeared in church in Calvin's Geneva. After Servetus was arrested and imprisoned, Calvin went to visit him, but gained no satisfaction, and left the "heretic who was self-condemned" to die by execution. With his book tied to his arm, Servetus was burned at the stake using unseasoned logs on October 27, 1553.[11]

This brutal execution brought to life voices that sought greater tolerance and understanding. Foremost among these was a French intellectual, Sebastian Castellio (1515–1563). Castellio had once worked in Geneva and sought out Calvin as a fellow scholar, but soon found he could not submit to Calvin's rigidity in matters of biblical interpretation. Many of the religious radicals of Europe fled to Basel for refuge from Calvinism, and Castellio did the same. He was horrified by Servetus' death because it marked the first time a Protestant had been executed for religious beliefs rather than political beliefs. His book *Concerning Heretics* soon appeared under a pseudonym.

Recognizing that Calvin would not tolerate any form of heresy, Castellio saw this extreme religious oppression destroying what the Reformation stood for. Thus, he helped create our modern understanding of tolerance. Earl Morse Wilbur (1866–1956), the great Unitarian historian, believed that Castellio, more than Servetus, deserves to be considered the true founder of liberal Christianity, as he argued for an ethical faith centered "not in dogma but in life and character."[12] Castellio wrote, "I do not see how we can retain the name of Christian if we do not imitate His clemency and mercy."[13] He argued that we cannot be sure if a person is a heretic or not,

---

[10] Bernard Cottret, *Calvin: A Biography* (Grand Rapids, MI: Eerdmans Publishing, 2000), p. 217.
[11] Bainton, *Servetus*, pp. 210–212. [12] Wilbur, *History of Unitarianism*, pp. 208–209.
[13] David B. Parke, ed., *The Epic of Unitarianism* (Boston, MA: Beacon Press, 1957), p. 9.

and regardless, this punishment was too severe. Most famously he declared, "to kill a man is not to protect a doctrine, but it is to kill a man." Calvin, responding to accusations of "blind rage" and torture, poured out venom on Castellio, calling him a poisonous beast, but Castellio remained safely in Basel until his death in 1563.

The glue holding Servetus and the future anti-Trinitarians in eastern Europe together was an Italian humanist/rationalist group, many of whom ended up in exile from their homeland. Several of these reformers attacked Calvin for his inhuman execution of Servetus, but they were also ready to defend Servetus' doctrines as well. Many of these humanists wanted to take radical religious thinking further than Servetus had.[14] Among these theological followers was Matteo Gribaldi (1506–1564) who was familiar with Servetus' writings, corresponded with him, and may even have tried to intercede with Calvin during Servetus' trial.[15]

Another radical writer was Laelius Socinus (1525–1562), who was born in Siena into a family of reputable jurists, but abandoned legal studies to pursue his interests in scripture. Perhaps due to fear of the Inquisition he left Italy, and traveled extensively in all the Protestant lands. He finally landed in Kraków, Poland where Italian culture was in vogue, and Servetus was much read. Although Socinus was reticent about expressing his theology, and was just beginning to formulate his ideas in writing when he died in 1562, the reputation of his extended family as possible followers of Luther[16] caused the Inquisition to monitor his activity. He had failed to secure his father's estate, but his writings and library passed on to his nephew Faustus, who would use them to inspire his own theological development, and that of the Polish anti-Trinitarians.

Liberal religion also emerged in eastern Europe because of geography and immigration routes. The rise of the Inquisition in Italy in the 1540s forced the religious reformers to leave or else face death. Some of these refugees traveled on old Italian trade routes as far north as Kraków. The severity of the Inquisition drove more and more Italian, humanist anti-Trinitarians towards Poland and the edge of the Habsburg Empire. Polish anti-Trinitarianism would also spread to Transylvania, its neighbor to the south. Both places had long histories of being religious border countries, representing dividing lines between Christian and Muslim with the Ottoman Empire on the south and east, and looking north to

---

[14] Wilbur, *History of Unitarianism*, p. 209.

[15] George H. Williams, *The Radical Reformation* (Philadelphia, PA: The Westminster Press, 1962), p. 623.

[16] Williams, *Radical Reformation*, p. 631; Wilbur, *History of Unitarianism*, p. 246.

Catholic Poland bordering Orthodox Russia. Historian Diarmaid Mac-Culloch believes it is no mere coincidence that here where Western Latin Christianity met Eastern Orthodoxy, the inhabitants had centuries of practice in making compromises.[17] Being on the frontier forced faith-based communities to deal with other viewpoints, and this created the possibility for Christianity to be more tolerant of a variety of perspectives and perhaps, because of the cross-cultural interactions with Islam, a type of Christianity could emerge whose prophet was not divine, but more like Mohammed. Furthermore, Poland and Transylvania were simply further away from the strong arm of the church, making direct control more difficult. This was especially true in Transylvania, which achieved autonomous status under the suzerainty of the Ottoman Empire, and paid tribute to the Turks. Without an ability to maintain ecclesiastical influence, Catholic power waned and Protestant preaching began to flourish.

Sixteenth-century Poland was an amazingly diverse place. The federal union of the Kingdom of Poland and The Grand Duchy of Lithuania in 1569 (Union of Lublin) replaced a personal dynastic union and created the largest kingdom in all of Europe. The Jagiellon dynasty was constitutionally based, with nobility that participated fully in the political process and elected the king. While Poland had Catholic monarchs, its aristocracy was a well-educated, politically powerful elite who were attracted to Protestant reform. A high level of lay participation in church corresponded well with the nobility's participation in government. But perhaps most critical was that it was a multilingual (at least six languages) and multicultural land, from Swedes in the north to Tartars in the south representing a faith spectrum ranging from Lutheran to Sunni Muslim, and including the largest Jewish community in all of Europe. Poland became a crucible of engagement for people who were very different from each other. The coexistence of these diverse religions with the Eastern Orthodox Church and its history of being less rigid about the Trinity, with a kingdom boasting an elected monarch, created a tolerant atmosphere in which Unitarianism could develop. The Confederation of Warsaw established religious toleration in Poland in 1573. Part of a new coronation oath stated, "I will preserve and maintain peace and quiet among those that differ with regard to religion, and will not in any way . . . suffer anyone to be influenced or oppressed by reason of his religion."[18]

---

[17] Diarmaid MacCulloch, *The Reformation: A History* (New York: Viking Penguin, 2003), p. 255.
[18] Phillip Hewett, *Racovia: An Early Liberal Religious Community* (Providence, RI: Blackstone, 2004), p. 49.

With Lutheran organizations already beginning to create a foothold in Poland, King Sigismund II Augustus came to the throne in 1548. He issued a royal edict against heresy, but it was generally not enforced, and toleration was granted to Lutherans in Royal Prussia. The King also declared that he was "king of the people, not of their consciences." With accumulating abuses in the Catholic Church, Lutheran writings became increasingly popular, especially "among the steady stream of students returning from abroad." A key figure in the establishment of the Reformed Church in Poland was Jan Laski. A former priest who spent several years at Basel learning from Erasmus, Laski had been head of the Strangers' Church in London, a home for all foreign Protestants. Back in Poland in 1556, he spearheaded the Reformation by preaching, organizing congregations, overseeing the Bible translated into Polish and holding synods.[19] Radical theological opinions were first publicly voiced at a joint synod of Polish Calvinists and Bohemian Brethren who met in synod at Secemin in 1556. Peter Gonesius (1530–1571), who had read Miguel Servetus and been influenced by the Italian humanist Matteo Gribaldi, got up to speak with a wooden sword strapped to his side, the symbol for pacifism. Gonesius shocked the assembled body by denying Jesus' divinity, and by declaring that infant baptism was a sham. Not welcome in Poland, Gonesius returned to his native Lithuania, and helped establish the anti-Trinitarian movement there with his ministry in Wegrow.[20]

One of the central figures who provided the link between Miguel Servetus and the rise of an organized anti-Trinitarian movement in both Poland and Transylvania was yet another Italian humanist, Giorgio Biandrata (1516–1588). A follower of Gribaldi and a physician, he became an expert on women's diseases, and wrote extensively on the subject. This specialty brought him to the Polish court of the Milanese Queen Bona Sforza in 1540, where he treated both the Queen and her daughter Isabella, the future Queen of Transylvania. Queen Bona brought a large group of Italian courtiers with her, contributing to a flourishing Renaissance cultural influence. A brief return to Italy led to an interest in the emergent Protestant faiths, but this conversion made Biandrata a target of the Inquisition. Finally, he came to permanently settle in Poland in 1558, just after Calvin

[19] Wilbur, *History of Unitarianism*, pp. 273, 280–281; MacCulloch, *Reformation*, p. 187.
[20] Lewis W. Spitz, *The Protestant Reformation, 1517–1559* (New York: Harper and Row, 1985), p. 232; MacCulloch, *Reformation*, pp. 256–257; Charles A. Howe, *For Faith and Freedom: A Short History of Unitarianism in Europe* (Boston: House Press, 1997), pp. 63–67. After Gonesius, the leadership in Lithuania eventually fell to Simon Budny, who Wilbur calls the "most fearless and consistent" of the Unitarians produced in Polish lands. See Wilbur, *History of Unitarianism*, p. 378.

called him a "monster" that would create more of the same ilk.[21] His role became especially crucial in Transylvania, where he was called to care for Isabella in 1560.

Within the Polish Reformed Church during the next few years there was a growing split over the Trinity. When Biandrata arrived in Poland in 1558, the matter was being hotly debated. During the height of the controversy, anti-Trinitarians attributed divine affirmation to a bolt of lightning, which struck the steeple of the Catholic church in Kraków while the liberal Gregory Paulus (1525–1591) was preaching against the Trinity elsewhere in the city. A permanent schism within the Reformed Church had been building for a few years, as the Calvinists refused to meet in synod with the liberals or accept the liberal view that it be one undivided church, which tolerated divergent views on the Trinity, and this split finally occurred in 1565. The anti-Trinitarians were rejected by the majority and forced to form their own synod, the Minor Reformed Church, which met for the first time in June at Brzeziny, the historic beginning of Unitarianism as an organized movement.[22]

Feeling persecuted for their heretical views, many members of the Unitarian Polish Brethren migrated to a new community called Raków, which was created in 1569 under the benefactor, Jadwige Gnoinskiej, a sympathetic Arian, whose coat of arms was the crayfish or rak, thus the name Raków. Her husband, Jan Sieninski, who held the land around Raków, declared: "I will not rule over the religion of the aforesaid Rakovians in which they differ from one another... nor will I permit agents to rule the same, but each of them, as the Lord gives him grace, and as his knowledge of the truth leads him, shall cherish his religion in peace with himself and his descendants."[23] After the establishment of the community, they opened a printing press and founded the Academy of Raków, which eventually had 1,000 students. Following the example of Plato's Republic, they seriously pondered whether they needed to create a separate utopia apart from the world. They believed in living out the true Christian non-violent path of meeting revenge with forgiveness, and hatred with love. They wondered if, like the Hutterites, they needed to create a separate, purified community apart from the state. After a period of struggle where they held all property in common and social rankings were barred, the Racovians reorganized

[21] Wilbur, *History of Unitarianism*, p. 303.
[22] Wilbur, *History of Unitarianism*, pp. 328–331. The church was first described as "the brethren in Poland and Lithuania who have rejected the Trinity," but most of their opponents usually referred to them inaccurately as Arians, while they preferred to be called Christians.
[23] Owen Chadwick, *The Reformation* (Baltimore, MD: Penguin, 1964), p. 200.

under Simon Ronemberg, who reinstituted the ordained clergy. For the next sixty years, Raków was the center for Polish Unitarianism.[24]

Many of the humanists who fled Italy and found their way to such outposts as Transylvania and Poland have been called "evangelical rationalists," one of three groups who constituted the Radical Reformation. The rationalists often shared positions with two other groups of radicals, the Anabaptists and Spiritualists. The common views with the latter included adult baptism and pacifism, while the former eschewed the need for communion or other outward signs of dogmatic Christianity. All of the groups wanted more than mere reform, and advocated radical change either with the restoration of the primitive church or a completely new church, often reflecting an eschatological intensity for change.[25]

One of most significant refugee Italians was a lawyer named Faustus Socinus (1539–1604), the nephew of Laelius Socinus (1525–1562). He became the true leader of the Polish Reformers, and eventually gave them his name as the identifying mark of Unitarians. The name Unitarian was commonly used in reference to Muslim doctrine. Those Christians who denied the divinity of Christ were always called Socinians until the end of the eighteenth century when the word "Unitarian" began to be generally applied. Socinus said that the idea of Jesus as God is "repugnant to sound reason." He believed that Jesus was totally human, but that God shared his divine power with him, making him an adopted deity who could be worshipped. Many of Socinus' views were embodied in the *Racovian Catechism* (1605), which was published the year following his death.

Called the "most influential document in Unitarian history," this catechism was a summary of church beliefs in question and answer format. Its content reflected a strong emphasis on following the ethical teachings of Jesus and the Ten Commandments, and also commented extensively on social relations, including a stance against capital punishment and an embrace of pacifism. The catechism declared God is one in His essence and not three. Jesus Christ is depicted as a real man with only a human nature, but is God's son by his utter obedience, resurrection and ascension. Only one sacrament, the Eucharist, is recognized. The catechism affirms that man as created by God, "is endued with free will," and this leads to an understanding that: "There is no such thing as Original Sin, wherefore neither can it deprave free will. For that Original Sin cannot be proved out of the Scripture... And the fall of Adam being one act, could not have such power as to deprave his own nature, much less the nature of all his

---

[24] See Hewitt, *Racovia*.   [25] Williams, *Radical Reformation*, p. 857.

posterity."[26] This catechism continued to be an influential statement of Unitarianism even after the Brethren were forced to flee from Poland after 1658. The Brethren or their sympathizers issued at least fifteen editions of the new catechism in Latin, Polish, English, Dutch, and German.

Socinus permanently settled in Poland in 1580. Even though he assumed a leadership position, he never became a communicant member at Kraków because he thought adult baptism unreasonable, and therefore not a prerequisite for membership in the church. This went even further than the Anabaptists who believed that only adults could make a faith choice, and thus opposed infant baptism. Socinus affirmed the belief that prayers could be addressed to Jesus, and that he could be worshipped, a different position from the Lithuanian and Transylvanian Unitarians.[27] During subsequent years of rising Catholic fervor, Socinus endured literary attacks, and finally in 1598 a physical assault by students who burned his books, and probably would have drowned him, if he were not rescued by a university professor. The Unitarians soon began to lose the protection of the Confederation of Warsaw; a religious liberty the Jesuits claimed should never have been extended to "Arians." In 1611, Iwan Tyskiewicz was beheaded in Warsaw because he would not renounce his heretical beliefs.[28] In 1638, a boundary dispute in Raków led to the closing of the press, and the banishment of all Unitarians from the city. By 1660, Unitarians were either forced to convert or go into exile. The oldest Unitarian movement in the world, born in a place once known as the heretic's asylum, had failed to survive.

The Unitarian Churches in Hungary and Romania today have evolved from one continuous tradition, mostly the descendents of the Szeklers, Hungarian-speaking descendants of Hun invaders. Unlike Unitarianism in much of the rest of the world, these Unitarians do not struggle with rampant pluralism and identity problems. They have a strong attachment to their history and its liberal Christian faith, made tolerant by their ethnic independence, and their geographic placement in a pluralistic environment. Waves of ethnic migrations in eastern Europe created a greater mix of "nations" than was true in western Europe. The Reformation replicated these ethnic splits religiously – all the Unitarians were Szeklers, and most Magyars were Calvinists. It seems possible that this correspondence

[26] George H. Williams ed., "The Polish Brethren, Documentation of the History and Thought of Unitarianism in the Polish-Lithuanian Commonwealth and in the Diaspora, 1601–1685," *The Proceedings of the Unitarian Historical Society*, XVIII, Part 1 (1976–1977), p. 229.

[27] David E. Bumbaugh, *Unitarian Universalism: A Narrative History* (Chicago, IL: Meadville Lombard Press, 2000), pp. 37–38.

[28] Howe, *Faith and Freedom*, p. 80.

between nation and religion helped bring toleration to Transylvania, it being natural for each group to govern its own affairs. After 1545, that portion of Hungary called Transylvania became an independent country, providing a political and religious buffer between Islam and Christianity. The relationship between the tolerant Unitarianism that developed there and the Muslim faith to the east is made intriguing by the presence of Suleiman I of the Ottoman Empire, and his support for the monarchy of John Sigismund, the only Unitarian king in history. Suleiman sent an emissary to witness Queen Isabella nursing the young prince after he learned of his birth in 1540. Then the following year, the sultan sent troops to rescue Isabella's army in Buda as it was about to be defeated by Ferdinand of the Habsburg Empire. Suleiman then controlled much of lower Hungary, but allowed Isabella and her son to rule Transylvania. He likely preferred a small independent country on the border to a much stronger empire that might threaten him militarily. A further relationship has been suggested by the British Unitarian historian Alexander Gordon, who claimed the word "Unitarian" was commonly applied to Islam, and may have been used to associate the anti-Trinitarians with the Muslims as believers in "an onely Soveraign God," or Unitarian in "its broadest scope."[29]

The infant heir to the throne of Transylvania, John Sigismund (1540–1571) was recognized by Suleiman I, but the royal child's father, John Zapolya, died suddenly two months after his son's birth, and political turmoil ensued. The boy's mother, Isabella, who was the daughter of King Sigismund I of Poland, succumbed to the political machinations of Bishop George Martinuzzi during her regency, and ended up losing her throne temporarily, going into exile in 1551. Hostilities between the Habsburgs and the Ottoman Empire resumed with a decade-long sea war. During the conflict over who controlled the throne of Transylvania, King Ferdinand had Martinuzzi assassinated. Suleiman wanted Isabella restored, and this process began in 1555. Escorted by Turkish troops, the Queen returned from Poland with Prince John after five years of exile. During her absence, the Protestant Reformation had made significant gains. Almost immediately, the Diet of Kolozsvár[30] in 1557 made a request that the two Protestant faiths, Lutheran and Reformed, be given equal worshipping

---

[29] Benjamin J. Kaplan, *Divided by Faith* (Cambridge, MA: Harvard University Press, 2007), pp. 248–249; Alexander Gordon, *Heads of Unitarian History* (Bath: Cedric Chivers Ltd, 1970), pp. 22–23.

[30] When the church wanted to consider matters essential to the faith, they assembled legislative bodies comprising officials from across a large geographic area. These meetings, and the edicts resulting from them, are referred to as "diets" and named for the city in which the meetings took place, such as the Diet of Worms and the Diet of Torda.

rights with the Catholics. Isabella supported this arrangement, thus setting a precedent that would lead to even broader tolerance under her son, who renewed this edict in 1563. Unitarianism was able to make significant gains in Transylvania due to the presence of Giorgio Biandrata, who had already made his mark in Poland. Biandrata had King John's ear as personal physician and counselor, and he represented King John in mediation when the Reformed Church unsuccessfully attempted to settle its divisions.[31]

The future founder of the Unitarian faith, Francis Dávid (1510–1579), was born in Kolozsvár. As a young man, he went through a rapid series of conversions from his inherited Catholic faith. He had seen the fruits of both the Renaissance and the Reformation at the University of Wittenberg. After his return home he became a Lutheran pastor and, eventually, the Bishop of the Lutheran Church in Transylvania. Some Lutherans objected to his rejection of the belief in the bodily presence of Christ in the sacraments. Peter Mélius helped convert him to the Reformed side, and he soon emerged as the head of the Calvinist churches in Transylvania as well as being named court preacher to John. His own personal reformation continued under the tutelage of Biandrata, who had been drawn to Dávid's debating skills, and after Dávid became the Reformed bishop, counseled him on a new way to understand the Trinity. Dávid seems to have become an avowed Unitarian in 1565, and debates over the issue began in earnest. In February 1567, at a synod in Torda, Dávid and Biandrata revised the catechism to reflect an Arian position. Dávid argued, "The eradication of the doctrine of the Trinity should be considered the consummation of the Reformation."[32]

Dávid also advanced religious toleration with King John's approval of the adoption of the Edict of Torda in 1568. In January of that year, the king called for a Diet where the four faiths of Transylvania – Catholic, Lutheran, Reformed, and Unitarian – assembled with debaters to argue for their respective viewpoints. These religious conclaves were like sporting events with scholarly judges and published arguments representing each perspective on truth, while each side sparred with the opposition. Dávid and Biandrata were among those who represented the anti-Trinitarians. The king finally adjourned the event after many days, and declared that tolerance for all four faiths was mandatory. It appeared by this decision that the Unitarians had won. The older edicts were renewed, and this newest

---

[31] Williams, *Radical Reformation*, p. 716; Earl Morse Wilbur, *A History of Unitarianism in Transylvania, England, and America* (Boston, MA: Beacon Press, 1945), pp. 18–20.

[32] Williams, *Radical Reformation*, p. 718.

and most advanced act included the Unitarians, as one of the four received faiths. The decree affirmed that "in every place the preachers shall preach and explain the gospel each according to his understanding of it, and if the congregation like it, well; if not, no one shall compel them, but they shall keep the preachers whose doctrine they approve."[33]

Historian Susan Ritchie argues that there is a direct influence of Islamic tolerance on the Edict of Torda, which was the "first modern articulation of the principle of religious toleration by Europeans at the level of state rule."[34] She says the reformation in Transylvania would never have developed to the radical degree that it did without the political protection of the Ottoman Empire. Ritchie also cites the example of an edict of toleration issued by the Pasha of Buda in 1548 in response to Catholic authorities that wished to condemn a Protestant pastor. This edict stated that Protestants "should be allowed to preach the Gospel everywhere to everybody, whoever wants to hear, freely and without fear."[35] There was a general climate of understanding between Christians and Muslims that may have set a precedent for the kind of free conscience and tolerance that was advocated twenty years later.

Perhaps the most significant debate on the Trinity took place less than two months after Torda at Gyulafehérvár. Dávid defended the Unitarian views, invoking the Bible alone as his authority. The adversaries began daily at 5:00 a.m. and continued for ten days, until finally the king ended this debate by offering the advice that the two sides seek harmony. The king favored the Unitarians, who were considered the victors. Dávid immediately returned to his home town of Kolozsvár. Tradition holds that the townspeople greeted him at the entrance to the city. From a large boulder, which became a Unitarian shrine, he told the assembled group that the king had affirmed their position, and they would not be persecuted as heretics. In response, the exuberant crowd carried Dávid on their shoulders into the town square, where he finished his speech with such eloquence that they were all converted to Unitarianism.[36]

The Unitarians in Transylvania had a short-lived period of triumph. The Trinitarian and Unitarian arms of the Reformed Church officially split after a debate at Nagyvarad in 1569. In contrast to the situation in

---

[33] Williams, *Radical Reformation*, p. 719.
[34] Susan Ritchie, "The Pasha of Buda and the Edict of Torda: Transylvanian Unitarian/Islamic Ottoman Cultural Enmeshment and the Development of Religious Tolerance," *Journal of Unitarian Universalist History*, Volume XXX (2005), p. 37.
[35] Ritchie, "Pasha of Buda," pp. 48–49.
[36] Wilbur, *History of Unitarianism in Transylvania*, p. 38; Williams, *Radical Reformation*, pp. 719–720.

Poland, the Unitarians in Transylvania had both the majority of reformed Protestants and the monarchy behind them. About this time, Dávid and Biandrata published a work, *The False and True Knowledge of God*, which showed their intellectual debt to Michael Servetus as it reprinted sections of his *Restoration*. They also appended a paper affirming their opposition to infant baptism, and the doctrine of Original Sin. Unitarianism received a constitutional affirmation in 1571 when it was given legal equality with all the other churches in the realm, and it was decreed that, "no one shall be harmed for any creed."[37] This timing was fortunate because King John, who had assured the Unitarians equal rights by his own conversion, fell from his horse, and subsequently died that same year.

This friendship between Dávid and Biandrata, which had fostered the Unitarian movement in Transylvania, soon came to a tragic end when Dávid realized his search for truth could not be suspended. The new election in Transylvania brought Stephen Báthory, a Catholic, to the throne. Stephen affirmed the general rule of tolerance, but also decreed that if any Unitarians introduced innovations to the faith, they would be excommunicated. Dávid's belief in "Semper Reformanda," or a continuing Reformation that was God's will, meant that there must always be space for reform. He began to preach that invoking Christ in prayer was no different than the Catholic practice of worshipping saints or the Virgin Mary. A Unitarian synod was held in Torda in March 1578 with Dávid and Biandrata opposing each other on the issues of infant baptism and the adoration of Christ. Biandrata asked Faustus Socinus to mediate, and convince Dávid to renounce his unwillingness to worship Christ.[38] Socinus stayed with Dávid, but was unable to change his mind, and this led Biandrata to decide that Dávid's innovations must be stopped. In short order, Dávid was placed under house arrest. Eventually he appeared at the royal court, and although the nobles supported him, there was pressure from the Jesuits and the Calvinists alike to condemn him. He was pronounced guilty and thrown into prison, where, because of his already weakened condition, he died on November 15, 1579.

The Golden Era of Unitarianism ended with the death of Dávid. Within the next year, the majority of clergy accepted Biandrata's plan to affirm infant baptism and communion, and his candidate for the superintendency of the church, Demetrius Hunyadi. Over the next several centuries, developments within Transylvanian Unitarianism could be characterized in these words of Hunyadi: "My friends, be adaptable. The condition of

---

[37] Williams, *Radical Reformation*, p. 725.   [38] Howe, *Faith and Freedom*, p. 105.

our continued survival is constant adaptation."[39] Many of the clergy were compelled to adopt Socinus' views on the worship of Christ rather than Dávid's. The movement was reorganized by Hunyadi, so that by the time of his death in 1592, there were 400 Unitarian churches in Transylvania. Yet, the compromises that occurred in the wake of Dávid's death were not enough to prevent persecution by the Jesuit leaders of the Catholic Counter-Reformation. Thirteen members of the Diet who were Unitarian were seized in 1594 and accused of conspiracy; five were beheaded, four killed, and the rest banished.[40]

As the seventeenth century dawned, many Unitarians were in rebellion against the prevailing government. Mózes Székely became the leader of a revolt and had some success, including the political support of the Turkish sultan, but he and many other nobles were all killed in battle. After 1608, Calvinist princes who tried to find ways to impose strict standards upon the Unitarians ruled the government. This culminated in the Accord of Deés, which was signed in 1638. The Unitarians agreed to invoke the name of Christ, practice baptism and communion, and also win approval for all of their writings from the prince. The signed agreement meant that political suppression could be legally practiced against the Unitarians. This document also marked the first time that the word "Unitarian" was used in print.[41]

For much of the remainder of the seventeenth century, church life remained in turmoil, as the Turks and the Austrians fought over Transylvania. In 1691, another Catholic Counter-Reformation resulted in the confiscation of schools and churches. The nadir of this period occurred when government forces occupied Kolozsvár in 1716, and seized the Unitarian mother church, which was converted to a Catholic edifice, and never returned to the Unitarians. Two years later, the college was seized as well. Seizures of buildings and attempts to convert Unitarians to Catholicism, or force their children to go to Catholic school, especially in the villages, were common. This was somewhat abrogated by the strong leadership of Michael Lombard Szentábrahámi (1683–1758), who became superintendent in 1737. Called the "second founder of the Unitarian church," his greatest strength was in building up the Unitarian schools, so that there was a strong base for the future of Unitarianism. This was essential since Maria Theresa's reign over the Austrian empire began another period of repression for the Unitarians. Fortunately, her son Joseph began to listen to the some of the Unitarian concerns, and in 1781 declared an edict of

---

[39] Ibid., p. 111.   [40] Ibid., p. 114.   [41] Wilbur, *History of Unitarianism*, p. 118.

toleration, whereby the rights of Unitarians to publish, preach and educate their children as they wished were returned to them after two centuries of oppression. They were even able to erect a church in Kolozsvár again.

Despite another period of repression in the mid-1800s, the Unitarians were able to form a synod in 1861, and chose a new leader, Janos Kriza. At this time, the title of "Bishop" was first used for the leader of the Unitarian Church in Transylvania. Kriza helped establish affiliations with both the American and British Unitarians. József Ferencz, who remained bishop for fifty-two years, followed him. Ferencz preached the first Unitarian sermon in Budapest in 1869, stimulating the return of organized Unitarianism to that part of Hungary for the first time in over 150 years. At this time Transylvania was reunited with Hungary, but this was short-lived. The first Unitarian congregation in Hungary was organized in 1873, and soon more congregations were founded. After World War I, the Unitarians in Hungary were forced to organize their own bureaucracy separate from the Transylvanian church, which then became part of Romania.[42] Prior to the split there were 163 churches, greatly reduced from the 500 congregations that existed at the time of Dávid's death. The vast majority of the churches in Transylvania suffered under both Nazi and Communist regimes throughout much of the twentieth century. The ethnic, cultural, and religious identities of the Unitarians were offensive to the government of Nicolae Ceauşescu (1974–1989), who wanted to make everyone Romanian. Despite the loss of funds and resources confiscated by the state, and clergy, who were torn between collaboration and resistance (one quarter suffered imprisonment), their strong faith tradition helped them survive this deprivation.

[42] Howe, *Faith and Freedom*, pp. 111–112.

CHAPTER 3

Great Britain

Unitarian history in Great Britain often begins with the "father of English Unitarianism," John Biddle (1615–1662), but the faith goes back much further, beginning with the translation of the Vulgate at the end of the fourteenth century. The Vulgate, a fourth-century Latin translation of the books of the New Testament and the Hebrew Bible, was, by the thirteenth century, both the official and the commonly used version of Christian scripture. John Wycliff (*c.* 1330–1384) developed a vernacular Bible to deepen a personal relationship with God, from whom all rights flowed to those who were in a state of grace. Wycliff then interpolated this belief into an attack on the institutionalized Catholic Church, which he believed had fallen into a state of sin. The Church could not claim rights that were only available as a gift of God. Wycliff proposed that the Church abandon all its property, require priests to live in poverty, and that the king eradicate the Church's endowment. He very quickly brought together the issues defining Unitarianism even today: locating authority; individualism both in piety and in the use of reason; and the relationship between assets and influence on the law.

Initially, Wycliff's radical theology, which dispensed of the pope and taxed church properties, appealed to the royalty. However, when he applied reason to the doctrine of transubstantiation, and stated his belief that the bread did not disappear through the act of consecration, Wycliff lost any royal support, and was removed from his teaching post at Oxford. In 1382, after the Peasants' Revolt, his writing was banned. Wycliff's vernacular Bible both implied a belief in freedom of conscience, and inspired a new religious movement that undermined the ecclesiastical structure of the British church.[1] The Lollards, members of this new religious movement, insisted that the true church was of the "Saved," and that salvation depended upon

[1] "Unitarian Missionary," *The Unitarian*, Vol. III, No. 9 (September 1908), p. 314.

adherence to scripture, rather than doctrine. Followers were encouraged to study the Bible. This practice led to anti-Trinitarianism, and in 1401, the Crown joined the Church in attempting to rout out religious dissent. Bishops were granted the right to arrest those deemed suspicious, or to call upon civil authorities for aid. The Heresy Acts were the first pieces of civil legislation regarding religious belief, and they declared Wycliff's theology of Unitarianism punishable by burning at the stake. Indeed, the first person put to death for religious beliefs in England, William Sawtrey, was a Unitarian and a Lollard.[2] The Archbishop of Canterbury condemned him as a heretic. Sawtrey appealed to the king and Parliament but the appeals were denied and, eight days later, the civil government enacted the statutes sanctioning death at the stake for heretical religious beliefs. Wycliff was condemned posthumously by the Council of Constance in May 1415, which required that his books be burned and his body exhumed. Because he had been declared a heretic, he was unwelcome in the church yard, even in death. In 1428, his body was exhumed and burned, and the ashes thrown in the River Swift.[3]

There is evidence that Jan Hus, a renowned faculty member at the University of Prague who is claimed as an ancestor by Unitarians, read Wycliff carefully.[4] The flaming chalice is intended to recall Hus' death at the stake for believing that the communion cup should be shared by all, and not only offered to the priestly class. Although these are seen as Czech or Bohemian roots, there is no mistaking the British influence. Hus, quoting Wycliff, ran afoul of the Inquisition when he criticized the Church's hierarchy. His death in 1415 marked the beginning of decades of religious warfare in Bohemia, and some accounts of the event report that Wycliff's treatises were used as kindling.

The story of Hus' martyrdom can help make clear the need for distinctions between Unitarianism as a theology, and institutionalized religion, which is not necessarily based on theology. In England, the struggle for Unitarians was not nearly as much about the nature of God as it was about having a place in the national Church. For some, this meant that a Unitarian theology would not be persecuted, and that the national Church would be broad enough to include diverse beliefs. For others, it meant the

---

[2] Earl Morse Wilbur, *A History of Unitarianism in Transylvania, England and America* (Boston, MA: Beacon Press, 1945), pp. 167–168.

[3] Gary Macy, "John Wycliff," in An Introductory Dictionary of Theology and Religious Studies, Orlando Espin and James B. Nickoloff, eds. (St. Benedict, MN: The Liturgical Press, 2007), p. 1500.

[4] S. Fletcher Williams, "John Huss and Jerome of Prague: A Sketch," *The Unitarian*, Vol. 6, No. 10 (October, 1891), pp. 448–452.

national Church needed to be organized locally, to prevent tyranny. There were Unitarians in Great Britain who wanted the king to be the head of the national Church, and there were Unitarians in Great Britain who wanted Parliament to have control over the state religion. It is not clear that there were Unitarians in England who wanted to create a separate religion based on their theology. That this ended up happening was a matter of force, rather than choice.

Close to a century and a half passed from the time of Wycliff's challenge to Church hierarchy and subsequent ex-communication until Henry VIII's initiation of the English Reformation. Civil rule and religious authority had already been fused, when Henry was named Defender of the Faith in exchange for denouncing Martin Luther and the Reformation. This changed heresy from a matter of church authority to one for the state. But Henry soon separated from Rome, refusing to recognize the existence of the pope, while keeping the Catholic system of bishops.

By creating the Church of England, Henry VIII inadvertently drew attention to the small Protestant groups that had not aroused much interest beyond intellectual circles. He participated in the spread of heretical views, including anti-Trinitarianism, by bringing Socinian scholars from Poland into the English universities in the hope of undermining Catholicism. Instead, the concept of religious education changed to include the use of reason, and exposed students not only to differences in forms of worship, but to new forms of organization. Ecclesiology became a major concern. When intense fighting in Holland led Anabaptists to flee, many joined the existing groups in England. The fledgling Church of England was united with anti-papal views that masked a variety of theological positions within the Protestant world. Real power relied primarily on financial incentives: the monasteries Henry VIII closed were sold off to the land-owning class, in order to gain their loyalty.

After Henry's death, Edward VI helped to develop liturgical stability through *The Book of Common Prayer* (1549), but the theology varied widely. A self-governing Strangers' Church, which was open to immigrants who had been involved in the Reformation, indicated a degree of tolerance, but was followed by Edward's half-sister Mary's attempt to return the country to Catholicism. Elizabeth's coronation in 1559 brought with it a restoration of the Church of England, and the forging of a national identity centered on the authority of the monarch and a broad church. The theological spectrum ran from conservative to radical, but the Anabaptists were considered a threat, and ordered out of the country. Secret congregations were established, particularly in Norfolk, England, which sixty years later would be the area from where massive numbers migrated to the New England colonies. By rejecting the connection to both the religious past and the Reformist impulse, a somewhat unified social landscape under the authority of both church and state suddenly became a diverse country in which leadership and authority were openly being questioned. These are the roots of institutional Unitarianism.

Because he was King of Scotland, James I's ascension to the English throne in 1603 made him the head of a national church that encompassed two entirely different religious traditions. A revival of theological warfare accompanied James to the throne. While the English were anti-papist, the Scots were truly anti-Catholic. They had already had a successful Reformation, and were offended that James, who had been raised in Scotland, chose the Church of England, which granted him the divine right to rule. The Irish, however, were hopeful that James was signaling a tolerance for Catholicism. Although the English generally wanted to retain the Episcopal system, many of them, especially those who gained property through the monasteries taken by the Crown, were allied with the Scots in their fears of Catholicism. And there were some Protestants in England who actually had a great deal in common with the Scottish Calvinists, and were hopeful of more serious reform of the Church of England. James I met with these Puritan Anglicans at the Hampton Court Conference in 1604, but he rejected their requests for change in the local churches, and banned all religious meetings taking place outside of the Church of England.

James I attempted to build a coherent religious identity through exclusion and punishment, and by ruling without Parliament. He burned scholarly works with which he disagreed, including the Racovian Catechism, and then burned Anabaptists and anti-Trinitarians at the stake for heresy. These public executions lasted for the first decade of James' reign, during which time the Pilgrims fled to Holland. Over time, James' cruelty made those defined as heretics appear instead as martyrs. Similar fragmentation was caused by the King James Bible (1611); intended to eliminate the use of vernacular translations, it nevertheless promoted direct, personal use of scripture among all classes. Direct reading of the Bible posed a threat to a tradition based on liturgy and creed, and led to dissent. The existence of the King James Bible implied a centrality that had previously only been expected in radical Protestant sects. In Scotland, the translation was a tyrannical removal of their language. By alienating the Scots and preventing the new Protestant landowners from representation in Parliament, James I sowed the seeds for Civil War.

Fifteen years into James' reign, he requested that representatives of foreign Reformed Churches be invited to help resolve theological and governance issues within the Church of the Netherlands. This resulted in the first ecumenical synod in history (Dort, 1618), and it met James' goal, which was to eject the liberal Arminians from the Dutch Church, keeping the Netherlands' Reformed Church as conservative as England's. Yet James' ambassadors were radicalized at Dort. They returned to England committed to a broad church and embraced a form of ethical humanism in place of theology, because they had been horrified by the behavior of those on their own triumphant side. These men expected people, especially clergy, to behave in accord with the stated beliefs, and wanted nothing to do with those who used their power to demonize others. A broad church would keep faith alive; fighting over minor differences would kill it. These Anglicans wanted to purify the Church of England by liberalizing the theology while maintaining the structure. Over the next twelve years, various strands of British Protestant faith battled over governance until their fragmentation allowed the Presbyterian forces to gain power in Parliament. James I's rule gave way to that of his son, Charles I, who continued the solitary rule.

When Charles I chose an Archbishop of Canterbury who established the Church of England as an authoritative arm of a centralized government, the Scottish overthrew the royal government, forcing Charles I to recall Parliament. He requested funds for an army, but received an imprisoned archbishop. The Parliaments of England and Scotland then negotiated the Solemn League and Covenant (1643), creating a Presbyterian–Parliamentary system, and giving England the resources of the Scottish Army as they fought against Charles I. As the new legal head of the Church of England, Parliament needed religious advisors, so it called together over a hundred Puritan clergy, who developed the Westminster Confession of Faith. This very conservative Confession alienated the Independents and those Anglicans interested in a broad church, and set the stage for Oliver Cromwell's military state. Anti-Catholicism and the Presbyterian Parliamentary system combined to make Ireland, which had remained royalist, the target of violent action.

Cromwell, whose family status was directly tied to land confiscated from Catholics, used the Scots to help subdue the Irish by claiming land held by Catholics and installing paid protectors, and then purging the Scots from positions of power. By 1648, he succeeded in destroying the monarchy and abolishing the House of Lords. It took three years to defeat the Scots and become the chairman of the executive body of the Parliament. His

New Model Army occupied Ireland, and developed a penal code against Catholics that resulted in the death or exile of approximately 15 percent of the population.

The years of Cromwell's rule in England represent a brief period of Puritan ascendancy in which neither royalty nor Presbyterians ruled. While the constant warfare drove some religious Dissenters to flee, it also enabled Unitarianism to spread within England. John Biddle had openly rejected the doctrine of the Trinity in 1644, and was charged with heresy, then released, whereupon he wrote a detailed statement against the Trinity and circulated it among his friends. His pamphlet was burned; he had it reprinted. He was imprisoned, then released to await a hearing. In 1646, as Britain entered the Commonwealth period, Parliament referred his case to the Assembly of Divines. It dragged on for five years without resolution, even as Cromwell was gaining power to separate theological issues from affairs of state. Instead of establishing a modern republic, Cromwell became autocratic. He signed the warrant for the beheading of Charles I, and assumed religious authority by issuing the Ordinance against Heresy (1648). Biddle remained confined to the Gatehouse at Westminster. In 1652, just before Parliament was expelled and Cromwell became Lord Protector, Biddle was released. He immediately organized the first anti-Trinitarian congregation in England, and made the Racovian Catechism available in English. Two years later, his Two-Fold Catechism (1654), advocating a very simple Christianity based on scripture alone, was seen as an attack on the Westminster Confession. He was thrown back in jail, and eventually banished to the Scilly Isles. Released in 1658, he was free for four years before being arrested again, while teaching a Bible class in his own home in London. This last arrest resulted from the Act of Uniformity (1662), and led to Biddle's subsequent death in prison.

After Cromwell's death, Parliament and the New Model Army asked Charles II to take the throne. At this point, any hope of religious reform was effectively over. The restored monarchy was extremely antagonistic to non-conformist clergy. The year 1662 is commonly referred to as The Great Ejection: 2,000 Independent Puritans lost their pulpits due to their refusal to sign the Westminster Confession of Faith. Additionally, worshippers were prevented from gathering in one another's homes, and ejected clergy were forced to relocate at least five miles from their former churches. Despite the punitive nature of these acts, non-conformists were strengthened by the acknowledgement that dissent was powerful enough to require legislated conformity. Charles II forced the hand of those who had wanted to work within the Church of England but did not conform to the

Articles of Faith, effectively joining them with all those who had already dissented.

In Ireland, land was confiscated from Presbyterians who had supported the Crown. Forced to relocate to Northern Ireland in 1648, they created a fairly strong community of Presbyterians with a Unitarian theology, which became a home for the Dissenters who were ejected from the Church of England in 1662. But Presbyterians in Ireland still persecuted heretics. The non-subscribers were not allowed to participate in the government or own property. Thomas Emlyn, a popular minister at a Presbyterian church in Dublin, was jailed for blasphemy in 1702, after a parishioner noticed that Emlyn never mentioned the Trinity. This imprisonment caused explosive debate about the Trinity, and the Belfast Society (1705) was formed in order for the Presbyterian ministers in the north to discuss the nature of God. Many among them grew convinced of the humanity of Jesus, leading the General Synod of Ulster to create the Presbytery of Antrim (1725) specifically for those who did not accept the Westminster Confession of Faith. In 1806, a group in Munster that had grown from the Scottish Seceders joined them. In 1824, the General Synod again required that ministers subscribe to the Confession of Faith, and seventeen congregations in Ulster responded by seceding. They formed the Remonstrant Synod of Ulster in 1830; and in 1910 these two groups, the Presbytery of Antrim and the Remonstrant Synod of Ulster, joined to form the Non-Subscribing Presbyterian Church of Ireland, which is part of the General Assembly of Unitarian and Free Christian Churches, while remaining a separate church. In 1910, there were thirty-eight congregations; there are currently thirty-four.

Other disenfranchised Presbyterians fled Ireland, and began migrating to the mid-Atlantic colonies. They formed independent congregations, and some of their first ministers were New England Congregationalists. In 1706, the first American presbytery was formed, and became the first synod in 1716, in Philadelphia. In the American colonies, no one had to sign the Confession as a whole. Each separate presbytery was allowed to judge Articles of Faith within the Westminster Confession as to whether or not they were "essential and necessary" to Christian faith. This created a system in which what was considered bedrock to the understanding of Christianity differed by region, giving a sense that those who gathered set the terms of the faith. It was not congregational polity, but it did institutionalize and democratize a debate about what is essential to the faith. This, in turn, fostered strong relationships with other Dissenters who had found no home in the Commonwealth, particularly since many of the English Presbyterians had Unitarian theologies.

Charles II ruled until 1685, and managed to keep the Church of England safely Episcopal: Protestant, but not particularly touched by the Radical Reformation. When his brother James II succeeded him, the fragile peace between Parliament and the Crown was shattered. Fears of Catholicism were so intense that Parliament orchestrated a coup, in which James II's daughter Mary, and her husband William, would take the throne. British history refers to this as the Glorious, or Bloodless, Revolution, a description which belies the reality in Ireland and Scotland, where major battles were fought. No blood was shed in London because the city was under the control of the Dutch, who ushered in William and Mary at the behest of both the House of Commons and the House of Lords. Ironically, as the backgrounds and experiences of those who were British citizens and British subjects grew ever more diverse, the middle way that Elizabeth had tried to create became increasingly narrow, through a process of legislation that had more to do with Parliament than royalty. James II's attempt to incorporate all people into the civic structure was met with huge opposition from those who supposedly represented the people.[5]

In 1687, James II passed the Act of Indulgence, which had three points: attendance at the Church of England would not be required; there would be freedom to conduct services in homes or in chapels; and civil or military offices would no longer require the pledging of a religious oath. The rights and protections for bishops and priests would remain in place. The goal was social peace achieved through personal freedom, rather than by forced conformity. The language introducing this Act foreshadows the American Declaration of Independence, ninety-two years before it was written. James II's removal from the throne was orchestrated within months of his Declaration of Indulgence, which was rescinded. The freedoms extended to Catholics, Unitarians, Jews, Muslims, and people of any or even no faith, were not put back into British law until 1969. John Locke's Letter on Toleration, often cited as a source for the United States Constitution, was written soon after this Act, and mentioned specifically the need to keep the affairs of the state separate from religious beliefs. But Locke was one of those who actively justified the removal of James II from the throne, an act that was motivated completely by religion; and more specifically, by anti-Catholicism.

William and Mary were ushered in to lead, and passed the Act of Tolerance. Generally, this is seen as a repeal of the Act of Uniformity, marking the beginning of a progression that inevitably led to more, if gradual, freedom.

---

[5] "Graduate Student Scott Sowerby Finds Surprising Side to King James II," *Harvard Science* (Cambridge, MA, April 17, 2003).

In reality, it and the Bill of Rights, which quickly followed, were regressive political bills that gave more control to the civil government and instituted the monarchy as a figurehead, at the expense of a more diverse social landscape. The Bill of Rights restated laws that already existed, but took away royal power that James II had used to grant freedom of conscience to all people. The Act of Toleration was an attack on James II's brief rule, and the beginning of a government that legislated doctrine rather than polity. The non-conformists only had the freedom to worship again if they would teach the correct doctrine, which explicitly excluded Catholics and non-Trinitarians. Services that differed from the Church of England's were tolerated, meaning that one could wear a robe, like preachers in Geneva, or a surplice, like the Catholics and Anglicans; that the prayers could be prescribed or voluntary; that there might or might not be a set liturgy, but the doctrine was fixed. This limited freedom essentially transformed a varied religious culture – even if some groups were illegal, they did exist in protective cells and had even been recognized by King James II – into one in which all roads led to Anglican doctrine. It was legislation that freed the government from prosecuting non-conformists while restricting their opportunities for education and public service. Unitarians were forced to provide their own schools, in the form of Dissenters' Academies, and a later Blasphemy Act prevented them from public office. These barriers were in full effect until 1813, and complete freedom for non-Trinitarians was not achieved until 1844. Even then, there was opposition. The conflict between the Crown and Parliament that started with James I in 1603, was decided in favor of Parliament, but not for liberty or democratic rule. It was a rejection of genuine leadership relating to religious freedom.

The meaning of this history is contingent upon one's beliefs in the purpose of religious institutions. For those who are institutionalists and who are Unitarian, the actions of William and Mary paved the way for the religion to develop, and perhaps even provided much of their purpose in the form of a fight for legitimacy. But for those who did not want to further divide Christianity, and who had sincerely hoped for an established church that had room for them, this was an unspeakable loss. These were people for whom the Bible was central, as was a kind of truth telling that relied upon being open. Being forced out was not an impetus to establish a sectarian faith; it signaled a failure of the church to ever be meaningful, and created a permanent double bind. What would a successful Unitarian movement look like if it did not happen within the established or legitimate church? As a foundational part of the institutional background, this continues to haunt Unitarians and Unitarian Universalists, and it explains some of the frustrations and complications of charismatic leaders who promoted anti-institutionalism.

For thirty years, these non-conformists had been classified as Dissenters, but the Independents generally wanted to dissent, while the Presbyterians were forcibly ejected. In 1691, they joined in an agreement called the Happy Union, but these Dissenters were tied together by decree more than desire. Although they were clergy centered, the Independents were organized as small groups of like-minded people who believed in making decisions together and without the interference of imposed authority. They practiced congregational polity, but in this union the concept of covenant was broadened to include all members of the faith, not only the specific gathered community. Now a minister who was ordained by one congregation could legitimately serve another. The Presbyterians dropped their system of governance, and both groups began practicing congregational polity that allowed ministers to move among the faithful.

The Happy Union broke down over education. The Independent tradition did not require formal training. Ministers came out of congregations and were ordained because of the relationship developed with the people. The Presbyterians wanted more doctrinal control, achieved through strict standards of ministerial training. The Independents were not interested and left the joint fund behind, then prevented the Presbyterians from attending their annual lecture. The Presbyterians soon created their own lecture at Salters' Hall. This became a site of historic significance to Unitarians in 1719, when 110 ministers met to discuss the nature of the Trinity. The meeting was an attempt to provide guidance to Presbyterians in Exeter who were struggling with the issue raised by Samuel Clarke's revision of the Book of Common Prayer. In a 57:53 vote, the gathering refused to interpret scripture, but the losing side met again and subscribed to a declaration of the Trinity. Thus the Dissenters formally split into Subscribers (generally made up of Independents and Particular Baptists) and non-Subscribers (Presbyterians and General Baptists). Unitarianism would grow from the latter.

The Universalists were brought into the non-Subscribing fold through this split at Salters' Hall. Universalism had its roots in the General Baptists, who were found primarily in the south of England and in Wales. Welsh tradition was to hold regular meetings at home, with monthly church gatherings. House churches, illegal elsewhere, were allowed and unsupervised in Wales. The General Baptists were radical: a church was created by free and equal relationships with each other and with God, and not by doctrine. The Bible was the only authority in religion, and the same study that led them to reject infant baptism caused a realization that the idea of an elect and the doctrine of predestination were non-biblical. According to Scripture, all people could be saved. These Baptist Universalists gained legitimacy by filling vacant pulpits during the English Civil War, and in 1649, the first official Baptist Church was organized. By the time the Crown was restored, and Charles II began persecuting them, there were over 20,000 Baptists, most of whom were Universalists. When the Baptists were driven underground, along with the ejected Puritan clergy, the language and the tradition of meeting at home meant that Wales was particularly well suited to preserve the religion. Baptist Universalists became anti-Trinitarian through association with other persecuted Dissenters, so that by 1750, most Baptists were also Unitarians. In 1802, the Welsh Unitarian Society was formed. Those Baptists who held more orthodox beliefs split off and formed the New Connection.

The Unitarians were seen as a central destabilizing force during this period of upheaval in Great Britain. The promotion of equality, individual freedoms, and the use of reason threatened the British social order. Just as the government associated the Peasants' Revolt with Wycliff's theology, Unitarianism was believed to incite revolution. This was especially true after the Cookites – Methodist Unitarians who created co-operatives and promoted economic reform favoring laborers – joined with the various other Dissenters who helped form the fledgling denomination. After the American Revolution, the attacks on Unitarians intensified. Great Britain's status as a world power had begun eroding and the exchange of ideas between liberal religionists in England and America was hazardous. And England had provided the seeds for this threat to grow: Thomas Emlyn's pamphlet was printed in America in 1756, and John Murray fled England in 1770 and arrived in an area of New Jersey that had been profoundly influenced by Dissenters who had left during the last round of religious persecution.

In 1772, Theophilus Lindsey (1723–1808) drafted the Feathers Tavern Petition, requesting that Parliament accept a declaration of belief in the Bible for Anglican clergy, instead of forcing them to subscribe to all thirty-nine Articles of Faith. His petition was denied. Lindsey did not consider himself a Dissenter, but by Parliament's definition, he was. He conducted a Unitarian worship service at Essex Street in 1774. Among the 200 people in attendance were Benjamin Franklin and Joseph Priestley, who had long been friendly with Franklin. Priestley (1733–1804) came into Unitarianism from the other branch of Dissent: he had been born to an Evangelical family, but as he reached adulthood found he could not subscribe to

Calvinism. After attending a Dissenters' Academy in Daventry, Priestley settled into the Presbyterian ministry, and into an active teaching career in the sciences. As Lindsey began at Essex Street, Priestley was on his way to serve in Birmingham, a move necessitated when his support of the colonists in the American Revolution cost him his teaching job. It was from Lindsey that Priestley learned the name "Unitarian"; and later it was Lindsey who publicly supported Priestley when he was attacked for his writings.

Essex Street Chapel was founded as the colonies in America won independence. In 1783, the British Unitarian William Hazlitt was preaching along the Atlantic seaboard. As the French Revolution began, Emlyn's pamphlet was reprinted in America. Rational Dissenters were enthusiastic about the Republic of Virtue, of society being rebuilt without land ownership as the mark of citizenship, or of a person's worth. Some British Unitarian writers were particularly exhilarated by the events of 1789 and joined the Jacobins, among them William Blake[6] and Mary Wollstonecraft, who was enraged that Edmund Burke, a passionate supporter of the American Revolution, called the Unitarians traitors and, more tellingly, Levelers. A level society was a threat to and a rejection of the British hierarchy.

Burke's assessment of the Rational Dissenters was the logical outcome of a process begun by Henry VIII, and continued by Elizabeth: the equation of heresy with treason. Dissenters believed that the truth was rational, and what was spoken in the religious sphere was applicable to all of life. By connecting the English Revolution, the American Revolution, and the French Revolution as a united, progressive movement, they were protesting an expanding global economy that trafficked in human lives, with trade routes and colonization efforts across Africa, Asia, Australia, Nova Scotia, and Jamaica.

By 1791, the English had embraced the label of traitor for these people; Wollstonecraft moved to Paris; Priestley was burned out of Birmingham and fled to Pennsylvania; and Joseph Johnson, who published many Dissenters, including Erasmus Darwin, Anna Barbauld, Mary Wollstonecraft, and William Godwin, was thrown in jail. Nevertheless, unity was achieved at the beginning of the nineteenth century. Thomas Belsham (1750–1829) went to Essex Street and spread Unitarian information in an organized and

---

[6] William Blake was born into a Moravian family that was also interested in Swedenborgianism. He was buried in the Dissenters' Burial Ground in Bunhill Fields. As Magnus Ankarsjo details in *William Blake and Religion: A New Critical Review* (Jefferson, NC: McFarland, 2009), the Unitarian connection was important, as they were the largest of the non-conforming groups during Blake's life, and many of the people Blake socialized with in the 1780s and 1790s were Unitarians. Joseph Johnson was perhaps the most important of these contacts.

purposeful way. He began providing a structure and a presence that invited like-minded people to join. In 1789, at the time Belsham became Unitarian, there were two congregations in England. In 1825, there were over 200, no doubt helped by the 1813 Trinity Bill that finally made Unitarianism legal.

At the time Priestley was fleeing England, the British East India Company was establishing itself as the ruler of the Indian subcontinent. Five hundred years after having been invaded by Muslims (*c.* 1000 CE), the Mogul Emperor Akbar (1543–1605) achieved a kind of unity among the native Hindus, the Muslim rulers, and the newly arrived Portuguese. But his successors became increasingly rigid towards non-Muslims, so that in the seventeenth century, religious tension was fierce and interfered with leadership. When the British East India Company moved to Bengal in 1698, and created settlements in Madras and Bombay, it developed its own local government, unlike the Dutch and Portuguese, who ruled their colonies from home. This position allowed the British to take over as internal forces jockeyed for power, and in 1800 they won control.

Because the British endeavor in India was a business, dedicated to exploiting the land for revenue, missionary activity was actively discouraged. Yet this climate was perfect for intellectual, academic interests, and led to the field of comparative religions. Joseph Priestley's 1799 book, *Comparison of the Institutions of Moses with those of the Hindoos and Other Ancient Nations*, was written twenty years before any other study of religion written without a missionary agenda, and it re-awakened an interest in India's medieval culture, long suppressed by Muslim rule. This, combined with the British East India Company's need to develop an elite cadre of civil servants, resulted in the new field of Orientalism. The British who became interested in Sanskrit, Persian, and Arabic worked to create schools in India that taught ancient texts. Although Orientalism was initiated and controlled by the British, it became an avenue for the Hindu majority to learn their own cultural history. Orientalism also led to the Bengal Renaissance and a vision of religious liberalism that continues to be part of Unitarian Universalism today.

The story of Unitarianism in India offers an opportunity to examine the role of romanticism and class issues as blinders to reality, and it may illuminate some of the reasons that Unitarianism began declining almost as soon as it was institutionally formed. It also makes clear the fundamental association of reason and texts for Unitarians. Moodelliar Vellazha was born a Tamil Hindu in 1768. After his parents were both killed in religious warfare, he was taken at the age of 9 by a Muslim trader, who sold him as a slave to a European ship officer. When his owner died, Vellazha was freed. He converted to Islam. However, in 1789, while working as a servant in England, he was baptized at St. James' Church and changed his name to William Roberts. The following year, back in Madras (now Chennai) and still a servant, he discovered that Dutch missionaries had translated the Bible into Tamil. Roberts read carefully, and could find nothing supporting the creeds taught in church. In 1793, living in England again, a servant working in the same household read Unitarian tracts to Roberts. Unitarian books accompanied his return to Madras in 1794.[7]

Over the years, Roberts ordered more books by Unitarians, as well as an English translation of the Qur'an, and when he traveled to England in 1806 he purchased copies of works by Priestley and Lindsey. Roberts created a Tamil prayer book based on Lindsey's, and in 1813 opened a Unitarian worship center in Madras. He wrote to Thomas Belsham for help and support of any kind, but there was minimal interest. For Roberts, having been born low caste, orphaned, and sold into slavery, Unitarianism created coherence from religious experiences in Hinduism, Islam, and orthodox Christianity, and provided a path towards self-determination rather than rigid social role. He dedicated his life to this faith, and was inspired to educate poor children in Madras. The British Unitarians never paid much attention. Yet the Madrasi Unitarians continue to this day. It is simultaneously an indigenous group, and a group that would not have existed were it not for the British Empire. Founded as a Unitarian Christian worship center, it remains Christian, with native leadership.

By contrast, the Calcutta-based Brahmo Samaj was of enormous interest to the British Unitarians, despite the deep ambivalence of its founder, Rammohun Roy, about Unitarianism as a religion. Roy had been working on a Bengali translation of the New Testament with the Baptist William Adam, and both became convinced that the doctrine of the Trinity was not biblical.[8] The interest the men shared led them to form the Calcutta Unitarian Committee in 1821. The British Protestant idea of religion was simultaneously validated and challenged by Roy's work: texts were the source of authority, but he studied the Vedas and the Upanishads, not the Bible. The truth and morality he was interested in matched the British Unitarian definition of Christianity, generating excitement about universality and anxiety about religious identity. By 1828, the Calcutta Unitarian Committee was gone, and the Brahmo Samaj had begun. Roy allowed only

---

[7] Spencer Lavan, *Unitarians and India: A Study in Encounter and Response* (Boston, MA: Skinner House, 1972), pp. 24–31.
[8] Lavan, *Unitarians and India*, p. 41.

Bengali to be spoken. It is clear that Belsham knew Roy was not Christian, yet he remained more excited by this connection with "opulence" and "elegance"[9] than in a Christian church formed by the believer, William Roberts.

Roy's work exploited some British prejudices. His rejection of current Hindu practices by defending tradition against false interpretation was a product of the Bengal Renaissance, and did not signal a conversion to Christianity so much as to the Enlightenment. He wanted to see more teachers, especially of science and literature. Roy's programs were designed to promote cultural exchange between the upper-middle-class liberals from both England and India; between dignitaries with a common interest in social reform. Roy started an independent press in Calcutta, promoting the values of literature and justice as rooted in ancient culture, and as purer than any particular religious practice. By joining with the British Unitarians, Roy was finding a way for the Hindus to stand up to outside influence.

The Bengali Renaissance has a great deal in common with the revival of Welsh culture, which happened at about the same time, and had similar entanglements with Unitarianism. During the Napoleonic Wars, there was also a deep interest among the Welsh in maintaining the past, even as their exposure to radical ideas through Belsham and Lindsey increased. Many of the English Romantic poets were champions of the Revolution, but in Wales romanticism took a slightly different turn. It looked back, as the Bengalis did, while relying on the written word in a fairly modern way that ignored the oral tradition of their own cultures. Edward Williams, or Iolo Morganwg, was an anti-clerical Unitarian from South Wales who fused Christianity with Arthurian legends and essentially recreated a modern bardic philosophy. His conceit was that the native druidic culture of Wales had survived the persecutions of Edward I, and that the rituals he promoted dated from these earlier Welsh people of faith. Williams produced hymns and poems, and claimed that they were newly discovered old texts. He also began a revival of Welsh culture and crafts that has had lasting influence, although it is now known that most of his "discoveries" were forgeries. Even as he reveled in the principles of the French Revolution and in associations with the most aggressive of the Rational Dissenters, Williams had an almost desperate fear of losing the Welsh language and culture, and instead of appealing to reason or freedom in an effort to preserve it, he turned to a mythic past. Rights and justice were posited as universal, yet geography,

---

[9] Lavan, ibid., p. 36.

language, history, and a clannish loyalty were what provided sustenance. Faith was rooted in nature, in the ties between a people and their home. This could simultaneously make a religion universal and particular, and it provided an effective model of pastoral care by making the tribe the healing community.

This romantic combination of tribalism and universalism sometimes caused arguments among liberals and reformers. Just as Lindsey had been calling for tolerance and a broader faith within the Anglican Communion, William Ellery Channing was calling for tolerance and a broader faith within the Independent (Congregational) Standing Order of Massachusetts. Both ended up with the label "Unitarian" – a label that had Socinian associations in Britain and in the mid-Atlantic states, but Arian ones in New England. Ironically, Arians were specifically excluded from British Unitarianism, and the New England liberals found the Socinians far too political. When Belsham wrote the *Memoirs of Theophilus Lindsey* in 1812, he called the Congregationalists in New England "Unitarian," providing material with which conservative Unitarians could attack liberals. Yet war soon united them: Gearing up to fight Napoleon's France, England took American ships. British Unitarians were against the war itself, American Unitarians were against the financing of the war, but they were both united in their opposition to the actions of the British government. By the time the British burned Washington, DC in 1814, the Unitarians in Britain had civil rights, and free interchange between them and American Unitarians existed at diplomatic levels. Although New England clergy continued to divide over theology and tradition, issues of civil liberty, intellectual debate, and literature quickly identified a global Unitarianism.

Periodicals helped strengthen Unitarian identity and extended the rational Christian principle of debate into the public domain.[10] Robert Aspland began the *Monthly Repository* in 1806. He fused an anti-authoritarian philosophy with a belief in rational theology by writing narratives of significant religious figures. The journal had exemplary stories of conversion or martyrdom that gave power to Unitarianism. He helped the religion achieve some legitimacy in society by building numerous internal supports. Although Unitarianism came first for Aspland, it was somewhat defined by its status as persecuted, and when the British and Foreign Unitarian Association was formed (1825), reform politics and institutional base building did not seem

---

[10] Isobel Armstrong, "The Monthly Repository and Unitarian Chronicle," *Nineteenth Century Serials Edition*, www.ncse.ac.uk/headnotes.

as necessary. He left the *Repository*, and served as a minister until his death in 1845.

But internal forces undermined the institutions he built. Under the new editor, William Fox, Unitarianism in the *Repository* came second to controversial articles on religion, poetry, education, and the emancipation of women. Dissenting intellectuals (not just clergy) began writing for the magazine, which was directing religious energy into reshaping civil life. Religion was seen as the source of a just society, which inevitably required networks of trust, not authority. The need for a solid institutional basis to this vision was minimized. When Fox abused that trust by separating from his wife and engaging in an affair with his ward, the *Repository* folded.

Some within Unitarianism had always wanted a broad church. Institution building was seen as sectarian, associated with missionaries. James Martineau (1805–1900) did not believe congregations should be called Unitarian, and worked instead to affirm reason alone, although he expanded the definition to include intuitive understandings. His approach was individual, ethical, and, he believed, devotional; but his listeners found him self-involved and disinterested in their needs. Martineau's broad-church approach to worship demanded that he rigidly isolate areas of ministry: education was distinct from social reform, as it was from worship. Religion could motivate service: Martineau had been a student of Lant Carpenter, and later taught in the Ragged Schools for children of the poor. Worship, however, was not aimed at social change.

Martineau had a public dispute with Anglican clergy in Liverpool, debating the nature of the Trinity, which led to his 1840 appointment as Professor of Mental and Moral Philosophy at Manchester New College. Later, he devoted himself to the training of clergy, and was Principal of the College from 1869–1885. Martineau had earlier been instrumental in passing the Dissenters' Chapels Act (1844), which protected the funds and meeting places of the Unitarians. For over fifty years, students for the ministry worked with him directly, and his influence lasted beyond those decades. He was the author of many hymns and prayers, and is celebrated as a luminary in British Unitarianism. Yet Martineau insisted that identifying congregations as Unitarian was dogmatic and narrow. He wanted the name "Free Christian" instead, and in fact organized a Free Christian Union to serve the same purpose as the British and Foreign Unitarian Association.

Martineau reveals the costs of a dream of a broad church for England; one based solely on the word of God. Martineau's sermons were very popular among the Anglican clergy with whom he was friendly, and therefore gave theological Unitarianism some positive social recognition. His insistence upon diversity and openness was limited to an Anglican Christian setting. He presented a double bind that permanently inhibited growth: If he followed ethical ideals and his conscience, the institution would suffer; if he did not, then the institution was corrupt. Even University College London, founded as a school for non-Anglicans in 1828, and with which Manchester College (now Harris Manchester College) was affiliated from 1854, was affected. Early on, the non-conformist view that all were welcome no matter what their religious views was dominant. But by 1866, the more radical understanding of non-sectarianism that Martineau championed was in place. Leaders could not have a specific religious identity. Instead of creating freedom, this requirement prevented Unitarian clergy from being professors.

William Gaskell (1805–1884), minister in Birmingham for over fifty years, provides a contrast to Martineau. Gaskell came from a Unitarian family with multiple lines of connections to other Unitarian families. His father taught theology at Warrington Academy, the precursor to Manchester College, where Gaskell himself became a Professor of Literature. But when the College moved to London and emphasized the non-sectarian view of Martineau, Gaskell remained in Manchester. He helped form the Home Missionary Board and, with John Relly Beard (1800–1876), developed the Unitarian College, Manchester, claiming both the name and the social purpose of the faith, with no division among worship, education, and reform. The Unitarian College, Manchester was devoted to serving those who traditionally had no access to education: women and mill workers, many of them displaced crofters sent from Wales to work in the mills. Gaskell's sermons were short and practical: he served the people. But Martineau was affiliated with a university that could grant degrees. The non-conformists had never been allowed to achieve this status; thus, Martineau symbolized a new possibility for Unitarians – the possibility of acceptance.

The Unitarians in Great Britain had long been defined by those who persecuted them, and by what they failed to believe in rather than the truths they celebrated. Not even one generation had been raised within a legally existing institutionalized faith when the Industrial Revolution completely changed the social order and created an atmosphere in which Unitarians were disproportionately influential.[11] Yet social influence due to business success or Parliamentary position did not necessarily lead to a coherent internal identity. In fact, Unitarians were uniquely positioned to

[11] D.W. Bebbington, "Unitarian MPs in the 19th century," *Transactions of the Unitarian Historical Society*, Vol. 24, No. 3 (April 2009), pp. 153–175, plus supplement.

be further divided by the development of big cities with economies based in production. Although the industrialized economy led to a significant rise in stature and power, the ideals of the religion also allied Unitarians with the poor, the disenfranchised, and the exploited workers who staffed the mills and plants. Those committed to a Unitarian faith saw the owners as the lords who controlled the land. Their allegiance was with those who toiled in a landscape that had been given to all. Broad-church enthusiasts saw instead that as lords, or captains of industry, individuals with Unitarian theologies had a chance to improve society. It was an opportunity for acceptance and inclusion, eliminating the need to claim an identity separate from the rest of the Anglican Communion.

From the beginning, institutionalized Unitarianism walked a precarious line of claiming legitimacy, yet fearing the constraints of any affiliations. The British and Foreign Association began as one that accepted membership from both individuals and congregations, but such a small minority of congregations ever joined that, in 1867,[12] the category was abolished, and membership was restricted to individuals. About 100 congregations developed over the nineteenth century, and there was optimism for the future. But the theological and organizational issues that plagued the Unitarians from the beginning continued to impede their progress, and the twentieth century was devastating. World War I was demoralizing, particularly for progressives who had held a positive view of human nature; and then, during the reorganization efforts in 1928, the four clergy leaders who were supposed to write the Unitarian vision statement could not agree. Although the number of congregations has decreased relatively slowly, the membership loss has been dramatic. When buildings were lost or damaged due to bombs in World War II, neither funds nor people existed to rebuild them all. In 1945, there were 25,000 Unitarians in Great Britain. In 1995, there were 7,000;[13] the General Assembly figure for 2009 states 5,000. At the end of the twentieth century, the Council of Churches denied the Unitarians both associate membership and observer status. Perhaps this external judgment on Unitarians in England will rally the faithful together; joining to free themselves from external oppressors as they did in the beginning, so that the principal values embraced by Unitarians can be embodied, and visible to others.

[12] Charles Howe, *For Faith and Freedom*, (Boston, MA: Skinner House, 1997), p. 160.
[13] Howe, *For Faith*, p. 180.

CHAPTER 4

From revelation to reason
America 1630–1833

The winding pathway from the belief in total human depravity that characterized Calvinism to the free will espoused by the Unitarians can be found
in developments within Puritan faith and culture. While the first settlers
in America after 1630 ascribed to a faith in salvation by grace, these immigrants also included opportunistic capitalists who wanted to prove their
own worth by succeeding in business. Many of those who found the secular
life more appealing decided that a liberal faith placing fewer theological
demands upon them was more congenial to this world rather than the
next. Edward Johnson, a wealthy Puritan, reported, "our maritime towns
began to increase roundly." The prosperity of this "place of Merchandize"
was a sign that God favored them, and this made worldliness more and
more appealing.[1]

The context for the development of a frugal, industrious, and ultimately
successful life was within the confines of the local community where each
Puritan church was gathered. A Puritan desire for more local and simple
forms of worship was stated by Cotton Mather: "we would worship God
without that *Episcopacy*, that *common-prayer*, and those unwarrantable
ceremonies, with which the *land of our fore fathers sepulchres* has been
defiled; we came because we would have our posterity settled under the pure
dispensations of the gospel, defended *by rulers that should be of ourselves*."[2]
The Puritans agreed that individual churches had the "power to choose their
officers and ministers." Self-rule, an aspect of Puritan life that fomented the
growth of a Unitarian tradition, was codified in the Cambridge Platform
of 1648 as "a scriptural model of church government."[3]

---

[1] Edward Johnson, "Wonder-working Providence of Sions Saviour in New-England," *Puritans in the
New World, A Critical Anthology*, ed. David D. Hall (Princeton, NJ and Oxford, England: Princeton
University Press, 2004), pp. 334–335.
[2] Cotton Mather, *Magnalia Christi Americana: Or, The Ecclesiastical History of New-England* (Hartford,
CT: Silas Andrus and Son, 1855), pp. 240–241.
[3] Peter Hughes, ed., *The Cambridge Platform: Contemporary Reader's Edition* (Boston, MA: Skinner
House Books, 2008), pp. 26, 29.

Even more central to each congregation than political autonomy was a written covenant. The covenants stated that the people were in a continuing, supportive relationship with God and each other, and so their churches were not founded upon church traditions, but upon the mutual consent of the people. The covenants articulated the congregation's purpose, which was centered upon the relationships among the people, rather than upon a creed. The sentiment of these covenants was expressed by John Winthrop in the sermon he gave on board the ship *Arbella* before the passengers arrived in the New World: "the onely way to avoyde shipwreck is . . . [to] be knitt together in this worke as one man."[4]

After the first generation of immigrants, membership standards became a significant issue, as there were fewer and fewer conversions. Increasing the number of people who were welcome under the covenant became an option, when the Half-Way Covenant was adopted at a synod in 1662. Under this system, the unconverted could bring their children to be baptized. They affirmed the covenant of the church, and became half-way members who could not take communion or vote in church affairs. While the purpose was to stem the tide of declension, the effect was a liberalizing tendency to broaden church membership, sometimes bringing in people as full communicant members who had not experienced conversion.[5]

The new standards were taken to the extreme with the founding of Boston's Brattle Street Church in 1698, a group that would eventually be called "the most respectable body of heretics in the new world." In addition to the Half-Way Covenant, they also broadened voting privileges in the selection of ministers so that all who paid for the support of the church could now vote, not just church members. New members were admitted to the church without the need to publicly express their experience of grace.[6] The founding of Brattle Street signaled a continuing decline in piety that exploded in the Great Awakening.

The Great Awakening of the 1740s became a watershed event for the Standing Order of Congregational Churches of Massachusetts. Many settled Congregational ministers felt itinerant preaching and its passionate style signaled a breakdown of the social and religious order that marked the established church, from which there had never been any legal dissent. The Old Light (anti-revival) and New Light (pro-revival) schools

---

[4] Perry Miller and Thomas H. Johnson, eds., *The Puritans: A Sourcebook of Their Writings*, Vol. 1 (New York: Harper and Row, Publishers, 1938), p. 198.

[5] Edwin Scott Gausted, *The Great Awakening in New England* (Chicago, IL: Quadrangle, 1968), pp. 9–12.

[6] *The Manifesto Church: Records of the Church in Brattle Square, Boston, 1699–1872* (Cambridge University Press, 1902), p. ix; Edwin J. Lewis, Jr., "The Unitarian Churches of Boston in 1860," *The Proceedings of the Unitarian Historical Society* (Boston, MA: Beacon Press, 1928), Vol. I, Part II, p. 7.

of thought split the Congregational clergy into two parties. In his major attack against the revival, *Seasonable Thoughts on the State of Religion in New England*, Charles Chauncy (1705–1787) declared that there was a "dangerous Tendency" in these evangelical methods. He fumed that the revivalists rejected reason and judgment in favor of passions that produced "*Shriekings* and *Screamings*."[7]

A permanent bias against revivalism from some of the Old Light faction became a catalyst for the future growth of the liberal or Arminian position, which took its name from a Dutch theologian, Jacob Arminius, who believed salvation was something God offered, but that each person had to make the choice whether or not to accept the offer. Salvation for the Arminians consisted of a balance of faith and works.

During the remaining years of the eighteenth century, the Old Light and New Light parties began to develop distinct and contradictory theological systems. Unlike their European counterparts, the issue of the Trinity was not primary. Doctrines about human nature came under attack first. In response to the Calvinist belief in moral determinism, the early liberals began to argue that sin could be gradually overcome with the assistance of God, and that sin was a personal matter rather than a permanent condition of the entire human race. When John Bass in Ashford, Connecticut was asked, "Don't you think that a Child brings Sin enough into the World with it to damn it forever?," he defiantly answered No, and soon lost his pulpit.[8] The Arminians said humans are free moral agents who can choose the good solely as a result of training and experience. Ebenezer Gay (1696–1787), who served in Hingham, Massachusetts for seventy years, has been referred to as the father of Unitarianism in America. In his long life he witnessed the transition from Calvinism to "Natural Religion as Distinguished from Revealed." He denounced the revival, and also affirmed the importance of human capabilities in knowing how to make good ethical choices: "Man is not merely so much lumpish Matter, or a *mechanical* Engine, that moves only by the Direction of an impelling Force," but instead has a special natural endowment which gives him the "Power of Self-determination, or Freedom of Choice."[9]

These initial tendencies to reform Calvinism all pointed towards a redefinition of God. God's benevolence was seen in the works of creation, and

[7] Charles Chauncy, *Seasonable Thoughts on the State of Religion in New-England, a Treatise in Five Parts* (Boston, MA: Rogers and Fowle, 1743), Part I, pp. 76–77.

[8] Conrad Wright, *The Beginnings of Unitarianism in America* (Boston, MA: Starr King Press, 1955), p. 73.

[9] Sidney E. Ahlstrom and Jonathan S. Carey, eds., *An American Reformation: A Documentary History of Unitarian Christianity* (Middletown, CT: Wesleyan University Press, 1985), p. 49.

this meant an intended happiness for His creatures. John Tucker of New-bury, Massachusetts said that the obedience God requires of us is not that of slaves to a master, but rather "it must be *free*, – a matter of choice." Other liberal doctrinal affirmations included anti-Trinitarianism. The lib-erals mostly embraced an Arian position that Jesus, while subordinate to God, was nevertheless more than a mere man. Many years later, Francis Parkman wrote that all the liberals in greater Boston held "high and exalted views of the person and mediation of Jesus Christ" . . . and would "be very unwilling to be confounded with the followers of Dr. Priestley," who held a human view of Jesus.[10]

The liberal leaders in the eighteenth century were Chauncy, Gay, and Jonathan Mayhew (1720–1766), all of whom opposed the revival. Chauncy, minister of the First Church, Boston believed that "an enlightened Mind, not raised Affections ought always to be the Guide of those who call themselves Men." The liberals shunned a theological style that reflected an emotional conversion in favor of a slow, educational process that was devoted to the conduct of life.[11] While the Great Awakening was symp-tomatic of a radical division between those who wanted to re-emphasize the doctrines of Calvin, and those who wanted to subvert them, the leaders of both camps were responding to intellectual challenges fomented by the Enlightenment. The two sides struggled with how to appropriate natural religion. Those who wished to remake Christian theology to emphasize human abilities said that the revelation of God in scripture needed to be balanced by human reason, discerning the truth from personal experience and observation.

The most rational of all the liberals were the Deists, many of whom were the founders of the American nation. Deism was a philosophical position for individuals, not an organized movement, and its adherents mostly remained members of their traditional family churches. Nevertheless, they affirmed radical religious truths that rejected all manner of Christian rev-elation, and emphasized human sensual experience as the primary way to understand natural laws and nature's God.

The most renowned Deist was Thomas Jefferson (1743–1826). The heart of religion for Jefferson was not Christian dogma, but ethics: "It is in our lives and not our words that our religion must be read."[12] His most

---

[10] Wright, *Beginnings of Unitarianism*, pp. 177, 217.
[11] Gausted, *The Great Awakening*, p. 99; Jonathan Mayhew, *Seven Sermons* (Boston, MA: Rogers and Fowle, 1749), Sermon II, pp. 34, 38.
[12] Thomas Jefferson, *The Jefferson Bible: The Life and Morals of Jesus of Nazareth*, introduced by F. Forrester Church (Boston, MA: Beacon Press, 1989), p. viii.

comprehensive attempt to articulate his faith came with what was later known as *The Jefferson Bible*. When he excised all of the miracles from the Christian scriptures with a pair of scissors, Jefferson demonstrated his belief that it was only through their daily lives and works that humankind should be judged. While Jefferson once forecast that Unitarianism would "become the general religion of the United States,"[13] because its doctrine of the one God was the purest form of Christianity, and its "solidity" was restored and vindicated by the advocacy of "freedom of religious opinion" in the new nation, he was never able to join an organized congregation. Much of what Jefferson felt about religious beliefs he learned from "the great apostle," Joseph Priestley (1733–1804).

While Jefferson's Deism was an extreme understanding of Enlightenment rationalism, other liberal viewpoints embraced more distinctly Christian elements. The Unitarianism that was expressed most fully in the mid-Atlantic states was the transplanted English Socinianism, embodied by Priestley and his followers. Most recent historiography has downplayed Priestley's influence on American Unitarianism, and has promulgated a parochial view that Unitarianism in America was indigenous to the New World and grew out of Puritanism in New England. While this was the dominant expression of the faith, the English influence is far more significant than is generally recognized. The first attempts at evangelizing America occurred when William Hazlitt (1737–1820), a British Unitarian, arrived as an itinerant preacher in 1783. Hazlitt was surprised to find that Unitarianism was not embraced in New England. This may be attributed to its radical reputation, which made the liberals in New England reluctant to claim the Unitarian name, preferring to be called liberal Christians. Hazlitt found they were "already Arians . . . yet generally afraid to avow their sentiments."[14]

The most enduring contribution for Hazlitt came with his influence upon James Freeman (1759–1835). After Freeman became a reader at King's Chapel, Boston in 1782, he began to have reservations about the Trinity, and three years later the congregation voted to forego references to it in their liturgy. Hazlitt showed Freeman the prayer book that was used in Theophilus Lindsey's congregation in London, and it was used as the guide in preparing the King's Chapel prayer book. Thereafter,

[13] Adrienne Koch and William Peden, eds., *The Life and Selected Writings of Thomas Jefferson* (New York: Modern Library, 1944), pp. 703–704.

[14] J. D. Bowers, *Joseph Priestley and English Unitarianism in America* (Philadelphia, PA: Pennsylvania State University Press, 2007), p. 50.

the oldest Episcopal Church in New England became the first Unitarian church in America. Freeman said that, because of Hazlitt, "there are now many churches in which the worship is strictly Unitarian." But Hazlitt felt as though his mission was a failure and he returned to England in 1787.[15]

Joseph Priestley arrived in America in 1794, hoping to follow "my still favourite pursuit, the propagation of Unitarianism."[16] In Philadelphia he found a city with a strong scientific community, and much more religious diversity than in New England. As soon as he arrived, Priestley began preaching Unitarianism to all willing listeners. His first sermon, *A General View of the Arguments for the Unity of God*, expressed the "place and value" of "the proper Unitarian doctrine." Subsequent sermons and publications became the catalyst for the formation of the First Unitarian Society of Philadelphia in 1796. Priestley permanently settled on the frontier in Northumberland, Pennsylvania, where he founded a small society. A painful rebuff came from the Arians in New England, who at first were unwilling to accept the Unitarian name due to its radical reputation. They disavowed Priestley's influence when William Ellery Channing (1780–1842) wrote, "I have little or no interest in Unitarianism as a sect." And "With Dr. Priestley," Channing continued, "I have less sympathy than with many of the 'Orthodox.'" Channing characterized himself as an "independent Christian," noting "I am little of a Unitarian," and "have little sympathy with the system of Priestley and Belsham."[17]

It is significant that several English Unitarian immigrants exerted influence in the extension of Unitarianism. James Kay, a disciple of Priestley, tried valiantly to spread the liberal message by itinerant preaching in twenty-four towns in Pennsylvania, but the American Unitarian Association was indifferent to this evangelism and preferred to support one settled ministry in Harrisburg. Kay influenced Robert Little, an Englishman who became the first Unitarian minister in Washington, DC; a congregation that included politicians John Quincy Adams and John C. Calhoun among its founders. John Campbell, who also came to America from England, became the first Unitarian minister in Pittsburgh. Towards the end of his life, Kay's isolation in Pennsylvania was alleviated by Harm Jan Huidekoper (1776–1854), a Campbell convert who was instrumental in founding first a church

---

[15] Bowers, *Joseph Priestley*, p. 51.   [16] Bowers, ibid. p. 66.
[17] William Henry Channing, *The Life of William Ellery Channing, D.D.* (Boston, MA: American Unitarian Association, 1882), p. 427.

in Meadville in the 1820s and then, in 1844, the Meadville Seminary, which became a training ground for clergy who would settle on the "frontiers" of Unitarianism.

While most of the English Unitarians felt that Boston Unitarians turned their backs on them because of the radical nature of their theology, the tune changed when the foundations of liberal Christianity were shaken to the core by a more radical movement, Transcendentalism. In the 1830s, when Henry Ware, Jr. (1794–1843) feared Unitarianism might abandon its Christian roots, he declared that they must "do something toward vindicating the character of an injured man."[18] Ware had come to feel that Priestley should be considered the founder of Unitarianism in America. The radical and evangelical trans-Atlantic spirit that Priestley infused into American Unitarianism resurfaced later in the westward expansion of the faith.

After the Great Awakening, certain Congregational clergy, especially those educated at Harvard College, began to gravitate towards liberal theological doctrines that were Arminian and Arian. This split among the ranks began to happen in isolated places when a new minister was called into service, or a conflict needed to be settled. An early example of this occurred with the settlement of Aaron Bancroft (1755–1839) in Worcester, Massachusetts. When Bancroft came to Worcester to try out his preaching skills, a majority of church members rejected him. Then, many of the prominent members decided to form a separate parish and call Bancroft to its ministry. Once Bancroft was settled in Worcester in 1786, he found that none of the neighboring clergy would exchange with him, and this remained true for the first seven years of his ministry. Most of the conservative Congregationalists felt the liberals were preaching heresy, and refused to exchange. Arminians were more willing to exchange pulpits because they wanted people to experience a variety of viewpoints and viewed Christianity in ethical rather than strictly doctrinal terms.

Shortly after Bancroft was installed, the local Worcester Association of clergy dissolved because its members refused to fraternize with a reputed Arminian. At the end of fifty years of service, Bancroft described how he was, "talked against, preached against, denounced and shunned," when he started his ministry.[19] Historian Conrad Wright divides the "Unitarian

---

[18] Bowers, *Joseph Priestley*, p. 190.
[19] Frederick Lewis Weis, *A Short History of the Worcester Conference and of the Worcester Association* (Worceste, MA: Worcester Conference, 1947), p. 14; Samuel Atkins Eliot, *Heralds of a Liberal Faith* (Boston, MA: American Unitarian Association, 1910), Vol. 3, p. 22.

controversy" into three ten-year segments, with each period having its own decided emphasis. The first ten years, 1805–1815, focused on what Channing later called "the system of exclusion and denunciation in religion."[20] The three ways in which the division of liberal and orthodox was made manifest were refusals to exchange pulpits, exclusion from Christian fellowship, and boycotting of ecclesiastical councils, all of which Bancroft experienced early in his ministry. These councils, whether for ordination examinations or to settle conflicts, were no longer unbiased, but were increasingly composed of ministers and parishioners who followed a particular theological position, and invitations were extended on a partisan basis.

The "capture" of Harvard by the liberals in 1805, occurring with the election of Henry Ware (1764–1845) to the position of Hollis Professor of Divinity, has usually been characterized as the precipitating event to the Unitarian controversy. A vacancy existed in the Professorship, but President Willard had delayed the discussion of a successor because Ware's candidacy made him proclaim, "he would sooner cut off his hand, than lift it up for an Arminian professor." Then Willard died, too. Jedediah Morse called Ware's doctrinal views into question, stating that he did not possess "sound and orthodox principles."[21] Nevertheless, Ware, who had been minister in Hingham, Massachusetts for seventeen years, was elected to the Hollis Chair in February 1805. When a liberal was elected president of the college the following year, Morse interpreted it as a revolution in the affairs of the college and determined that a new school must be established to train clergy who were sound in the Calvinist faith. Andover Seminary was established in 1807.

The second ten-year period (1815–1825) of the controversy was dominated by theological wrangling. The publication of a pamphlet called *American Unitarianism*, by Jedediah Morse, inaugurated the struggle. The pamphlet reproduced a chapter of a biography of Theophilus Lindsey written by Thomas Belsham, two luminaries in the emergence of British Unitarianism. This chapter described the expansion of liberalism in New England, but it appeared as though the theological orientation was the same as the more radical Socinians. When the pamphlet was reviewed in the *Panoplist*, Jeremiah Everts reported that there had been a "defection from those doctrines of the Bible," and this "defection had proceeded in the downward

---

[20] Conrad Wright, "Institutional Reconstruction in the Unitarian Controversy", in Conrad Edick Wright, ed. *American Unitarianism, 1805–1865* (Boston, MA: Massachusetts Historical Society and Northeastern University Press, 1989), p. 3.
[21] Wright, "Institutional Reconstruction," pp. 3, 13.

course to the lowest degrees of Socinianism, and to the very borders of open infidelity."[22]

The high point of this second decade occurred on May 5, 1819, when William Ellery Channing delivered "Unitarian Christianity" at the newly formed Unitarian church in Baltimore, Maryland. Channing, a native of Newport, Rhode Island, and the minister of the Federal Street Church in Boston, had become the leading liberal voice. This address was an acknowledged manifesto of the liberal Christians in New England to both claim the Unitarian name, and also to signal that they were planning to spread their particular gospel message outside the confines of greater Boston. Channing began by defining how liberals interpret scripture: "Our leading principle in interpreting scripture is this, that the Bible is a book written for men, in the language of men, and that its meaning is to be sought in the same manner as that of other books."[23]

Channing elucidated the distinguishing marks of Unitarianism by protesting against "the irrational and unscriptural doctrine of the Trinity," and declaring his allegiance to the unity of God. He understood God as a being of moral perfection, who created "this world as a place of education" and human beings for "good and holy purposes." This idea was embodied in "self-culture," a belief in ever-expanding abilities for self-improvement. Finally, Channing protested how other Christians have made humans seem impotent, as "they subvert our responsibility," and "make men machines."

Feeling the sting of being excluded from the broader Christian fellowship that once existed, Channing suggested that intolerance is the most significant way in which Christians have departed from their faith. "We read with astonishment and horror, the history of the church; and sometimes when we look back on the fires of persecution, and on the zeal of Christians, in building up walls of separation, and in giving up one another to perdition, we feel as if were reading the records of an infernal, rather than a heavenly kingdom." After years of refusing to accept the Unitarian name, this sermon finally gave the liberals a platform to stand upon. Following its publication, the sermon became the second most widely circulated pamphlet ever, trailing only Thomas Paine's *Common Sense* in sales.[24]

In the early years of the Unitarian controversy, Joseph Stevens Buckminster (1784–1812) was the rising star of the liberals. A brilliant scholar, he graduated from Harvard at 16, and became minister at the Brattle Street

---

[22] David B. Parke, ed., *The Epic of Unitarianism* (Boston, MA: Beacon Press, 1957), pp. 85–86.

[23] William Ellery Channing, *The Works of William Ellery Channing, D.D.* (Boston, MA: American Unitarian Association, 1875), pp. 367–368.

[24] Channing, *Works*, pp. 371, 376, 377, 382–383.

Church in Boston before he turned 21. His major contribution to the movement came in his knowledge and dissemination of the new German biblical criticism in America. Unfortunately, Buckminster succumbed to a fatal attack brought on by epilepsy, and he was dead at the age of 28.

Buckminster also best exemplified the social and economic elitism that has sometimes been associated with what would later be called the Boston Brahmin culture, a name derived from the Hindu caste system which labeled the community leaders as Brahmins, or those closest to the one true God (Brahma). In India, the Brahmins were the caste from which the Brahmo Samaj drew most of its members; however, the Brahmo Samaj represented a tiny fraction of the Hindu upper caste. In Boston, families of British Protestant origin created an East Coast establishment that discreetly but effectively dominated academia, trade, politics, and the arts. This group of elite community leaders functioned as an enlightened aristocracy, and became associated with the "Boston Religion" of Unitarianism. The liberal ministers of greater Boston purposefully moved away from pietism and transformed religious expression into an "indigenous high culture." This became a religious substitute as it sought to refine the person and elevate the mind. In 1862, *The Christian Examiner* quoted a minister who said that it was necessary for ministers to draw upon all kinds of literature to create refined essays because "the most intelligent and earnest men and women will go to literature instead of to church for inspiration, guidance and culture." While the dream of a literary flowering was realized, it was centered on what Ralph Waldo Emerson called "radical antitraditionalism."[25]

The second phase of the Unitarian controversy (1815–1825) has been defined as a time of theological controversy, exemplified by the Wood 'n' Ware Debate, a pamphlet war of more than 800 pages of theological opinion on the doctrine of human nature between Henry Ware and Leonard Woods, a professor at Andover Seminary. Yet, the most significant institutional event during this period was the Dedham decision. Handed down in 1820, this court case redefined the power of a parish, and gave many of the liberal congregations an opportunity to control the property in nearly one quarter of the parishes in Massachusetts. This case began when the parish (all the voters in the town) in Dedham, Massachusetts called Alvin Lamson, a young liberal, to be its minister. A majority of the church members objected. Historically, a parish would usually abide by a church

[25] Ann Douglas, *The Feminization of American Culture* (New York: Alfred A. Knopf, 1977), p. 11. See Peter S. Field, *The Crisis of the Standing Order: Cultural Intellectuals and Cultural Authority in Massachusetts, 1780–1833* (Amherst, MA: University of Massachusetts Press, 1998).

veto, but in this case they refused. The orthodox members then withdrew and took the church records, the silver and the deeds with them, and a lawsuit ensued. The Dedham decision established that even a minority of church members was a "creature of the parish," and therefore had the legal right to the property. It also gave the parish the right to call the minister. All precedent was destroyed in the case when the separate nature of the church was completely neglected. This decision had repercussions in many communities, as Trinitarians withdrew from parishes dominated by Unitarians and formed new societies, while in others the Unitarians withdrew.[26]

Building an independent ecclesiastical organization was a bitter pill for the Unitarians to swallow. They had hoped that the Standing Order of Congregational Churches of Massachusetts could remain a broad, tolerant, ethical group that was not divided by dogmatic truths, but this proved impossible. In January 1825, forty-four ministers and laypeople met to consider a plan for organization. Aaron Bancroft wanted Unitarianism to spread "slowly and silently." Some of the clergy considered the proposal "very dangerous," or were reluctant "taking any name." These divisions proved difficult to overcome, but a group of younger ministers presented a plan to the Berry Street Conference of ministers in Boston on May 25, 1825. The next day, the American Unitarian Association (AUA) was formed. While the purpose of the new association was "to diffuse the knowledge and promote the interests of pure Christianity," it was an organization that had only individual members rather than congregations, and its purpose was primarily to publish tracts as a proper means of spreading Unitarian principles. Yet the AUA acknowledged the need for ecclesiastical authority in its first report: "The circumstances of the times require a more systematic union, and a 'concentration of labors, by which interest may be awakened, confidence inspired, and efficiency produced.'"[27]

Channing, who seemed to be the logical leader for the new movement, refused the presidency of the AUA. Setting a benchmark for an aversion to centralized power that has always characterized Unitarianism, Channing feared associations because they "injure free action," and especially because "they accumulate power in a few hands."[28] Divisions had occurred and doctrinal differences were debated, and finally, the Unitarians concluded

[26] Conrad Wright, *The Unitarian Controversy* (Boston, MA: Skinner House Books, 1994), pp. 111–135.
[27] Parke, *Epic of Unitarianism*, pp. 101–102, 104; American Unitarian Association. First Annual Report of the Executive Committee of the American Unitarian Association (Boston, MA: Isaac R. Butts and Co., 1826), p. 14.
[28] Channing, *Works*, pp. 148–149.

"that we are a community by ourselves." In his *Sober Thoughts on the State of the Times* (1835), Henry Ware, Jr. remarked: "It is a crisis of unspeakable interest to us." He further wondered what would be "the character and power of those institutions," and the "nature" of the faith, and concluded that he was "oppressed" by the "magnitude" of this question. This was a particularly heavy burden on Ware as he was engaged in training future ministers at Harvard, a position to which he brought renown for pastoral skills, and a personal piety that balanced the rational faith with some emotional fervor.

Disestablishment has been called the most important event in Unitarian history. After this, the freedom to not affiliate with any church became a viable option, and people left in droves. Support by compulsory taxation may have fooled the Unitarians into believing they were leading a large, growing movement. Ware said people attached themselves to Unitarianism because they "dislike Calvinism, but like nothing else." A characteristic of the liberal faith has been the rejection of traditional theological formulations, making it difficult to articulate a positive faith: "They are anti-Calvinists, anti-orthodox, anti-zealots, anti-everything severe and urgent in religion."[29] While Baptists, Universalists and others were struggling to define their faiths and reach out to new converts as they battled the establishment, their Unitarian counterparts were enjoying the fruits of a steady stream of tax-paying parishioners, and felt no urgency to be evangelical.

Since Puritan times, most Congregationalists of both Unitarian and Trinitarian stripes maintained that there was a direct relationship between religious instruction and a moral civic order. Universalists, like the Baptists before them, believed that the support of religion was not a civic duty, but a spiritual obligation. Since many of the converts to Universalism came from Baptist backgrounds, there was already an inbred hostility toward an ecclesiastical establishment that wanted to coerce payments, threaten imprisonment or seize property. There was supreme irony that the Unitarians, who joined the Universalists in calling for freedom of thought and conscience, ended up "being the only party in favor of *compelling people by law to support religion.*"[30]

Thomas Whittemore (1800–1861), minister, historian, businessman and politician, became the Universalist leader in the fight to ratify the Eleventh

---

[29] Richard Eddy Sykes, "Massachusetts Unitarianism and Social Change: A Religious Social System in Transition, 1780–1870" (Ann Arbor, MI: University Microfilms, 1968), p. 173; Henry Ware, Jr., *Sober Thoughts on the State of the Times* (Boston, MA: Isaac R. Butts, 1835), pp. 10, 13–14.

[30] William G. McLoughlin, *New England Dissent, 1630–1833: The Baptists and the Separation of Church and State*, Vol. 2 (Cambridge, MA: Harvard University Press, 1971), p. 1187.

Amendment to the Massachusetts Constitution. Whittemore not only organized the Universalist clergy against the establishment, but also edited the *Universalist Trumpet*, a newspaper that railed constantly against the "tyrannical" system. As a state representative, Whittemore led the attack in the Legislature: "Religion to do any man good must operate in his heart . . . and a mere artificial support can never do."[31] In November 1833, a constitutional amendment to end compulsory religious taxes received overwhelming support from the voting public.

This fight against the establishment began with John Murray (1741–1815), an Englishman, who is often called the father of Universalism in America. Yet he was one of four significant progenitors of Universalism. Murray was a leader in the Methodist Church when he first encountered Universalism while visiting a woman from his church who had been converted to the new heresy. Murray decided to read James Relly's pamphlet, *Union*. Eventually, this led to an awareness that "*if Christ died for all men, then assuredly all men must be saved*."[32] Murray's faith was sorely tested when first his infant son and then his wife, Eliza, died within the same year. The expenses he incurred in trying to care for them led to his incarceration in debtors' prison. After he was released, he vowed to begin a new life in America.

It was the landing of his sailing vessel in 1770, and its unanticipated resting place on a sandbar off the coast of southern New Jersey, which began his journey toward Universalist leadership. Once on dry land, Murray met a man named Thomas Potter, who told him, "I knew that God, who put it into my heart to build a house for his worship, would send a servant of His own to proclaim His own gospel." Then Potter tried to convince Murray that he was the man God sent to fill the pulpit. This was not what Murray had in mind, but they finally struck an agreement. They decided that if the ship remained stuck on the sandbar, then it would be a sign from God that Murray was meant to preach there. If the ship became free, then Murray would proceed on his journey. When the prevailing winds did not change, and the ship remained stuck after two days, the Sabbath arrived and Murray agreed that God had brought him "into this new world to make known unto this people the grace and the blessing of the new covenant."[33]

During the next several years, Murray preached up and down the East Coast. Finally, in 1774, he arrived in Gloucester, Massachusetts, where a group had already been converted, as "The writings of Mr. Relly were not

---

[31] McLoughlin, *New England Dissent*, pp. 1231–1236.
[32] John Murray, *The Life of John Murray*, ed. L.S. Everett (Boston, MA: A. Tompkins, 1844, eighth edition), p. 111.
[33] Murray, *Life*, p. 144.

only in their *hands*, but in their *hearts*." Murray's preaching of "damnable doctrines" was attacked in the local paper. Not long thereafter, an evening lecture provoked many people to throw stones through the windows. One large stone just missed hitting Murray, provoking him to comment that, "This argument is solid and weighty, but it is neither rational nor convincing."[34] Eventually, a vote was "surreptitiously obtained" at a town meeting that Murray should "depart from the borders of Gloucester."

Yet, Murray's small band was not deterred, and on January 1, 1779 a group of sixty-one people formed the Independent Christian Church in Gloucester. The town taxed them for the support of the parish, and eventually some goods were seized and sold at auction. Murray was persuaded to put his name on a lawsuit to recover the property, so that all dissenting religious groups "were known in law," and that their teachers were considered legitimate teachers of "piety, morality and religion." This law suit was finally settled in 1786. The Universalists won the right to have their tax dollars support the Universalist Church. This lawsuit gave other dissenting groups the same right – to direct any taxes to their chosen institutions, rather than the established church.[35]

One of the ardent followers of James Relly's teachings was Judith Sargent Stevens. She struck up a friendship with Murray and eventually, after she was widowed, they were married in 1788. Stevens was an early advocate of women's rights and education, and she joined her future husband in evangelizing for Universalism. The Murrays left Gloucester in 1793 to settle at the First Universalist Church in Boston, where John Murray remained until his death in 1815.

Murray was also active in the earliest attempts to organize Universalist churches. A group in Oxford, Massachusetts issued invitations to New England Universalist congregations in 1785 to be "cemented in one body . . . bound by the ties of love to assist each other." Yet these meetings did not convene every year, so the founding of the New England Convention in 1793 is considered the true, uninterrupted institutional founding date. Murray also attended a Philadelphia Convention in 1790, along with delegates from Pennsylvania, New Jersey and Virginia. This group adopted both "Articles of Faith" and a "Plan of Church Government," which proved to be models for later documents, including the Winchester Profession of Faith. The convention also adopted a resolution against slavery, composed

[34] Murray, ibid., pp. 203, 205, 209, 212.
[35] Thomas Whittemore, *The Modern History of Universalism. From the Era of the Reformation to the Present Time* (Boston, MA: Thomas Whittemore, 1830), pp. 352–357.

by patriot and Universalist, Benjamin Rush (1745–1813). It stated that holding slaves was "inconsistent with the union of the human race in a common Saviour."[36]

The convention meeting in Philadelphia was held in a meetinghouse bought for a society of Universal Baptists led by Elhanan Winchester (1751–1797). Originally from Massachusetts, he became a Baptist itinerant preacher, settling in Welsh Neck, South Carolina in 1775. In a successful revival in 1779, he not only brought in nearly 150 white members to the church, but also converted 100 black slaves. No preacher had ever openly shared the Gospel with slaves, but Winchester said that while professing Christians might have prejudiced the slaves against religious instruction, "they had no prejudice against me on this score, as I never had any thing to do with slavery, but on the contrary condemned it; and this being generally known . . . they shewed a disposition to attend my ministry." After this, Winchester ministered to both a white church and a black church.[37] It was at about this time that Winchester read Paul Siegvolk's *The Everlasting Gospel*, a Universalist import from Europe. After settling in Philadelphia, Winchester became aware of German Baptists, or Dunkers, in Pennsylvania and adjacent states who believed in the "doctrine of the Universal Restoration." Winchester began to waver, and soon came to believe that as a result of God's benevolence, the consequence for mortals is "perfect and universal salvation."[38] A new Society of Universal Baptists was formed in Philadelphia from 100 members who were ex-communicated from the Baptist Church.

Winchester became friendly with George deBenneville (1703–1793), a physician, and visited him frequently. For several years they conducted missionary tours together in Pennsylvania and Virginia. Winchester called him a "humble, pious, loving man," and was later responsible for publishing deBenneville's *The Life and Trance of Dr. George deBenneville.*[39] Winchester also spent six years in England preaching and working with William Vidler to transform the General Baptist Assembly, forming many new, inclusive Baptist–Universalist congregations that eventually joined with the Unitarians.

[36] Russell E. Miller, *The Larger Hope, The First Century of the Universalist Church in America, 1770–1870* (Boston, MA: Unitarian Universalist Association, 1979), pp. 70–71, 76–79, 80–81, 579.

[37] Edwin Martin Stone, *Biography of Rev. Elhanan Winchester* (Boston, MA: H. B. Brewster, 1836), pp. 26–27.

[38] Elhanan Winchester, *The Universal Restoration: Exhibited in Four Dialogues Between a Minister and His Friend* (Philadelphia, PA: Gihon, Fairchild & Co., 1844), pp. 3, 12.

[39] George deBenneville, *The Life and Trance of Dr. George deBenneville, The Annual Journal of the Universalist Historical Society,* Vol. 2 (1960–61), p. 73.

George deBenneville was Universalism's earliest preacher in America. As an adult, deBenneville heard a voice telling him to "preach the gospel in France," but this was a difficult decision to heed, "fearing persecution." This fear proved valid when deBenneville was thrown in prison. While his cellmate was hanged, deBenneville escaped with his life thanks to a reprieve from Louis XV. After that, he preached in many places, especially in Germany, where he was exposed to several radical pietists, including Johann Conrad Beissel, who later emigrated to American and founded the Ephrata community in Pennsylvania. Near the end of his sojourn in Germany, deBenneville became seriously ill, and experienced an ecstatic vision of the truthfulness of "the restoration of all the human species without exception." A messenger told him that he must return to his "earthly tabernacle to publish and proclaim" a "universal gospel."[40] Once he settled in America, deBenneville traveled with the Ephrata missionaries, including trips to the coast of New Jersey, where he may have met Thomas Potter. In his medical practice, deBenneville began to use Native American herbal remedies. His friendliness with the tribes reflected his willingness to facilitate a religious dialogue with them. While deBenneville never founded any congregations, he helped spread the Universalist gospel in many mid-Atlantic locations, and also proved an inspiration to others. His sharing of Radical Reformation and pietistic views from Europe in America indicates how cross-cultural and international the early Universalist faith was.

When Universalism was developing in the late eighteenth and early nineteenth centuries, the greatest force behind its expansion was Hosea Ballou (1771–1852). His father, a native of Rhode Island, had moved the family to the backwoods of New Hampshire, and Ballou was raised Baptist, the son of a "pious and devout preacher." Not long after he was converted to Universalism in 1789, Ballou admitted to his father one day that he was reading a Universalist book. His father then observed the boy hiding it in the woodpile, and he went to retrieve it that he might destroy it, only to discover that this Universalist book was the Bible. Early in his career, Ballou closely followed the Calvinism of John Murray, but this quickly changed. In a letter to Thomas Whittemore in 1795, he wrote: "I had preached but a short time before my mind was entirely freed from all the perplexities of the doctrine of the Trinity, and the common notion of the atonement."[41]

The preacher with the most profound impact on Ballou was Caleb Rich (1750–1821). Rich's rebellion from orthodoxy began when he founded

---

[40] deBenneville, *Life and Trance*, pp. 74–83.
[41] Maturin M. Ballou, *Biography of Rev. Hosea Ballou* (Boston, MA: Abel Tompkins, 1852), pp. 23, 36, 42; Whittemore, *Modern History*, pp. 437–438.

a "new religious society" in Warwick, Massachusetts in 1773, and subsequently became a professed Universalist. Rich found Universalism by way of ecstatic experiences after he began to hear voices telling him that his motive for seeking salvation came from purely selfish principles. He has been called the most important indigenous Universalist in New England.[42] Ballou fell under the sway of Rich's preaching, and began a circuit-riding ministry in 1791, often preaching in houses to extended kinship groups.

Ballou's thought could be characterized as an unusual mix of pietism and rationalism. The rationalism came from reading Ethan Allen's *The Oracles of Reason* (1785). Allen, the Revolutionary War hero, taught Ballou how to use reason in the interpretation of scripture. Still, reason and reliance upon the authority of the Bible reinforced his basic belief that understanding Christianity did not require academic training. He tried to appeal directly to people in informal, homespun, and emotional ways, promulgating a populist theology. Many new sects surfaced in the revolutionary period, and most of these, including Universalism, reflected a radical evangelicalism.[43]

During his ministry in Vermont, Ballou wrote *A Treatise on Atonement* (1805). It was his greatest work, and perhaps the most influential theological book in Universalist history. Traditional Christian theology stated that God was owed an infinite debt because of human sin, and God's reconciliation to humanity can come only through Christ's death on the cross. Ballou believed, "It was not the removal of God's dissatisfaction with humanity, but a manifestation of God's love to us. It was the effect and not the cause of God's love." The *Treatise* was also the first book printed in America to state a Unitarian conception of God. Ballou wrote, "Jesus is a created, dependent being, the beginning of creation."[44] He is not sacrificed to appease God, Ballou thought, but created to bring humans to God.

Ballou's grounding in Calvinism was evident in his emphasis on the sovereignty of God: "We are nothing only as we exist in God." His theology also reflected a strong determinism where individual merit played no role in salvation. He wrote that whatever "blessings were intended by these promises, there is not the least intimation that they were promised on any conditionality... The fulfillment of them" depends "entirely upon the will and power of God." His was a classless vision of heaven, without pedigrees

[42] Stephen A. Marini, *Radical Sects of Revolutionary New England* (Cambridge, MA: Harvard University Press, 1982), pp. 72–73.

[43] Mark A. Noll, *America's God: From Jonathan Edwards to Abraham Lincoln* (New York: Oxford University Press, 2002), p. 153.

[44] Hosea Ballou, *A Treatise on Atonement*. Edited with a new introduction by Ernest Cassara, based on 1886 edition (Boston, MA: Skinner House Books, 1986), pp. 100, 111.

or genealogies, where salvation was union with others, not personal fulfillment. "The main object in all that we do is happiness," Ballou declared, and "knowing that his own happiness is connected with the happiness of his fellow-men, which induces him to do justly and to deal mercifully with all men, he is no more selfish than he ought to be."[45]

Over time, Ballou became what was called an ultra-Universalist, or one who believed that immediately upon death every human person achieved salvation, and that any punishment for sins occurred during human life. Orthodox opponents had always attacked the Universalists due to the perception that universal salvation led to immorality. They believed that the threat of hell was necessary to make people behave. Ballou served on the committee that drafted the Winchester Profession (1803), but its primary author was Walter Ferriss. Its first three paragraphs became the primary Universalist faith statement for the remainder of the nineteenth century. It affirmed the efficacy of scripture as a revelation of the final destiny of the human race, a God of love who will restore the entire human family to happiness, and that people should practice good works. A key addition to the Winchester Profession was a statement that came to be known as the "liberty clause." It allowed for latitude of belief among Universalists, so that groups could be open about the subject of punishment after death, and could adopt such Articles of Faith as fit "their particular circumstances."[46]

While the Profession left open the question of punishment after death, Ballou increasingly favored the truth of the "death and glory" position, fully adopting it by 1817 when the Restorationist controversy began in Universalist ranks. Proponents of Restorationism posited that there was a period of punishment following death before individuals were to be restored to full holiness. Much of the factional infighting took place in the burgeoning number of newspapers. Thomas Whittemore articulated the ultra-Universalist viewpoint, and became known as Ballou's "attack dog," as he defended the "ultra" position in the *Universalist Magazine*, a publication founded by Ballou in 1819. The controversy raged for more than a decade and was marked by personal insults and threats of separatism.

At first, Universalist schisms were prevented because the sect was small in numbers and grounded in friendship among the clergy, plus its very survival was constantly threatened by attacks on its legitimacy so that differences could be overlooked. This changed after the group began to experience rapid growth. While more far-flung areas of expansion like Maine and New York were less likely to experience divisions, the relative strength in

---

[45] Ballou, *Treatise*, pp. 33, 34, 199, 217.   [46] Miller, *Larger Hope*, pp. 44–49.

numbers in greater Boston meant they had more opportunity to exploit previously hidden conflicts. The Restorationist controversy featured two of the more significant Universalist clergy of this period: Abner Kneeland (1774–1844) and Adin Ballou (1803–1890). In 1826, David Pickering wrote that Kneeland and other "ultras" proved that Deism had "taken a deep root" in Universalist minds, and he was "determined to gird on the sword ... for the express purpose of hunting the enemy out of the ranks."[47] This was only the beginning of trouble for Kneeland, who later became the last person jailed for blasphemy, and served a sixty-day sentence in 1838 for articles published in his newspaper. In a statement, Kneeland wrote: "Universalists believe in a god which I do not; but believe that their god, with all his moral attributes (aside from nature itself), is nothing more than a chimera of their own imagination."[48]

The controversy reached a climax when the Southern (New England) Association feared that a new Providence Association was a separatist movement and they forced the clergy to either resign from the new group or face removal from fellowship. This action led to a permanent schism, so that when the Providence Association met in 1831, it formed a new denomination, the Massachusetts Association of Universal Restorationists, to defend their doctrine. Adin Ballou became a public spokesperson for the Restorationists that year, when he started editing a paper calling for total separation from the main body of Universalism. By then, he was serving a Unitarian parish in Mendon, Massachusetts. It was not unusual for Unitarian churches to consider Universalist candidates who were Restorationists. Later in his career, Ballou founded the Hopedale Community, a utopian society that articulated his philosophy of Christian non-resistance.[49]

Hosea Ballou's disciples maintained organizational control until mid-century, but Restorationists steadily increased in influence as their faith in free will, and the potential of punishment for sin, made them more like other mainstream faiths. Restorationism gave the Universalists a more explicit moral dimension, but also undermined Ballou's radically egalitarian faith. This institutional strife among Universalists may have helped foment

---

[47] Peter Hughes, "The Second Phase of the Restorationist Controversy: Disciplinary Crisis and Schism, 1824–1831," *The Journal of Unitarian Universalist History*, Vol. XXVIII (2001), Part 2, p. 52. See also Peter Hughes, "The Origins and First Stage of the Restorationist Controversy," *The Journal of Unitarian Universalist History*, Vol. XXVII (2000), pp. 1–57.

[48] Ernest Cassara, ed., *Universalism in America: A Documentary History* (Boston, MA: Beacon Press, 1971), p. 166.

[49] Hughes, "Second Phase," pp. 70–77.

the formal organization of State Conventions and a United States Convention in 1833.[50] Many of Ballou's disciples, including the ultra-Universalists Nathaniel Stacy and Stephen Smith, organized and spread Universalism institutionally. Smith, who preached throughout the infamous "burned-over district," reported that "the progress of Universalism in the State of New York was relatively rapid." In the course of twenty years, he said it went from one preacher to thirty, and from no congregations to upwards of seventy.[51]

Stacy was one of the most active and effective itinerant preachers, spending his career spreading the Universalist gospel in New York, Pennsylvania, and Michigan. As a young storekeeper in Dana, Massachusetts, he was tricked into preaching his first sermon one Sunday when Ballou feigned a headache.[52] Stacy went on to organize many congregations and local associations, including playing an influential role in the formation of the New York State Convention in 1825, the first Universalist ecclesiastical body of its kind.

Stacy also witnessed the remarkable preaching of Maria Cook, the first woman to excite crowds with the message of universal salvation. Universalism proved to be a gospel that invited the equality of the sexes by the very nature of its message that God loves and saves all. This message of moral and intellectual equality meant that barriers to certain professions would be breached. When Stacy heard Cook in 1811, he reported that "there was not a sermon delivered with more eloquence, with more correctness of diction, of pathos, or one listened to with more devout attention."[53] Perhaps the frontiers of faith provided more such opportunities for innovation. In Maine, Lucy and Sally Barnes, daughters of Thomas Barnes, the earliest Universalist preacher there and a disciple of Caleb Rich, established preaching and publishing firsts. Sally, whose married name was Dunn, became a preacher of some renown, "who could preach as good a sermon in ten minutes as most ministers could in an hour." Lucy was one of the earliest women to write about Universalism. In *The Female Christian* (1809), she described human relationships as a metaphor for her own relationships with divinity. Jesus became a "heavenly friend," God a loving parent, and

---

[50] Ann Lee Bressler, *The Universalist Movement in America: 1770–1870* (New York: Oxford University Press, 2001), p. 42; Hughes, "Second Phase," pp. 81–82.

[51] Thomas Jefferson Sawyer, *Memoir of Rev. Stephen R. Smith* (Boston, MA: Abel Tompkins, 1852), p. 155.

[52] Nathaniel Stacy, *Memoirs of the Life of Nathaniel Stacy: Preacher of the Gospel of Universal Grace* (Columbus, PA: Abner Vedder, 1850), pp. 71–72.

[53] Stacy, *Memoirs*, p. 223.

all people were united in one family. Every person was "born into the glorious liberty and spirit of the gospel."[54] In a Republican America, this gospel of liberty and equality was a natural avenue to women's liberation and the abolition of slavery.

[54] George Quinby, as quoted in Charles A. Howe, "Under Orders from No Man: Universalist Women Preachers Before the Civil War," The John Murray Distinguished Lecture for 1989, p. 35; Laura Horton, "Lucy Barns' *The Female Christian: A Universalist Treasure Rediscovered (Again)*," in *The Unitarian Universalist Christian*, Vol. 58 (2003), p. 84.

CHAPTER 5

From reason to intuition to freedom
USA 1833–1894

The Universalists survived the Restorationist controversy and compensated in 1833 by creating a central ecclesiastical body, the United States Convention of Universalists. That same year, the Unitarians faced telling evidence of an organizational vacuum when the Standing Order of Massachusetts was disestablished. A lack of centralized authority, coupled with an insistence on freedom of conscience, meant the two churches – Universalist and Unitarian – would find themselves in the ensuing decades riddled with conflict over relationships to revelation, miracles, scientific truth, and ultimately Christianity itself.

Nothing is more celebrated in American Unitarian history than the revolt of the younger generation of Transcendentalists from their Unitarian parents. Agitated for religious reasons, they longed for a direct and immediate relationship with God, as experienced through nature. Even before the publication of his essay *Nature* in 1836, Ralph Waldo Emerson (1803–1882) had rejected the rational "corpse cold Unitarianism of Brattle Street and Harvard College" for a "return to reason and faith." In the spring of 1827, Emerson found himself torn between the family profession of parish ministry modeled by his father, and the poetic muse of "feeling" inspired in him by his Aunt Mary Moody Emerson.[1] Emerson chose ministry, but soon gave up the social world of his father, his attachment to Christianity, and his formal affiliation with the church. His public reasons for the resignation were explored in his essay, *The Lord's Supper*. Emerson argued, "Jesus did not intend to establish an institution for perpetual observance."[2]

The Transcendentalists flourished during a time of intellectual and social reform, when a democratizing and experimental spirit seemed to pervade

---

[1] Robert D. Richardson, *Emerson: The Mind on Fire* (Berkeley, CA: University of California Press, 1995), pp. 78–83.

[2] Ralph Waldo Emerson, *The Complete Works of Ralph Waldo Emerson* (Boston, MA: Houghton, Mifflin and Co., 1876), Vol. XI, pp. 4–5, 18, 21.

every aspect of American culture. First and foremost, they were Unitarians. They had learned to study scriptures using the newest criticism, and concluded, like their "bishop" William Ellery Channing, that Jesus was not God, and human beings were not born sinful. They drank from the cup of Channing, who Van Wyck Brooks described as having "a vision of human nature, which seemed to him a godhead in the making," or as Channing said in *Likeness to God*: "In ourselves are the elements of the Divinity."[3]

Samuel Taylor Coleridge's *Aids to Reflection* appeared in 1829, and began a thirst for European literature among the Transcendentalists that would never be quenched. The word "Transcendental" derived from Immanuel Kant's idealism, whereby he taught that humans understand the universe through transcendental forms that are inherent in the mind. The German theologian, Friedrich Schleiermacher, had a system, Andrews Norton said, of "pantheism," in which religion was nothing more than a "sense of union of the individual with the universe, with Nature." In addition to the German idealists and the English Romantic poets, Platonism and the thought of Emmanuel Swedenborg also influenced Emerson's idealism. Finally, all of these influences were capped by texts from other world religions. In Hinduism, Emerson found affirmation for the idea that there is a fundamental unity to all human experience, and he believed the Bhagavad-Gita to be "a transnational book."[4]

The Transcendentalists have a reputation for suspicion of inherited traditions and forms, but many did not debase the church as a lifeless institution. Some of them reformulated congregational life and faith in dynamic new ways. Others discovered additional institutional incarnations, including discussion groups, publications, schools, and utopian societies. The Transcendental Club or "Hedge's Club" met when Frederic Henry Hedge (1805–1890) traveled to Boston from his congregation in Bangor, Maine. Hedge found that his "historical conscience" kept him "ecclesiastically conservative." At one of the last meetings of the Club, he defended the American Unitarian Association from attacks by others. In "Antisupernaturalism in the Pulpit" (1864), Hedge wrote, "Whoever would build permanently must build on the past."[5]

[3] Van Wyck Brooks, *The Flowering of New England* (New York: E. P. Dutton & Co., Inc., 1936), p. 13; William Ellery Channing, *The Works of William Ellery Channing D. D.* (Boston, MA: American Unitarian Association, 1875), p. 293.

[4] Philip F. Gura, *American Transcendentalism* (New York: Hill and Wang, 2007), pp. 110–111; Richardson, *Emerson*, pp. 4–5, 18, 21.

[5] Barbara L. Packer, *The Transcendentalists* (Athens, GA: The University of Georgia Press, 2007), p. 166; Sidney E. Ahlstrom and Jonathan S. Carey, eds., *An American Reformation: A Documentary History of Unitarian Christianity* (Middletown, CT: Wesleyan University Press, 1985), p. 429.

Among the first women to attend Hedge's Club was Margaret Fuller (1810–1850). Fuller also moderated her own discussion groups, "Conversations," which proved liberating for many women. Fuller brought her demand for women's equality to bear in *Woman in the Nineteenth Century*, which called for women "to be free from compromise, from complaisance, from helplessness."[6] Fuller and Elizabeth Palmer Peabody (1804–1894) first expressed their voices through teaching, with Peabody later transforming European educational ideas into the American kindergarten movement. She was impressed with Bronson Alcott's (1799–1888) teaching methods, and together they opened the Temple School in 1834.

The school at Brook Farm (1841) was the utopian community's greatest success. The founders were George Ripley (1802–1880), the former minister of the Purchase Street Church in Boston, and his wife Sophia (Dana). Ripley became more concerned about the laboring classes in the wake of the panic of 1837, a serious financial crisis followed by an economic depression. In "The Temptations of the Times," he expressed dismay over "the inordinate pursuit, the extravagant worship of wealth" founded upon "temptations to an excess of selfishness." Then in his "Letter of Intent to Resign," he indicated how he sometimes avoided preaching on certain subjects for fear of parishioners' response. Faith, he believed, could not simply be the improvement of personal character, but individuals needed to confront the "evils of society."[7]

Ripley's advocacy for the reform of society over the reform of self is what historian Philip Gura defines as the central conflict within the Transcendentalist movement. This conflict has continued as a central issue within Unitarianism. The promotion of individual transformation means that, while there may be personal efforts at reform, there is no corporate vision for fundamental social change. Ripley saw his colleagues as conservative preservers of the order of things, complacently at ease with the status quo.

The Ripleys had a vision that people of all stations and classes could be educated so as to "prepare a society of liberal, intelligent and cultivated persons, whose relations with each other would permit a more simple and wholesome life, than can be led amidst the pressure of our competitive institutions." Brook Farm adopted Charles Fourier's brand of socialism, but struggled financially and then failed in 1846, mostly due to a devastating fire.

---

[6] Perry Miller, ed., *The Transcendentalists, An Anthology* (Cambridge, MA: Harvard University Press, 1950), p. 461.

[7] Gura, *American Transcendentalism*, p. 141; Lawrence Buell, ed., *The American Transcendentalists* (New York: Modern Library, 2006), p. 104.

After the demise, Ripley wrote that the Unitarians were "too fashionable, too aristocratic, too well to do in the world . . . [to ever be] in favor of any radical social changes." The remnants of Brook Farm coalesced around a new religious institution, the Boston Religious Union of Associationists, started by William Henry Channing (1810–1884) in 1847. Although the new church did not last many years, the idea of creating a religious institution that welcomed all faiths and advocated the social reform of society remained a liberal vision.[8]

Channing moved on to Rochester, New York, where he became active in abolitionism. His radicalism made it hard to secure pulpits. Thomas Wentworth Higginson (1823–1911) also knew the consequences of political preaching, after he was called to serve the Unitarian congregation in Newburyport, Massachusetts in 1847. He only lasted two years there, preaching once too often against slavery for the ears of the shipowners who earned their living from the export of cotton. After the passage of the Fugitive Slave Law (1850), he said: "DISOBEY IT . . . and show our good citizenship by taking the legal consequences." He lived out a vision of "resistance to tyranny," when he and five cohorts, including Theodore Parker and educational reformer Samuel Gridley Howe (1801–1876), teamed up to become "The Secret Six." They agreed to support abolitionist John Brown's plot to attack the arsenal at Harper's Ferry and launch a slave revolt. Later, Higginson's essay "The Sympathy of Religions"[9] became an important contribution to Free Religion.

General interest in anti-slavery activity began expanding from 1830 onwards. A belief in the dignity of the human soul ignited the passion of humanitarians, who began to speak out. George Willis Cooke once said, "In proportion to its numbers no religious body in the country did so much to promote the anti-slavery reform as the Unitarian." But, in 1830, most Unitarian ministers were not abolitionists. They were gradualists who believed that slavery should be contained, and eventually abolished. There were active abolitionists, like Samuel J. May (1797–1871), who helped found the American Anti-Slavery Society in 1833. May was asked to deliver the eulogy for Karl Follen (1796–1840), the German–American abolitionist, but finding a Unitarian church that was willing to host the funeral of an

---

[8] Gura, *American Transcendentalism*, p. 208; Ripley to Emerson, in Joel Myerson, ed., *Transcendentalism: A Reader* (New York: Oxford University Press, 2000), p. 308; Sterling F. Delano, *Brook Farm: The Dark Side of Utopia* (Cambridge, MA: Harvard University Press, 2004), pp. 296, 336.
[9] Albert J. von Frank, *The Trials of Anthony Burns; Freedom and Slavery in Emerson's Boston* (Cambridge, MA: Harvard University Press, 1998), p. 27; Edward J. Renehan, Jr., *The Secret Six: The True Tale of the Men Who Conspired with John Brown* (New York: Crown, 1995), p. 147.

abolitionist proved difficult. Members of the Federal Street Church, where William Ellery Channing was minister, threatened to nail shut the pew doors rather than host such an event. After the Civil War, May asserted that too many of the Unitarians "were corrupted and morally paralyzed by our national consenting with slaveholders."[10]

Channing had felt increasing pressure over the years to speak out against slavery. Among those who convinced him to do so was Lydia Maria (Francis) Child (1802–1880). She had won considerable fame for her cookbook, *The Frugal Housewife*, but her economic and social fortunes fell when she published *An Appeal in Favor of That Class of Americans Called Africans* (1833). After Samuel J. May convinced Channing to admit, "I have been silent too long," he published *Slavery* (1835), in which he wrote, "God in making him [the slave] a rational and moral being, has put a glorious stamp on him, which all the slave legislation and slave markets cannot efface."[11]

The Universalist belief in freedom of conscience made it difficult for them to agree on abolitionism. There was also some question as to whether a religious group should be involved in political action, so while many Universalists opposed slavery on moral grounds, they were unwilling to upset the system. Even when they organized themselves to be more politically effective, Universalists were usually excluded from working with other religious groups who often labeled them infidels. During the revivals in western New York, new converts were often identified as former Universalists who had wallowed in sin. The press constantly labeled Universalists as criminals, as a result of their belief in there being "no hell." Public places were often closed to Universalist meetings, and their testimony was not allowed in courthouses.[12]

The early decades of the nineteenth century were a period of rapid expansion for Universalists, as they focused on spreading the gospel message of salvation rather than preaching social reform. In 1844, Robert Baird reported that the Universalists claimed 600,000 followers, but this was a vastly exaggerated number. Nevertheless, they had become a major sect in America, largely through evangelism. The assaults on their personal

---

[10] Donald Yacovone, *Samuel Joseph May and the Dilemmas of the Liberal Persuasion, 1797–1871* (Philadelphia, PA: Temple University Press, 1991), p. 80; Conrad Wright, *The Liberal Christians* (Boston, MA: Beacon Press, 1970), p. 62. See George Willis Cooke, *Unitarianism in America* (Boston, MA: American Unitarian Association, 1902), p. 353.

[11] Channing, "Slavery," in *Works*, p. 695.

[12] Whitney R. Cross, *The Burned-Over District: The Social and Intellectual History of Enthusiastic Religion in Western New York, 1800–1850* (New York: Harper and Row, Publishers, 1965), p. 44.

morality made speaking out on issues all the more complicated because Universalists were also seeking to be accepted in society.[13]

There were some Universalists, such as Sylvanus Cobb (1798–1866), the Spear brothers, and Mary Livermore, who became active in a variety of reform movements. Cobb started a newspaper in 1839 specifically to address social issues. Charles Spear (1801–1863), and his younger brother, John Murray Spear (1804–1887), were radicals on a number of fronts. They were prominent in organizing the first two Universalist anti-slavery conventions in Lynn, Massachusetts in 1840 and 1841. After serving in several parishes, Charles Spear became especially known for his efforts to abolish the death penalty, and urged Universalists to support outlawing "a relic of a dark, cruel, and barbarous age." He also spoke out against the treatment of prisoners, and published *The Prisoner's Friend*. His brother, John, was attacked by a mob in Portland, Maine after an 1844 anti-slavery meeting during which he had asked the audience "if they were afraid of free discussion." Then in 1851, he began to be receptive to "spirit messages," reflecting what would soon become a serious challenge to the entire Universalist denomination.[14]

The next year, John Murray Spear received numerous messages from the spirit world through his namesake, John Murray, who introduced him to "wonderful, mysterious powers." Eventually, Spear began to receive spirit directions for constructing the "New Motor." This was a machine that would absorb electrical energy by using magnets and metals to help bridge the gap between heaven and earth, and focus the divine energy of the universe. But the New Motor only absorbed scorn, and Spear was removed from ministerial fellowship. Concerns raised in one Universalist paper were that their clergy did not have rigorous enough training or examination, and the organization was "very loose." The report concluded that many ministers were attracted by "some novelty," and moved on because they did not have "any settled or well digested faith in religious principles."[15]

In the ensuing years, the challenge of spiritualism proved much more damaging to the Universalists than the Transcendentalist uprising did to the Unitarians, as many Universalist clergy left the denomination, and

[13] Russell E. Miller, *The Larger Hope: The First Century of the Universalist Church in America, 1770–1870* (Boston, MA: Unitarian Universalist Association, 1979), pp. 164, 617–619.

[14] Miller, *The Larger Hope*, 503; John B. Buescher, *The Remarkable Life of John Murray Spear* (Notre Dame, IN: University of Notre Dame Press, 2006), p. 39.

[15] Buescher, *Remarkable Life*, pp. 79, 96–104; John B. Buescher, *The Other Side of Salvation: Spiritualism and the Nineteenth-Century Religious Experience* (Boston, MA: Skinner House Books, 2004), pp. 44–46.

entire congregations were swept up with the "enthusiasms" and "strange doings" of spiritualism. On the Unitarian side, many of the Transcendentalists remained committed to the congregations, and the theological transition from liberal Christianity to a more inclusive humanistic faith took decades. Individualized experiences of transcendence did not revolutionize the congregational forms. But Universalism underwent wholesale conversions. Historian Winthrop Hudson later wrote that Universalism provided the greatest number of converts to spiritualism among all denominations, and, as a movement, never recovered from the experience.

In the late 1840s the northeastern US was replete with séances, trances and spiritual healings. The enthusiasm from the Second Great Awakening was being channeled in new directions, including mesmerism, phrenology, communism, and spiritualism. Central to an embrace of spiritualism was a belief in the power of science to explain the world. The invisible world of spirits could come into the material world of observation and experimentation. But the dream of spiritualism bringing understanding was divisive. Thomas Whittemore wrote: "We hope the time will come when the Universalist denomination will not be the receptacle of every strange thing under heaven."[16]

While some reformers were consumed by the radical spirit of their age, others helped initiate a new era of human rights. During the Civil War, Mary Ashton Rice Livermore (1820–1905) became a central figure in the work of the United States Sanitary Commission. She visited battlefields, raised vast amounts of money at fairs, and became a skillful public speaker. This experience was put to good use after the war, as she became active in the promotion of women's rights. Many Unitarian and Universalist women became prominent in this cause that was first energized by the 1848 convention in Seneca Falls, New York. Universalism had a natural affinity for women's equality, with its core message of spiritual equality and salvation of all people. Livermore helped organize what later became the Association of Universalist Women.

Livermore's new organization helped fund theological students. She believed that women must heed the call to ministry: "No power, ecclesiastical or other . . . has a right to hinder her." The first woman to enter the ranks was Lydia Ann Moulton Jenkins (1824–1874), as a co-minister with her husband in 1860, but Olympia Brown (1835–1926) is usually recognized

---

[16] Miller, *The Larger Hope*, pp. 223–224; John Greenleaf Adams, *Memoir of Thomas Whittemore, D.D.* (Boston, MA: Universalist Publishing House, 1885), p. 173.

as the first woman to be ordained (1863) with full denominational authority. In the meantime, Livermore became a committed suffragist, telling Brown, "You see where the tide has carried me – clear out to sea. I am in for the [suffrage] war, now." Livermore would devote the rest of her life to winning full voting rights for women, becoming a world-renowned speaker known as the "Queen of the Platform."[17]

The Civil War provided both a critical need and the opportunity for women to enter the clergy. Universalists were increasingly founding sectarian schools, including Tufts College (1852) and St. Lawrence (1855), where Olympia Brown was admitted. The president of the Canton Theological School at St. Lawrence, Ebenezer Fisher, attempted to dissuade her, as "he did not think women were called to the ministry."[18] He was not alone in his opinion. Once Brown entered the parish ministry she experienced the prejudices of many parishioners who voiced complaints against women entering the profession, including their weak voices, lack of reason and intelligence, and need to maintain domestic roles. Yet, over the years, Brown enjoyed success in several parishes including Bridgeport, Connecticut, where showman P.T. Barnum (1810–1891) was a member. Eventually, she entered full-time suffrage work. Brown suffered not only the prejudices women clergy usually endured, but also the stigma of being politically active. During her Bridgeport pastorate, she wrote that "I preached better... than at any other time in my life." This was not sufficient. A small faction began to stir up opposition to her ministry, including those who "had been opposed to a woman as minister."[19]

But there was support for the vision of equality. Adin Ballou (1803–1890), who shared in the reform work of abolition, temperance and women's rights, also had a broad plan for social change. He established the Hopedale Community in 1842 in Worcester County, Massachusetts. In the first half of that decade, more than forty utopian communities were begun in America. By the time of its demise fourteen years later, Hopedale had nearly 300 people living there. Ballou called it "a neat village of some fifty pleasant dwellings... with substantial manufacturing establishments along its western border."[20]

---

[17] Wendy Hamand Venet, *A Strong-Minded Woman: The Life of Mary A. Livermore* (Amherst, MA: University of Massachusetts Press, 2005), pp. 139, 147.

[18] Gwendolen B. Willis, ed., "Olympia Brown, An Autobiography." *The Annual Journal of the Universalist Historical Society*, Volume IV (1963) p. 27; Ann Lee Bressler, *The Universalist Movement in America, 1770–1870* (New York: Oxford University Press, 2001), p. 91.

[19] Willis, *Olympia Brown*, pp. 39–40. See A. H. Saxon, "Olympia Brown in Bridgeport," *The Proceedings of the Unitarian Universalist Historical Society*, Vol. XXI (Part 1), 1987–88, pp. 55–65.

[20] Adin Ballou, *History of the Hopedale Community* (Lowell, MA: Thompson and Hill, 1897), p. 345.

Ballou's utopian plan was based upon what he called Practical Christianity. Central to this vision was a belief in pacifism: "I do hold myself bound by its holy requirements, never, under any pretext whatsoever, to kill, assault, beat, torture, enslave, rob, oppress, persecute, defraud, corrupt, slander, revile, injure, envy, or hate any human being, even my worst enemy." Ballou corresponded with Leo Tolstoy about non-resistance, and developed an anarchistic philosophy. He felt all government was based in coercive powers, and people needed to withdraw from it as much as possible.[21] Even though the community ultimately closed, it became the foundation for the Unitarian church in Hopedale, Massachusetts.

The internal debate over Restorationism presaged continuing conflicts, especially over the boundaries of Christianity. Abner Kneeland, who became the last man jailed for blasphemy, tested the bounds with an 1833 article that questioned the existence of God and the resurrection of Christ. Kneeland also expressed doubts about the continued existence of human consciousness after death. His assaults on basic tenets of faith resulted in sixty days in jail in 1838, after which he moved to a free-thought community in Salubria, Iowa.

When the Boston Association of Universalists met in 1847, Thomas Whittemore reported that a "vigorous discussion came up in reference to the faith necessary to constitute a person a Universalist." Some members wondered if someone could remain a Christian minister if they "did not believe in the resurrection of Jesus" or "disavowed miracles." Some of the debaters thought the Winchester Profession was sufficient, but a vast majority of the clergy and laity felt their biblical faith was being assaulted by the "loose German Rationalism and speculative free-thinking and doubting then so rife in New England and elsewhere." In December 1847, the *Trumpet and Universalist Magazine* reported on the irreconcilable differences posed by a non-creedal free faith that also required a Bible-believing definition of Christianity. "We want a Christian believer for a pastor, not a skeptic. But the Universalists [grant] fellowship [to] believers and skeptics all alike."[22]

The "free-thinking and doubting" became worse after the publication of Charles Darwin's *On the Origin of Species* (1859). The initial reactions to Darwin were hostile, since Universalists believed that human beings were the creation of an intelligent God, and that species were immutable. By

---

[21] Ballou, *Hopedale Community*, p. 166.

[22] Thomas Whittemore, *Modern History of Universalism, From the Era of the Reformation to the Present Time* (Boston, MA: The Author, 1830), pp. 174, 177; Alonzo Ames Miner, as quoted in Ernest Cassara, ed., *Universalism in America: A Documentary History* (Boston, MA: Beacon Press, 1971), p. 170.

the end of the century, though, Universalists followed the lead of Orello Cone (1835–1905), who maintained a belief in God, and yet was an apostle of science. Cone was an inportant and influential pioneer in the field of biblical criticism. By this time, the Universalist message of salvation for all was appearing in other religions. There had been a gradual softening of Calvinism, so each faith offered salvation based on individual merit, much like Restoration Universalism. Universalists, hoping to achieve social acceptance, now generally rejected the "ultra" position, and, in the process, lost their unique reason for being.[23] They were less radical, and other faiths less conservative.

There had been a growing religious skepticism in the denomination, and, by 1870, many Universalist clergy and laity thought it was time to require a statement of belief. Since its adoption in 1803, the Winchester Profession had contained a "liberty clause," whereby Universalists had been free to interpret the Profession. Feeling that the traditional "creedless" faith had been subverted, the 1870 Convention passed a resolution that explicit belief in the Profession became required for fellowship. Herman Bisbee, serving in St. Anthony, Minnesota, was removed from fellowship in 1872 because of this resolution. In a series of lectures, Bisbee denied the miracles and said the Bible was not infallible. He was called an "infidel" in the denominational press. The Boston Declaration (1899), adopted almost thirty years later, restored freedom of conscience to clergy. This Declaration affirmed five principles: the Fatherhood of God, the leadership of Jesus, the trustworthiness of the Bible, certainty of retribution for sin, and "the final harmony of all souls with God." And importantly, no "precise form of words is required as a condition of fellowship." Fortunately, Universalists had finally agreed that belief was a private matter rather than something legislated for by ecclesiastical fiat or decree.[24]

Historian George H. Williams has suggested that there were three major expressions of Universalism in the latter part of the nineteenth century. While Bisbee's scientific naturalism was one of these, it was a tiny minority, and most Universalists continued to believe in a Christian Universalism. One of the old-fashioned Bible believers was Quillen Hamilton Shinn (1845–1907), the "Grasshopper missionary," who traveled an average of 700 miles a week and founded dozens of churches, chiefly in the South. He was also involved in the Norfolk and Suffolk, Virginia, missions, which

---

[23] Bressler, *Universalist Movement*, p. 125.
[24] Russell E. Miller, *The Larger Hope: The Second Century of the Universalist Church in America, 1870–1970* (Boston, MA: Unitarian Universalist Association, 1985), p. 89.

were established in 1889 by the first black Universalist minister, Joseph Jordan (1842–1901). Shinn disliked the word "liberal," and openly expressed disdain for Unitarians, who he described as the "go-as-you-please church." Finally, Mary Livermore represented a third group, who advocated for an American church of the future, or a religion of democracy. In 1870, she said that the world was moving toward a time "when we shall recognize the great tie of brotherhood the world over."[25]

Religious naturalism also caused a Unitarian institutional conflagration in the events and exchanges of the Miracles Controversy, initiated when George Ripley reviewed James Martineau's *The Rationale of Religious Enquiry* in 1836. Ripley declared that it was an "unsound method" to make a belief in miracles the "essential foundation of Christian faith." Rather than depending on scripture for truth, Ripley said "let us determine whether our nature has any revelation of the Deity within itself. . . " Then Ralph Waldo Emerson delivered his *Divinity School Address* in July 1838. He was disturbed by the current state of the ministry, and protested: "Whenever the pulpit is usurped by a formalist, then is the worshipper defrauded and disconsolate." The historicity of the miracles as a tool of conversion was described as a profanity, and ultimately Emerson challenged the new ministers to show "that God is, not was."[26] Andrews Norton (1786–1853), a professor at Harvard, claimed Emerson was proposing "to reject all belief in Christianity as a revelation."

The *Divinity School Address* provoked a firestorm within the denomination. Henry Ware, Jr. wrote to Emerson saying that the ideas "would overthrow the authority and influence of Christianity." In his *Discourse on the Latest Form of Infidelity*, Norton stated that the "mass of evidence" being rejected is what "establishes the truth of his religion," and that a rejection of the miracles was tantamount to a rejection of Christianity. In *The Latest Form of Infidelity Examined*, Ripley accused the Harvard faculty of condemning people for implementing the "spirit of freedom" in the "pursuit of truth." This part of the controversy concluded with an article by Theodore Parker, writing under the pseudonym Levi Blodgett, who said the truth of Christianity did not need to rest on miracles, but instead had to be innate in the soul.[27]

[25] Miller, *Second Century*, pp. 349, 352, 360, 369; *Proceedings at the Universalist Centennial*, Held in Gloucester, MA, September 20th, 21st, 22nd, 1870 (Boston, MA: Universalist Publishing House, 1870), p. 63; George H. Williams, "American Universalism: A Bicentennial Historical Essay," in *The Journal of the Universalist Historical Society*, Vol. IX (1971), pp. 29–30.

[26] Miller, ed., *Transcendentalists*, pp. 131–132, 195; Emerson, *Works*, Vol. I, pp. 135, 137, 138, 144–145.

[27] William Hutchison, *The Transcendentalist Ministers, Church Reform in the New England Renaissance* (Boston, MA: Beacon Press, 1965), p. 77; Miller, ed., *Transcendalists*, pp. 211, 217; Dean Grodzins,

Theodore Parker (1810–1860) had revolutionary blood in his veins, as the grandson of the captain who faced the British regulars on Lexington Green. Not long after the crisis stirred up by Emerson's *Address*, a sermon that Parker preached at the ordination of Charles Shackford in South Boston reinvigorated the debate and exposed Parker as a theological radical. The sermon, titled *The Transient and Permanent in Christianity* (1841), explained that Christian forms and doctrines were transient: they "change and perish, but the word of God cannot fail." The permanent in Christianity is what people "feel in the heart." In response, the Boston Association of Ministers tried to exclude Parker. This was difficult, since implementing a doctrinal test would violate their principle of free inquiry. Clergy resorted to social and professional snubs, refusing to exchange pulpits with Parker, and trying to force him into quiet disappearance. Parker did not co-operate. His fame grew, especially as he continued to be involved in abolitionism. This was according to historian Dean Grodzins, "the first and only time in American Unitarian history, [that] a body of liberal Christian clerics seriously considered dismissing a colleague solely on the grounds of doctrine."[28]

While the Transcendentalists in New England were trying to foment a revolution from within Unitarianism, religious liberals who emigrated west were attempting to expand the faith. The traditional interpretation of Unitarian growth has been that the Unitarians had little evangelical fervor, and refused to proselytize. In this view there was no intentional outreach, and growth was dependent upon Boston Unitarians moving west and establishing outposts. Yet evidence suggests that liberals were interested in extension, and that the faith that developed in the West was more in keeping with this dynamic culture. As early as 1835, Henry Ware, Jr. declared that "A great work is to be done there."[29]

In that same year, the *Western Messenger* was founded to "explain and defend the misunderstood and denounced principles of Unitarianism." It was intended as a missionary vehicle for the Unitarians when it was launched. Working closely with James Freeman Clarke (1810–1888) in Louisville, and William Greenleaf Eliot (1811–1887) in St. Louis, Ephraim

---

American Heretic: Theodore Parker and Transcendentalism (Chapel Hill, NC: University of North Carolina Press, 2002), pp. 196–198.

[28] Miller, ed., *Transcendentalists*, p. 278; Grodzins, *American Heretic*, p. 444.

[29] Henry Ware, Jr., "The Best Means of Bringing Our Lay Brethren to be More Useful in the Maintenance of Religious Institutions," Berry Street Essay, Boston, 1835. www.uuma.org/BerryStreet/Essays/BSE1835.htm.

Peabody (1807–1856) wanted the journal to educate the public about Unitarianism and cultivate a new following. The prospectus declared: "The ear of the public is open, but the tongue of the press, so far as Unitarians are concerned, is silent. We think the West demands and will support such a work." Indeed, the AUA missionary, Benjamin Huntoon, stated at the Association's 1837 Annual Meeting that the West was where "the destiny of Unitarianism is to be decided." But Boston's support eroded when the first issue of the *Messenger* attacked the "orthodoxism" of the Unitarians back East. The *Western Messenger's* prospects further declined when Clarke criticized the AUA for its apathy and its "cerebral, lethargic, negative" faith.[30]

During these formative years for Unitarianism in the western United States, no person stood taller than Harm Jan Huidekoper, a Dutch immigrant to Meadville, Pennsylvania. Huidekoper regularly visited the Unitarian Church in Pittsburgh (founded 1823), and was converted there by John Campbell, a British Unitarian serving as the minister. In Pittsburgh, Huidekoper befriended Benjamin Bakewell, another British import and a huge success in the glass industry. These relationships inspired Huidekoper to found an Independent Congregational Church in Meadville in 1825. Huidekoper was determined to spread his Unitarian faith. In *The Unitarian Essayist*, he wrote: "The religious opinions which we entertain, we esteem of priceless worth... These opinions we hear perpetually misrepresented... Men are warned against our places of worship and our books; our arguments are carefully evaded... Under such circumstances we cannot remain silent."[31]

Bakewell concurred with Huidekoper. There was "insistent prejudice which exists against our doctrines," and the Unitarians were in "want of a little more zeal amongst ourselves." New societies could not afford to pay for good preaching, and there were differences in style between East and West. Bakewell said the people needed "a more popular manner both in and out of the pulpit," noting that "extemporaneous preaching" delivered with a "greater degree of energy" was preferred.[32]

---

[30] Robert D. Habich, *Transcendentalism and the Western Messenger* (Cranbury, NJ: Associated University Presses, Inc., 1985), pp. 51, 71, 83, 105, 113; Miller, ed., *Transcendentalists*, pp. 201, 203.

[31] Nina Moore Tiffany and Francis Tiffany, *Harm Jan Huidekoper* (Cambridge, MA: Riverside Press, 1904), p. 220.

[32] Kathleen R. Parker, "Benjamin Bakewell and the Arrival of Unitarianism in Pittsburgh," unpublished paper, for Collegium: An Association for Liberal Religious Studies, 2008, p. 7.

Historian Charles Lyttle referred to Huidekoper as a "miniature Unitarian Association in himself." Huidekoper not only wanted to spread a sectarian faith, but also wanted to secure this by training preachers especially suited for the West. This came to fruition with the founding of Meadville Theological School in 1844. The charter stipulated that "no doctrinal test was ever to be made a condition" of receiving an education there.[33]

James Freeman Clarke returned east convinced that Unitarianism needed a new kind of church; one that would not completely forsake Christianity, and yet would speak to the progressive needs of the spirit. He founded the Church of the Disciples in 1841, and instituted the renewal with three major changes. Owning pews, Clarke said, was an undemocratic practice that shut out the poor from attending, and thus he proposed that all financial contributions to the church be voluntary, and seating be free. He also wanted to unite the church, "not on ceremonies, nor on a creed, but on study and labor, on loving and doing." He wanted the church to offer interest groups, classes, and social programs for the poor. Finally, his new model of church changed the traditional worship service, so that it became possible for lay members to give sermons. Clarke called for more active participation by all the parishioners.[34]

The Unitarian Association's leaders responded to these new ideas as a threat, and tried to consolidate their beliefs on a thorough-going Christian basis. Nathaniel L. Frothingham was part of a group that wanted "restraints on religious liberty," and said "by rejecting the precepts of our neighbors, we do not resign all precepts for ourselves." The impetus towards more doctrinal self-understanding was institutionalized at an annual meeting of the American Unitarian Association (AUA) in 1853. The Annual Report suggests that the church leaders were mindful that "some general statement of theological opinions" needed to be given, but they could not take the form of "an authoritative creed." They defined Christian as "recognition of the Messiahship of Jesus," including his "miraculous mission," and "especial divine revelation."[35]

---

[33] Charles Lyttle, *Freedom Moves West: A History of the Western Unitarian Conference* (Boston, MA: Beacon Press, 1952), pp. 55–66, 231–235.

[34] Arthur S. Bolster, Jr., *James Freeman Clarke: Disciple to Advancing Truth* (Boston, MA: Beacon Press, 1954), pp. 92, 125, 131, 140–141; Ahlstrom and Carey, *American Reformation*, pp. 293–294, 298–300.

[35] Octavius Brooks Frothingham, *Boston Unitarianism: 1820–1850, A Study of the Life and Work of Nathaniel Langdon Frothingham* (New York and London: G. P. Putnam's Sons, 1890), pp. 40–41;

Theological and institutional consolidation was more than a response to the Transcendental threat. It was an expression of hope that the denomination might grow. Henry Whitney Bellows (1814–1882), minister at the Church of All Souls in New York City, saw an opportunity for Unitarian expansion when he traveled to San Francisco to help the church there in the wake of the death of its minister, Thomas Starr King (1824–1864). King, who served both Universalist and Unitarian churches in greater Boston, went west in 1860. An unflagging supporter of Lincoln and the Republicans, he has often been credited with keeping California in the Union during the Civil War. He spread liberal religion throughout the state, and Bellows was excited by the possibilities. He envisioned a church organization that would be strong and active in promoting Unitarianism, but was confounded by a weak AUA that relied on individual subscribers who were both parochial and apathetic. Bellows wrote that the Boston Unitarians were spiteful towards the radicals, and would not support any initiatives "which don't originate in Boston." They were "sticklers for individual independence in the churches, and very little disposed to expect great things, or to undertake large enterprises." But a large enterprise was what Bellows wanted, and in December 1864, he proposed forming a national conference. This was to be a parish representative organization that would be infused with "bold energy."[36]

Bellows had been dreaming of this moment since he delivered his address, *The Suspense of Faith* (1859). He told his audience that churches had lost their faith, had become "lecture foundations," and were "less religious" and "more political, social and ethical." He feared that science and literature were becoming "substitutes for religion." Protestantism, he said, had brought individual freedom to faith with a mighty centrifugal force, but it had gone too far. Bellows worried that there was some denominational complacency among the Unitarians because their successful advocacy of "the rights of conscience, the rationality of method, the freedom of inquiry . . . had transformed all of American Christendom." Now, he said, society must turn back to "the existing religious institutions of Christendom."[37]

A national representative body was achieved in 1865 with the formation of the National Conference of Unitarian Churches. Clarke and Bellows were part of a group identified as the "Broad Church Movement."

Christian Examiner and Religious Miscellany. LV, Fourth Series, Vol. XX, July, September, November 1853 (Boston, MA: Crosby, Nichols and Co., 1853), pp. 158–159.

[36] Wright, *Liberal Christians.* pp. 86, 94.

[37] Ahlstrom and Carey, *American Reformation*, pp. 374–375, 378–379, 380, 394.

This group hoped to unite four Unitarian theological groupings, ranging from evangelical creedal advocates to traditional upholders of Brahmin self-culture, through the Broad Christian group to a radical fringe that considered Christianity to be one of many world religions. To a remarkable degree, they were able to organize a permanent ecclesiastical body with delegate representation from each congregation meeting annually to advise the AUA. But how inclusive would the group be?

While there was some controversy over the name of the organization, the theological implications of the preamble would prove to be an issue that produced serious divisions. The preamble stated that the members were "all disciples of the Lord Jesus Christ," who were doing the "service of God" by "building up the Kingdom of his Son."[38] This proved troublesome to many of the radicals who believed any Christian wording contained a taint of creedalism. When the National Conference met the following year in Syracuse, New York, the preamble was reaffirmed. Several disgruntled clergy left feeling as though the bedrock of free inquiry had been destroyed. William James Potter (1829–1893) fumed on the train ride home to New Bedford, Massachusetts that he was going to start a "spiritual anti-slavery society." He joined forces with Francis Ellingwood Abbot (1836–1903), who had brought an alternative preamble to the convention, which proposed the principles of "Love, Righteousness and Truth." This was soundly defeated. Feeling rejected, Abbot and Potter regrouped with others to form the Free Religious Association (FRA) in May 1867.[39]

In their articles of organization, the FRA stated that the basis for this group was something broader than anything attempted in religious history. Seeking the "common ground on which all religion rests," the founders sought an "ultimate union . . . of all religions, Christian and non-Christian." For the first time, a religious organization proposed that all faiths meet "on perfectly equal terms." The FRA also advocated the possibility of advancing truth with no sense of "finality in religious faith and practice." In its goal of professing the "pure religion" of Theodore Parker, the FRA was also formed to "encourage the scientific study of theology." While the FRA never amounted to much organizationally, its impact on the American Unitarian Association (AUA) and liberal religion was substantial.[40]

---

[38] David B. Parke, ed., *The Epic of Unitarianism* (Boston, MA: Beacon Press, 1957), p. 121.

[39] Wright, *Liberal Christians*, p. 104; Conrad Wright, *A Stream of Light* (Boston, MA: Skinner House Books, second edition, 1989), pp. 79–80.

[40] The Free Religious Association. *Freedom and Fellowship in Religion: A Collection of Essays and Addresses* (Boston, MA: Roberts Brothers, 1875), pp. 357–361.

Bellows' National Conference of Unitarian Churches was representative of his belief in formal, institutional networks among those who shared a specific religious identity. The FRA founders, by contrast, were supporters of broad theologies within individual congregations. They wanted to accept many faiths, and keep affiliations loose enough to prevent exclusion. John Weiss (1818–1879) feared strong, central institutions where, "The soul is weakened by learning to lean upon a go-between." Most of the radical leaders sought more democratic, universal expressions of faith, but did not quit the institutional church, as has sometimes been implied. They remained committed to Unitarianism, but were concerned about its direction. Historian David Robinson wrote, "Most of the radicals . . . were serving as Unitarian ministers or trying to negotiate a suitable alternative. The fate of the church, broadly speaking, and of their particular churches was thus of compelling interest to them, both philosophically and personally."[41]

The career of Octavius Brooks Frothingham, Nathanial Frothingham's son, embodies this tendency. As a parish minister, he served twenty years at Third Unitarian (renamed Independent Liberal Church) in New York City, where Bellows snubbed him for leading a "church of the unchurched," espousing a vague theology. His theology was called "too broad for Unitarianism or any mere theological creed." Frothingham believed that institutions were the focal point of historical change. He affirmed the church as an institution, but wanted to broaden it to include intellectual and social aspects that made it more of a community center. Frothingham said, "The future religion must be *social*."[42]

The FRA's radical elements that went west made the most enduring impact. William Channing Gannett (1840–1923), the son of a Boston minister, served parishes in Milwaukee, St. Paul, Hinsdale (Illinois), and Rochester (New York), where suffragist Susan B. Anthony (1820–1906) became his parishioner. When Gannett first settled in the West, he began a close association with Jenkin Lloyd Jones (1843–1918), the uncle of Frank Lloyd Wright, the famous architect with whom Gannett collaborated on a volume called *The House Beautiful*. This effort to sanctify the home mirrored the ideal church, which was a humble abode that was useful

[41] John Weiss, *Life and Correspondence of Theodore Parker* (New York: Arno Press and The New York Times, 1969), pp. 59, 62–63; David M. Robinson, "The New Epoch of Belief": The *Radical and Religious Transformation in Nineteenth-Century New England*," *The New England Quarterly*, Vol. LXXIX, No. 4 (December 2006), p. 561.

[42] Wade J. Caruthers, *Octavius Brooks Frothingham, Gentle Radical* (Tuscaloosa, AL: University of Alabama Press, 1977), pp. 181–184; Robinson, "New Epoch," pp. 570–572.

seven days a week to teach culture, provide community service and offer mutual care.[43]

This was a new vision of ministry that served people in many social, educational, and emotional ways. Women who entered the ministry in increasing numbers in the late nineteenth century enthusiastically adopted it. The Western Unitarian Conference (WUC), formed in Cincinnati in 1852, was a product of Huidekoper's evangelical spirit, and the organizational work of his protégé Augustus Conant. But the WUC was plagued by doctrinal and denominational conflict from the start. When Gannett formed alliances with the women ministers on suffrage, confrontations took place. The president of Meadville seminary said that a "company of women" had "ruined" the WUC, because they had been "controlled" by Gannett.[44]

The women who "ruined" the WUC were a significant evangelical force on the Great Plains, which their male colleagues usually avoided because of the extremely hard work of building new congregations, and the typically low pay. The shortage of men created an opportunity for women to break the stereotype of a traditionally male profession and provide leadership. Between 1870–1890, about seventy women joined the ranks of the liberal ministry, twenty of whom made up a support network called the Iowa Sisterhood. For a half-century, these women battled for respect from a denominational bureaucracy that was rarely supportive. Differences between Unitarians in the West and East were evident in many ways: The West had simpler church buildings, less concern for an avowed Christian basis for faith, and disregard for traditional hierarchical ways of conducting business. In 1889, Caroline Bartlett (later Crane) wrote to Jenkin Lloyd Jones, the secretary of the WUC, "The more I see of the spirit of the East, the more I feel that I am of the West – and that I am glad of it."[45]

Jones declared that women were crucial to the Western movement "quite as much if not more than the men." For many of the Sisterhood, the emotional center of their lives was found in their relationships with other women. Their sermons often celebrated friendship, and their style of ministry has been called maternal, because of the vision of the congregation as home-like, with programs that nurtured the whole person and ventured into all parts of community life. The acknowledged leader of the Sisterhood

---

[43] William Channing Gannett, *The House Beautiful* (Boston, MA: James H. West Co., 1885), pp. 17–18; Samuel A. Eliot, ed., *Heralds of a Liberal Faith* (Boston, MA: Beacon Press, 1952), Vol. IV, pp. 142–147.
[44] Cynthia Grant Tucker. *Prophetic Sisterhood: Liberal Ministers of the Frontier, 1880–1930* (Boston, MA: Beacon Press, 1990), p. 140.
[45] Tucker, *Prophetic Sisterhood*, pp. 3–4, 119–121.

was Mary Safford (1851–1927). Teaming with Eleanor Gordon (1852–1942), their work spread to the Iowa Unitarian Conference, where together they edited a journal, *Old and New*. Safford organized six congregations in Iowa. She wrote, "We have organized this church, but are we doing all we have the power to do to help it grow, to make it a center of light and warmth in this community?"[46] Safford eventually served as an AUA director, often battling with the AUA to maintain local control of funds and governance.

Jenkin Lloyd Jones embraced the Iowa Sisterhood as an embodiment of the impulse within Unitarianism to evangelize the West. Jones settled in Janesville, Wisconsin to spread the faith. He argued for a WUC that was more independent from the AUA, and, by 1875, was employed as a WUC Missionary Secretary, with annual contributions going to the WUC rather than the AUA. During Jones' term, the number of congregations increased from forty-three to sixty-one, and the number of state conferences grew from one (Wisconsin) to eight. In 1880, Jones traveled nearly 15,000 miles, driving him to the brink of "physical bankruptcy."

Free Religion caused some ministers to withdraw from the AUA, and the AUA to remove others. Octavius Brooks Frothingham (1822–1895) requested that his name be removed from the annual Yearbook, since he followed Free Religion. This led William Fox of the AUA to ask William J. Potter, the minister in New Bedford, Massachusetts, if he wished to remain on the list. When Fox wrote back expressing his relief that Potter still "calls himself a Unitarian Christian," Potter responded that he did not consider himself one. Fox thereupon removed his name. The WUC resolved to "protest against this erasure of names," saying that it was a "departure from Congregational and Unitarian principles." They then affirmed that the WUC "conditions its fellowship on no dogmatic tests."[47]

The controversial "Issue in the West" was summarized in a pamphlet of that name written by Jabez Sunderland, who succeeded Jones as secretary of the WUC in 1884. Jones had organized churches in the name of "Freedom, Fellowship and Character in Religion." Sunderland questioned whether Western Unitarianism was ready to give up its traditional character. He felt that a new order of Unitarianism based on principles was being created, without beliefs that would commit members to theism or Christianity. Historic Unitarianism was being sacrificed to a "Free or Ethical Religion."

---

[46] Tucker, ibid., pp. 81, 120; Dorothy May Emerson, ed., *Standing Before Us: Unitarian Universalist Women and Social Reform, 1776–1936* (Boston, MA: Skinner House Books, 2000), pp. 131, 498.

[47] Wright, *Stream*, pp. 82–85; Lyttle, *Freedom*, pp. 134–137. See Thomas Graham, "The Making of a Secretary: Jenkin Lloyd Jones at Thirty-One," *The Proceedings of the Unitarian Universalist Historical Society*, Vol. XIX, Part II (1982–83), pp. 36–55.

Gannett saw Sunderland's position as an effort to exclude those who did not take the name "Christian" or "Theist," and he offered three resolutions at the 1886 WUC meeting. The only one that passed stated there would be "no dogmatic tests," but that the conditions of fellowship would be "Truth, Righteousness and Love." At the end of the annual meeting of the Conference, the Christians responded by organizing a rival conference, the Western Unitarian Association.[48]

This issue of the theological basis of Unitarianism came to a head in 1887. The Christians feared that the radicals were trying to deprive them entirely of God and Jesus. The radicals feared the Christians only wanted uniformity of belief. Then Gannett proposed, "Things Commonly Believed Among Us" at the Conference meeting in Chicago. A large majority at the meeting in 1887 adopted his statement. True unity was achieved in 1894 when the National Conference found common ground. Martha St. John traveled from Pittsburgh to attend the meeting in Saratoga, New York and reported that "The most inspiring meeting was the one at which they adopted the new Preamble to the Constitution." The vote was taken after a long discussion, and then following a unanimous tally, "people jumped up, waved their hats and handkerchiefs and then they all sang the Doxology." She concluded, "It was feared that an agreement could not be reached, but Dr. M. [Minot] J. Savage's wording solved the difficulty."[49] The wording concluded: "These Churches accept the religion of Jesus, holding in accordance with his teaching, that practical religion is summed up in love to God and love to man." Finally, the Conference recognized that because of Congregational polity, "nothing in this Constitution is to be construed as an authoritative test."[50]

"Things Commonly Believed" provided the basis for this unity. It began by asserting: "The Western conference has neither the wish nor the right to bind a single member by declarations concerning fellowship or doctrine." It was centered on a broadly based, ethical faith: "All names that divide 'religion' are to us of little consequence compared with religion itself. Whoever loves Truth and lives the Good is, in a broad sense, of our religious fellowship."

---

[48] Lyttle, *Freedom*, pp. 182–186.
[49] Martha St. John, letter to her mother, September 30, 1894, typed copy provided by Kathy Parker.
[50] *Official Report of the Proceedings of the Fifteenth Meeting of the National Conference of Unitarian and Other Christian Churches* held in Saratoga, NY, September 24–27, 1894 (Boston, MA: George H. Ellis, 1894), pp. 19–20; See William H. Pease, "Doctrine and Fellowship: William Channing Gannett and the Unitarian Creedal Issue," *Church History*, Vol. 25 (Issue 3), September 1956, pp. 210–238.

The statement prefigured the broad-based free faith that developed in the twentieth century by declaring that "reason and conscience" were the final religious authorities. Moreover, the centrality of the Bible and Jesus were broadened to honor "all inspiring scripture" and "all holy souls" who were great religious teachers of "righteousness and love, as prophets of religion." "Things Commonly Believed" was later summarized and promoted by the American Unitarian Association with these words of process: "Freedom, the method in religion, in place of Authority; Fellowship, the spirit in religion, in place of Sectarianism; Character, the test in religion, in place of Ritual or Creed; Service or Salvation of Others, the aim in religion, in place of Salvation of Self." In *Freedom Moves West*, Charles Lyttle wrote of "Things Commonly Believed" that it "remains the most comprehensively and nobly conceived, the most justly and persuasively argued, the most ethically inspired and the most beautifully expressed document of its kind in all Unitarian history."[51]

---

[51] *Unity*, Vol. xix (June 4 and 11, 1887), Numbers 14 and 15, Tenth Annual Western Unitarian Conference Number and Year Book, p. 200; Eliot, *Heralds*, Vol. iv, p. 145; Lyttle, *Freedom*, p. 189.

CHAPTER 6

A religion for one world

In the summer of 1886, in the western New York State city of Jamestown, Unitarians and Universalists shared a lecture platform for the first time. To bolster growth for his new Independent Congregational Church, James Townsend planned a summer lecture course. For two weeks in July that year, the "brightest minds in the country" occupied a tent and entertained large numbers of people. Soon *The Unitarian* was advertising both The Lakeside School and the New Theology, which "would unite in the bonds of a common sympathy all those who . . . are seeking to preserve the truth that has found imperfect expression in ancient forms of faith, and to set it forth in a form which shall command the respect and reverence of the disciples of science and modern thought."[1] The following spring, railroad developers purchased land from Clara Wilcox, with a site on Lake Chautauqua carved out for the Lakeside School. By the summer of 1887, a beautiful, 9,000 square foot tabernacle had been built in Wilcox Grove, and the second season of the school began. It was an enormous success. But there was no third season. By 1888, Townsend had suffered a breakdown and resigned his pulpit, and it was discovered that the developers had cheated Wilcox. She was forced to foreclose upon the property, and the Lakeside School of New Theology found itself with a huge debt, no home, and no leader. It was never reconstituted.

Major themes for Universalists and Unitarians in the twentieth century are compressed into this story. Scientific discoveries, especially Darwin's theory of evolution, changed the abode of God, or at least demanded an examination of how science and nature lived alongside theology. A belief in progress challenged creedal faith. The personal faith development of religious leaders created confusion about theology and denominational affiliation. Education began to be seen as the new form of religious practice.

[1] Jabez Sunderland, Brook Herford, and Frederick Mott, eds., *The Unitarian* (Boston, MA, 1887, Volume 2), p. 112.

Capitalist expansionists cultivated relationships that created both opportunity and financial ruin, and complicated mission work throughout the world. Liberal women supported specific projects rather than the church in general, because the administrative infrastructure was both weak and unfair to women. Sympathies widened, but religious identity grew fractured.

By 1900, inter-faith co-operation was abundantly evident. The American Unitarian Association celebrated its seventy-fifth year by founding the International Council of Free Christians and Other Liberal Thinkers and Workers, a group that included Universalists. The largely ceremonial meetings soon had over 2,000 attendees, representing 88 different religious traditions. In 1910, women attending the congress formed their own group, and between the two World Wars, after the creation of a center in England, the name settled as the International Association for Religious Freedom (IARF). Charles Wendte (1844–1931), the secretary for twenty years, found that through the IARF he was able to make connections that had escaped him domestically. Universalists had consistently rejected overtures from Unitarians, and in 1897 had called for strict denominationalism. But in 1907, Wendte co-ordinated the Federation of Religious Liberals in America, and Universalists, Quakers, Reform Jews and Unitarians had a national inter-faith body.

The path to alliances among liberals was the 1893 World Parliament of Religions, which, in its validation of a bridge among all faiths, laid out the Universalist and Unitarian struggle for religious identity in the modern era. Jenkin Lloyd Jones (1843–1918) described the World Parliament as Pentecostal, as the unification of all people in all nations under the heavens in one holy enterprise.[2] He worked with civic leaders to keep the Exposition open on Sundays, arguing that the "material (was) so valuable that religion cannot afford to withdraw it from public study . . . any day of the week or any hour of the day."[3] Those with commercial interests were thrilled to have this rationale for remaining open. Liberal religion became identified with secular, cultural ideals that were communal in nature, yet tended to lead to more individualism and the undermining of cultural bonds.

Worldwide Universalism represented both fulfillment and irreparable loss for Protestants, who had always been defined by the Bible. Even the broadest of the liberal Christians had based their faith on reason as it applied to the Bible. This text prevented the faith from radical individualism and

---

[2] Thomas Graham, "Jenkin Lloyd Jones and the World's Columbian Exposition of 1893" (Collegium Proceedings, Vol. 1, 1979), p. 78.
[3] Graham, *Jenkin Lloyd Jones*, p. 66.

from an overwhelming diversity, by providing a common bond and some degree of shared authority. By subsuming other religious traditions into liberal Protestantism, sacred scripture was broadened to include religious texts from all faiths and the "book of nature." There could no longer be a separate Protestant religion. Many of those who protested the World Parliament understood this better than the organizers, who for the most part did not genuinely believe in parity. Genuinely held ideals of a universal religious impulse contrasted with strict sectarian divisions. Liberals wanted to deepen the spiritual life and promote a less materialistic culture. But common worship, in the midst of honoring the world's ten[4] great religions, was Protestant. The Lord's Prayer was used to begin every single day of the Parliament, and, preceded by Handel's Hallelujah Chorus, closed the event as well. The liturgist was a rabbi. Fewer than a quarter of the papers were by non-Christians. The universal spirit praised and sought after by liberals was actually a kind of unmoored, literate Christianity; and the purpose of gathering was to inspire a deeper, wider Christian faith.

Exposure to people of faith who were not Christian and yet upheld similar principles presented both a challenge and an opportunity to further embrace a natural theology. Exposure to Eastern religions, such as Buddhism or Shinto, reified the truths of science, gave people hope that a common humanity existed, and affirmed evolution as a progressive force that would lead inexorably to a higher culture; one that would reflect the values of liberal, educated Protestants, especially peace. Unitarianism and Universalism in the twentieth century were shaped by a dialectical legacy: the success of this vision in the public realm masked deep divisions about sectarianism within the institutionalized church, and both have effected identity and program development ever since.

Nowhere was liberal religion and social reform more entangled than in India. By the time of the World Parliament, Unitarians had been in India for an entire century, during which the British had established themselves as rulers, annexed Bengal, and established the social and legal order through business interests which precluded religious work until 1833, when missionaries were invited in to help create an elite native class to bridge the differing cultural expectations of the colonized and colonizers. Beginning in 1830, liberals began to factionalize, with all sides claiming the legacy of Rammohun Roy, the founder of both the short-lived Calcutta Unitarian Society, and the Brahmo Samaj, a Hindu reform group. Both British and American

---

[4] Hinduism, Buddhism, Jainism, Zoroastrianism, Taoism, Confucianism, Shinto, Judaism, Christianity, and Islam.

Unitarians described Roy as "the most advanced Christian,"[5] even as they acknowledged that he was maintaining his status as a Brahmin. Without any conversion, a Hindu was being incorporated into a vision of Christianity, in large part *because* he was a high-caste Hindu. The Brahmo Samaj splintered, with one branch defining itself as explicitly Hindu and non-textual, and another allying with Unitarians for social change. When an American Unitarian preacher, in India for health reasons, renewed interest in missionary work, a rift developed between the British and the American Unitarians. Each supported different leaders of the Brahmo Samaj. The entanglement of Hindu and Christian, of missionary activity and political reform, of personal goals and petty agendas mixed with religious vision, essentially strangled Unitarianism in India, while simultaneously keeping it more tantalizingly in reach there than in any other land.

The Orthodox Hindu backlash to missionary work in Bengal had deepened throughout the century, leading to reform groups being treated with suspicion. This was evident at the World Parliament, and was explicitly stated. Manilal Dvivedi said the Brahmo Samaj was the result of the intellectual impact of British rule.[6] Reformist Hindus were a colonial by-product and had a very narrow tightrope to walk, balancing issues of health, education, and poverty with tradition, identity, and status. For Unitarians and Universalists, identity continued to confound in much the same way as it had with Roy. Vivekananda (1863–1902), who represented Hinduism at the World Parliament, was a Brahmo and believed in Universal Religion. He was also a Unitarian, in that he believed in one God. But Vivekananda was a Hindu, and he was critical of Christianity. A Hindu fanatic might punish himself or might throw herself on a funeral pyre, he said, but he or she would never punish others, and could not have lit the fire of the Inquisition, because Hindus are tolerant of other religions.[7] Vivekananda's non-sectarian vision of religion included a belief in evolution and the importance of science, but was explicitly not Christian. Unitarians and liberal religionists praised Vivekananda himself, and his wisdom, without completely grasping the distinction between his vision and their own. He was merged into Christianity; his identity as a Hindu subsumed into a broader liberal Protestant view of universalized religion.

---

[5] Attributed to Joseph Tuckerman, quoted in Spencer Lavan, *Unitarians in India* (Boston, MA: Beacon Press, 1977) p. 70.

[6] Carl T. Jackson, *The Oriental Traditions in American Religious Thought* (Westport, CT: Greenwood Press, 1981), p. 248.

[7] John Barrows, ed., *The World Parliament of Religions* (Chicago, IL: Parliament Publishing Co., 1893), p. 977.

The theological confusion resulting from simultaneously embracing and misunderstanding a reformist Hindu as a liberal Christian was even more of an issue with Protap Mazumdar, who was at the World Parliament as a representative of the Brahmo Samaj. Mazumdar had been orphaned, and grew up reading Parker and Channing in Charles Dall's Unitarian mission in Calcutta. Mazumdar saw Asia as the birthplace of every important religious discovery; and the first value imported to the West was an elevated view of nature. He criticized Western religion's work ethic and its lack of visible practice, saying, "In the West you work incessantly; work is your worship. In the East we meditate; worship is our work."[8] Work as worship defined non-sectarian Unitarians. Mazumdar was appreciative of their efforts for social reform and was a zealous supporter of economic and educational opportunities for all. But he did not see work as worship.

The exposure to world religions generated interest in mission work, but it also undermined the concept. Missionary activity conveyed disrespect. This tension quickly became evident in Japan, where the Universalists had established a mission in 1890 when the American West and South, and Japan, were defined as the places most suitable for growth. Margaret Schuler and the Reverends George Perin and Wallace Cate arrived in Yokohama, and soon a church was erected, a theological school started, a magazine published, preaching outposts established, and English classes were offered.[9] The large number of people who wanted to go to Japan was not necessarily helpful. Repeated staff changes not only caused a lack of continuity in the program and in leadership, it also meant that missionaries were not fluent in Japanese. This automatically created a culture in which the mission staff could not communicate directly or on an equal basis with potential converts. Akashi Shigetaro (1872–1965) had already begun a Universalist church in Tokyo, primarily to address issues of poverty. Akashi did not believe Christianity was the only true religion. He found the Universalist missionaries too conservative, and his indigenous Universalist church remained distinct from the Universalist Church of America's mission.[10]

As more Universalist women arrived, there was a shift away from specific missionary work and towards education or social welfare projects. A home for girls escaping forced work as geishas was established and many American Universalist women contributors ceased sending funds to the

---

[8] Jackson, *Oriental Traditions*, p. 249.
[9] Carl Seaburg, *Dojin Means All People* (Boston, MA: Unitarian Universalist Ministers Association, 1983), unpaginated.
[10] Don McEvoy, *Credo International: Voices of Liberalism Around the World* (Delmar, CA: Humanity Press, 1983), p. 205.

Universalist Mission, favoring the specific work helping women.[11] Over time, self-supporting women's projects in Japan created a division, both financially and philosophically. There was potential for church growth: In 1912 there were five native Japanese preachers of Universalism and four American missionaries, and services were held weekly in four separate places for about 500 church members. But providing social services seemed to take precedence over worship: When the Perin–Cate Home for Boys opened, the minister of the Shizuaka church left to run it, and the church declined.

The mission in Japan was an intentional move into non-Christian lands, but instead of spreading the Universalist message, the experience in Japan began to transform Universalism itself. "Accustomed to proclaiming a gospel centered upon correcting the teachings of the Christian church regarding eternal punishment,"[12] the Universalists had not realized the irrelevance of this message to those who had never been taught they were damned. Universalists were forced "to confront the question of whether Universalism had any mission beyond that of correcting the teachings of other Christians."[13] In the process, the theological concept of salvation grew muddied. Instead of referring to an eternal life that was available to all, Universalism began to reflect a this-worldly component of including all people. As this more global and socially engaged sense of Universalism spread, Akashi Shigetaro, who explicitly linked socialism to Christianity, began working with the American Universalists.

The work in kindergartens and social service projects throughout the 1920s and 1930s partially reflected American Universalists' preference for funding small programs with personal connections rather than supporting centralized administration, but it was also the result of a social reality in Japan. The government grew increasingly conservative in the first decades of the twentieth century, and by 1928, all churches were controlled by the government, which was intent on keeping Japan both economically and administratively independent from foreign churches. In 1940, a law forced denominations with fewer than fifty churches to disband. The Universalists turned their churches over to the Congregationalists. The schools and homes, which had been the real Universalist mission, were removed from American control. Within a year, there were no American Universalists

[11] Seaburg, *Dojin*.
[12] David and Beverly Bumbaugh, "The New Universalism," A Sermon preached in Summit, NJ on Nov. 2, 1997.
[13] David Bumbaugh, "A Contemporary Evaluation of Universalism." *The Journal of Liberal Religion* (Chicago, IL: Meadville/Lombard, 2002), p. 3.

working in Japan, and the Japanese Universalists were now considered Congregationalists. When World War II ended, it was discovered that virtually all Universalist buildings had been destroyed.

Shortly before the Universalist mission began, Unitarians were invited to Japan. By the 1880s, Japanese intellectual leaders had come to see religion as "a pillar of the modern nation state,"[14] and if they were to compete economically on the world stage, the Japanese needed a religion. Christianity was a tool allowing access to the social network of world powers. However, the culture in Japan made supernatural beliefs unacceptable. In 1886, after studying in Britain, Yano Fumio recommended Unitarianism as the form of Christianity that would help Japan,[15] and other public leaders agreed. As a matter of national interest, the Japanese asked the American Unitarian Association (AUA) to send a representative to them. In 1887, Arthur May Knapp (1841–1921) arrived in Tokyo to aid in the development of a national religion for the purpose of economic and social competition.

Soon, Clay MacCauley (1843–1925), Saichiro Kanda, who had been studying at Meadville, and H.W. Hawkes, a British Unitarian minister, joined Knapp, along with three professors assigned to Keio University. The primary institutional connection of the Unitarians was to Japanese universities. There was no scripture associated with the Unitarians in Japan; no attempt to reform Buddhism or Shinto for the modern world. Instead, it was an application of the principles of reason, respect, science, and progress to a national ethos, and its impact was profound. The principled moral stance, divorced from tradition, is often cited as a source of Japan's nationalism, a tool in loyally binding the people to the government.

But the confusion as to the role of Christianity in a universal religion continued. Kinzo Harai, who had spoken as a Buddhist priest at the World Parliament, was a year later the Japanese Unitarian delegate to the AUA. He stated, "In Japan the people believe that at bottom all religions have the same truth in them." William Lawrence reported on the success in Japan in 1895, "the great mistake in general missionary efforts had been to establish on Oriental soil, . . . an Occidental institution . . . Unitarians had endeavored to harmonize all religion . . . Japan was . . . representative of Western advancement in the East. It had adopted American machinery, weapons, and philosophy, and was likeliest to accept the highest and purest

---

[14] Yamaguchi Aki. "Religious Universalism in Modern Japan: Unitarians as Mediators between Intellectuals and the West," *Japanese Journal of Religious Studies*, Vol. 32, No. 2 (Nanzan Institute for Religion and Culture, 2005), p. 305.

[15] Yamaguchi, "Religious Universalism," p. 308.

interpretation of Christianity as presented by Unitarianism."[16] Clay Mac-Cauley thought Christianity had little place in Japan, but that rational, naturalistic thought was congenial to the people.[17] As Universalist leaders in America resisted overtures from Unitarians, this statement was hauled out as a reason.[18]

The current tendency among American Unitarian Universalists to disparage the Universalist Church of America (UCA) and AUA for not persisting in these international efforts ignores history. The British recalled Hawkes in 1896, and the AUA ceased support in 1899. In a ten-year period, Japan had nationalized, industrialized in a manner that revolutionized the social order, renegotiated its treaties, warred with China, and gained Taiwan. These developments were precisely the goals of adopting a state religion. By 1905, with Japan's defeat of Russia, anti-Asian sentiment developed. The threat of Japanese military power conflated with fear of Chinese influence in America's newly acquired territories: Hawaii, Guam, Puerto Rico, Cuba, and particularly the Philippines. Japan's 1910 annexation of Korea provided a land buffer between the Russians and the rest of Asia. This protected US interests, but fed the fear of Asians. By the end of World War I, allied with Great Britain and the United States, Japan expected to be rewarded with new territory. Instead, European powers gained vast lands and the Americans refused to allow a racial equality clause in the covenant for the League of Nations. By 1924, the United States codified its racism into immigration policy.

The generalized anxiety about national identity that plagued the US in the wake of disruptive international experiences was compounded for the Universalists, who established their missionary goals just in time to experience major power shifts, both in the American South and in Asia. Before World War I, the Universalists had seemed to solidify around the broad Social Gospel leadership of Clarence Russell Skinner (1881–1949); but by the early 1920s, the growing conservatism of the country was reflected among the Universalists, too. Indeed, Universalists – who had always sought acceptance within the mainstream – retreated from the 1917 Declaration of Social Principles. Skinner, a pacifist and supporter of the International Workers of the World (IWW) was identified as an extreme liberal, and

---

[16] "Unitarian Meeting Over: National Conference in Washington Completes its Work," *New York Times*, October 25, 1895.
[17] Clay MacCauley, "Christianity in Japan," *Proceedings of the 17th meeting of the National Conference of Unitarian and Other Christian Churches* (Boston, MA: George Ellis, 1897), p. 183.
[18] Russell E. Miller, *The Larger Hope: The Second Century of the Universalist Church in America, 1870–1970* (Boston, MA: UUA), p. 546.

the British denied him a visa to visit India, out of fear that his interest in international peace would prove troublesome. The denomination ended up threatened from both within and without, as some embraced Skinner's leadership while others grew increasingly concerned with how the faith was perceived. Universalist membership shrank dramatically in the first quarter of the century. Abstract ideals of commonality were challenged by urbanization and immigration patterns that reflected shifting allegiances on the world stage. "White" could become a category which linked previously disparate ethnic groups by race, as global warfare and urbanization caused displacement. For African Americans, the immigration laws represented a huge loss as they categorized citizens and potential citizens by race first, then developed policies based on these categories. The limited freedoms that people of color had gained at the turn of the century were curtailed, and *de facto* racism became legalized.

Joseph Jordan (1842–1901), the first ordained African American Universalist, was challenged by urbanization. Jordan discovered Universalism through reading, and began a successful mission church in Norfolk, Virginia. He brought in a colleague to start a church in Suffolk. Quillen Shinn (1845–1907), who worked for the denomination as a missionary to the South, helped organize a youth program and Sunday School; then, an industrial training and a home economics program was developed, and a school built with funds raised by Shinn and Universalist women's groups. Although in 1901 there were 275 students enrolled, by 1904 it was closed. Most of the members had moved north.[19]

A second, unrelated Joseph Jordan (1863–1929) was brought into Universalism by Shinn. In 1904, Jordan reorganized the school in Suffolk and quickly built up both the church and the school. The school was consistently serving more students than it could hold, and was dependent upon tuition to operate, despite the fact that the students were impoverished. The lack of fundraising for the efforts among African Americans did not go unnoticed: After noting that missionaries had traveled across the globe and raised thousands of dollars, Shinn asked "Is the soul of the Negro worth as much as the soul of a Japanese?"[20]

The church in Norfolk died with Jordan, in 1929, but the school continued through the work of his daughter and granddaughter. In 1938, the school became a project of the Young People's Christian Union, and the following year programming shifted to social service work. The former school became a community center known as Jordan Neighborhood House, where

---

[19] Miller, *The Larger Hope*, pp. 361–365.   [20] Miller, ibid., p. 369.

Head Start programs were pioneered. Support and oversight came from a variety of Universalist sources, especially women's groups, until 1969, when all denominational ties ceased.

Even though the changing society was used as a reason to stop offering academic programs (public schools were forced to admit black students, therefore decreasing the need for the separate school), there was never any denominational agitation for integrated public schools, let alone an integrated church. The African American ministers were sent to preach in a separate environment, where they raised their own successors, or failed. A principal reason for failure was the role of economics in a tradition in which congregations are self-governed. The structural inability of a marginalized community to become self-supporting was never acknowledged. Universalists were loath to support a central administration, which was essential to real mission efforts; and they, like Unitarians, assumed that financial contributions by members reflected the value of the faith. When black leaders continued to need financial assistance, this assumption led to false judgments about work ethics and lifestyles, and about the value of the mission itself. There was no vision of a ministry that served people whose circumstances were not those of free, independent agents. Black leaders had to continually ask for handouts, and those continuing financial needs undermined confidence in the leaders. A belief in individualism, even an unconscious one, allowed denominational leaders to ignore the social reality of race. The practice of religion was in a world very different from the intellectual ideal of a broad sympathy.

As the United States became a colonial power itself, race became a factor in determining in what ways Americans were like the British and in what ways they were like other colonies. Did England represent home or tyrannical power? Among Unitarians, this question had the power to divide, by reviving the theological issues that had plagued the Church of England in the sixteenth and seventeenth centuries. Unitarianism in the US was an institution whose leaders had national administrative and military power. It no longer had the capacity to absorb radical political differences. Samuel Eliot (1862–1950) became executive secretary of the American Unitarian Association (AUA) in 1898, and by 1900 filled the newly created office of President. He is credited with centralizing the administration so that it could function in the world. Financial commitments were secured, church school curricula were developed, churches were started. The charter was amended to create an association of churches rather than individuals, headquarters were built and a system of departments created, leading to an assumption that corporate action would become easier and more effective.

But there was no leadership from a pastor or a theologian in this vision. Eliot's leadership shaped a presidential role reflecting a belief that what was truly valued was economic security and power. This institutional unifier, who made progress possible, used economic viability as a method to block the progress of women and people of color in the ministry.

Eliot declared Unitarianism a missionary association. Mission churches could neatly combine imperialism and a belief in racial purity by delivering a vision to others, rather than creating a community based on equality and freedom. During Ethelred Brown's (1875–1956) adolescence, the British colony of Jamaica gained some measure of self-government. The Civil Service created a burgeoning middle class, and Brown was part of it. But Brown discovered Unitarianism independently, by reading, and began pursuing the possibility of ministry in 1907. He was accepted at Meadville, and in 1912 was ordained as a missionary by the school, acting as proxy for a group of Unitarians in Montego Bay.[21] Both the British and Foreign Unitarian Association and the AUA supported this venture, and then almost immediately began a "policy of neglect" which "derailed the prospects of an indigenous Unitarian movement in the West Indies."[22] British Unitarian women raised funds for Brown, even though he was "not the type of man to entrust with the organization of a Unitarian church,"[23] and "the colored population of Jamaica was not intellectually fit to receive Unitarianism."[24] In November 1917, as revolts broke out in Jamaica and emigration began in earnest, Eliot ended all programs of church subsidy because the practice made local churches weak and dependent. Additionally, "foreign missions were an impertinence as well as a waste of effort and money." The shift in vision was remarkable: a direct result of American expansionism and the incorporation of a business model into the church structure. By 1920, the Jamaican church was closed, and Brown had moved to New York City.

Immediately, Brown formed the Harlem Community Church, with the main body of membership comprising other Jamaican exiles. Almost all official AUA energy directed toward this church, founded by an ordained Unitarian in a large city, was aimed at its demise. The fact that Brown earned money outside of ministry was used as a reason in the repeated attempts to remove him from fellowship. His interest in socialism, which tied him to John Haynes Holmes and Clarence Russell Skinner, was confused with

---

[21] Mark Morrison-Reed, *Black Pioneers in a White Denomination* (Boston, MA: Skinner House, 1980), p. 51.
[22] Juan Floyd-Thomas, *The Origins of Black Humanism in America* (New York: Palgrave-Macmillan, 2008), p. 39.
[23] Morrison-Reed, *Black Pioneers*, p. 57.   [24] Floyd-Thomas, *Origins of Black Humanism*, p. 39.

Communism, even though his calls for justice were based almost entirely on the writings of Unitarianism.[25]

The Unitarian and Universalist claim that all of humanity was the same, and shared a vision of justice and freedom, made it impossible to recognize experience that derived from national and racial identity. The Immigration Acts excluding Asians also restricted blacks from Jamaica and the Bahamas,[26] which was a call to action for recent immigrants. The Unitarian Church was a center from which they could agitate for their rights. African Americans were more likely to join integrated congregations, such as the Community Church of New York. Immigrants of color from British colonies, including India, were perceived as competition for limited work opportunities. The broad, idealistic identity crumbled in the pedestrian world, and made the liberals susceptible to endless internal processing, as well as to a religious practice that was continually subservient to special-interest groups, which defined people by their social experiences of oppression rather than by theology. Projects and missions were established and funded based upon the ability of a minister to garner support, and criteria for success reflected a business understanding of what qualified as worthy. This model could not help but perpetuate racism, even as ecumenicism and global ties were championed. While preaching "sympathy" and "universalism," the Unitarian and Universalist leaders tended to practice tribal warfare, fighting intensely with those whose visions were most closely aligned. Commissions formed to study merger and promote co-operation spawned more organizations instead: The Free Church Fellowship (1933–1937) was seen as a restriction being imposed upon people, rather than an opportunity for like-minded people to work together more effectively. Freedom gave license to retreat from connections and actions that would extend that freedom to others.

When it was published in 1933, the *Humanist Manifesto* reflected the consolidation of a plateaued movement.[27] The humanist–theist controversy, which defined twentieth-century liberalism, especially in the US, was not just a theological, academic debate; rather, it was a dialogue about the role of political activism in a global religious life, and the role of science in defining our deepest beliefs about who we (and who others) are as human beings. Science was used to uphold humanism theologically, and racism socially, in both denominations. This made global ethics impossible to practice, and besieged the liberal church from every direction,

[25] Morrison-Reed, *Black Pioneers*, p. 95.   [26] Floyd-Thomas, *Origins of Black Humanism*, p. 44.

[27] William F. Schulz, *Making the Manifesto: The Birth of Religious Humanism* (Boston, MA: Skinner House, 2002), p. 18.

and is at least in part why debates about the role of humanism, institutional racism and international involvement continue to this day. Humanism could have produced a liberation theology instead of retreating into individualism.

However, American or British racism was not always the reason projects ended. A 1997 Commission on Appraisal report mentions the work of a Japanese Universalist who began a Sunday School in Korea in 1928[28], then cites the failure to provide ongoing support as indicative of both the lack of interest in mission work and a sign of racism. In reality, this work could only have been attempted during a very brief period in the 1920s, and was a sign of Japanese imperialism more than liberal religion. Korea had been taken in 1910, and for a dozen years was subjected to severe restrictions. Rebellions in the early 1920s helped the Koreans gain a degree of intellectual freedom, but by the end of the decade, Japan began an explicit program of forced assimilation. Shinto worship was mandated; Korean names were changed to Japanese ones; the land was appropriated to produce rice for the Japanese; the native Koreans were starved. Those who see the demise of a Universalist Sunday School in this context as an American institutional failure believe that the Universalists had far more power than they did; and simultaneously do not recognize the power of the Japanese.

Just prior to the United States joining World War II, Robert Cummins became the General Superintendent of the Universalists. Cummins (1897–1982) had directed collegiate inter-faith activities and then been "revolutionized" by living and working in the "tropical Orient with people of many nationalities, races and religions."[29] An inclusivist, he did not participate in doctrinal controversies about the role of humanism, but part of his central plan to revive Universalism was to join the Federal Council of Churches. Because this effort failed, it has been interpreted as a step backward; part of a futile attempt to be accepted by the mainstream Christian denominations.[30] But the Federal Council's rejection led to the creation of a formal identity: The *Christian Leader* became the *Universalist Leader*, clergy began requesting ordination into the Universalist rather than the Christian ministry, and the General Convention of Universalists reformed as the Universalist Church of America (1942). Universalism was no longer a

[28] Commission on Appraisal, *Interdependence: Renewing Congregational Polity* (Boston, MA: UUA, June 1997), pp. 5, 164.
[29] Robert Cummins, *Excluded: The Story of the Council of Churches and the Universalists* (Boston, MA: UUA, 1966), p. 3.
[30] See Clinton Lee Scott, *The Universalist Church of America – A Short History* (Boston, MA: Universalist Historical Society, 1949).

sect within Christianity, but a religion of its own, free to pursue a relationship with another independent church. The Council of Liberal Churches was formed in 1953, and led to the vote for merger with the Unitarians in 1959.

In Japan, Universalism had continued under Akashi Shigetaro, who used his church as the headquarters for the Social Democratic Party. But following World War II, Akashi left Universalism behind. As Japan reopened, fundamentalist Christians were moving in, which mobilized the Universalists and allowed them to continue defining Universalism strictly as a theological correction. Working through the Service Committee, Carlton Fisher and John Shidara recruited students to prepare for the ministry at the Theological School at St. Lawrence University in Canton, New York, beginning in 1950. One of these ministers, Toshio Yoshioka, contacted the Philippine Universalists in 1958, a group that practiced a very similar form of Universalism.

Akashi, meanwhile, founded the Japanese Free Christian Church (Unitarian). He reported that an American Unitarian assigned to the International Military Trial in Tokyo sought him out, having heard about the presence of liberal Christians in Japan.[31] Akashi Shigetaro was also the principal founder, along with Shinicharo Imaoka, of the Japan Free Religious Association. Imaoka (1881–1988) was a graduate student at Harvard before World War I, and was intensely interested in promoting religious dialogue. Active in the International Association for Religious Freedom his entire life, he practiced a syncretistic faith with a small group at Unity House (Unitarian). It is through Imaoka that the Unitarians developed a relationship with the Rissho Kosei-Kai, a liberal Buddhist organization. Currently, the former Dean of the Meadville Lombard works in Japan, as a consultant to the Rissho Kosei-Kai.

"Unitarian Universalist International Engagement," a document on the Unitarian Universalist Association (UUA) website, says that John Nicholls Booth was sent by the American Unitarian Association (AUA) to reorganize Unitarians in Japan in 1948, reforming the Japan Unitarian Association.[32] Although Booth (1912–2009) was in Japan in July 1948, he makes clear in his book, *Fabulous Destinations*, that he was not supposed to be, and he does not mention Unitarianism at all. One point of the document is that Unitarians and Universalists have a history of not following through on mission work. It may be that in attempting to demonstrate this failure, missed opportunities have been dramatized and political realities have

---

[31] McEvoy, *Credo*, p. 208.   [32] See: uua.org/documents.uu_international_history_01.pps.

been ignored. Japan was under military control in 1948. Akashi Shigetaro's two sons, Michio and Shigeo, studied at Meadville Lombard and Starr King respectively, and returned to lead both Dojin and the Free Christian Church, suggesting that liberal Japanese religion was a family affair. If the statement posted at the UUA is true, the denomination had to be working secretly through the US military, and with the Akashis. At question in the end may not be whether the Universalist missionaries were supported, or whether the AUA abandoned a potential source of church growth, but whether the progressive religion, embracing science, progress and the use of reason, ended up contributing more to the military–industrial complex than to the spiritual life of the Japanese.

Although a military connection to the expansion of liberal religion may sound unlikely, it is undoubtedly true in the case of the Philippines. The legacy of political involvement between the Unitarians, colonial authorities, and the founders of the Philippines Independent Church is unavoidable. The Universalist side is more straightforward: The Universalist Church of the Philippines was first recognized by the government in 1955, the same year that Toribio Quimada received help from the American Universalists, when Carlton Fisher responded to Quimada's inquiry about a connection between his own church, Iglesia Universal de Cristo, and Universalists in America. A relationship developed. Quimada had become a Protestant as a teen and was ordained in 1943, but was excommunicated because of his liberal views. Fisher helped Quimada achieve standing as a Universalist minister, with congregations rooted in the traditional, theological conception of universal salvation. But Quimada's ministry was radical, and he was murdered in May 1988. The following month the UUA bylaws were changed so that foreign churches could join. The Unitarian Universalist Church of the Philippines (the name changed from Universalist to Unitarian Universalist in 1985) became a member congregation of the UUA in June 1988, representing 25 churches and 2,500 members. As with the Japanese Universalists, the faith is familial: Quimada's daughter, Rebecca Quimada Siennes, graduated from Meadville Lombard Theological School in 1999 and led the denomination after her father's death.

The only Christian nation in Asia, the Filipino population is 85 percent Roman Catholic and has a strong Muslim population in the south. Sunni Muslims have lived in Mindanao and surrounding islands for more than six centuries, and were not part of the Philippines when Spain colonized and Christianized most of the 1,000-mile archipelago in the mid-sixteenth century. Yet the United States included these southern islands when taking the Philippines from Spain, adding a formerly independent Muslim nation to a Roman Catholic Spanish colony which believed it had just won independence. The nationalist movement in the Philippines arose immediately, and was suppressed by the US during a guerilla war that continued until 1913. Filipino military deaths were counted at 20,000; civilian estimates ranged from 250,000 to one million; American casualties were 4,000 in number.

The liberal church in the Philippines dates from this period, and developed with Unitarian assistance. William Howard Taft (1857–1930), an extremely active Unitarian lay leader, was sent to the Philippines as the first Governor General. A government that separated church and state was an immediate necessity. Since the Catholic Church had possessed much of the country, Taft needed to settle land-ownership disputes. The land-reform program kept the vast independence movement under American colonial control.[33] First, in 1903, all Moro (Muslim) land holdings were declared void, and Christian Filipinos from the north were encouraged to take advantage of this chance for indigenous ownership. Gregorio Aglipay, a Catholic priest, was leading an independence movement that included separation from the Pope and ecclesiastical authority. Millions of Filipinos followed Aglipay's movement, remaining in their churches but redefining them as independent. Taft volunteered to serve as the Vice President of the Philippine Independent Church, and allowed the members to remain in Catholic buildings on Catholic land, even though the Pope was demanding restitution. By the time the legal suits were resolved, in 1908, in favor of Rome, the Independent Church had been working with Taft for close to a decade, and the independence movement was undermined from within. Taft appointed constables to travel with Aglipay, spreading disinformation and gathering intelligence. His tenure as Governor General included the passage of laws criminalizing vagrancy and tribal affiliations, and the elimination of groups of people through starvation.

American military officers built a new police force, comprised of Filipinos who were sent out to put down rebellions. The Muslims who would not acquiesce to foreign rule were massacred, simultaneously instigating both a civil war and a caste system in which natives of the islands could achieve the most personally, by policing their community based upon American business and political interests. When Taft became President of the United States, he appointed William Cameron Forbes as the Governor General of the Philippines. Forbes, a fellow Unitarian and the grandson of

---

[33] David Barrows, *A Decade of American Government in the Philippines, 1903–1913* (Yonkers, NY: World Book, 1914).

Ralph Waldo Emerson, was the direct beneficiary of his father's investment in the China trade, a business for which the Philippines were a strategic investment. Forbes pushed through laws that gave both American corporations and Christian settlers greater entitlements. Forbes accessed millions of dollars for private roads at the expense of general education and public developments for the people who lived mainly on the coasts, without vehicles or draft animals. These are areas where, in the twenty-first century, Islamic terrorism has grown into a worldwide threat.

Taft's collaboration with Aglipay reflected a form of Unitarian ideology rooted in Social Darwinism, allowing him to embrace expansionism. Samuel Eliot's controlling, capitalist behavior as AUA president had already irritated John Haynes Holmes (1879–1964), but his collaboration with Taft drove Holmes out of institutional Unitarianism. At the 1917 General Conference, Holmes proposed a ministry rooted in peace and the establishment of God's law. Taft denounced him and worked with Eliot to rout out seditious clergy through financial means. Denominational funds became unavailable to congregations whose leadership did not support the war. Holmes, a founder of the National Association for the Advancement of Colored People, supported Ethelred Brown and became a promoter of Gandhi.

This argument was not about pacifism. It was a conflict between a form of Unitarianism rooted in dissent, and a form of Unitarianism based upon a Protestant standing order in which the church was an arm of the state. The Philippine Independent Church was government work, not a missionary effort. Louis Cornish, the AUA President following Eliot, did not know the group existed. When he learned of it and sent John Lathrop to visit, a letter from Jabez Sunderland arrived: "My dear Lathrop, You speak as if you were the discoverer of the Filipino Church. Many years ago I discovered this church and wrote a full report to the Unitarian Association, but they never did anything about it."[34]

Cornish tried very hard to establish an institutional connection with the Filipino group.[35] Aglipay was invited to the United States, awarded an honorary degree from Meadville Lombard, and spoke in a variety of Unitarian churches in the United States and Canada. Aglipay died in 1940, six years before the Philippines gained independence, at which point the Independent Church was factionalized. The largest group, with legal

[34] Nym Wales, "The Church in Asia" in Stephen H. Fritchman, ed., *Together We Advance* (Boston, MA: Beacon Press, 1946), p. 139.
[35] Frederick Muir, *Maglipay Universalists* (Annapolis, MD: The Unitarian Universalist Church of Annapolis, 2001), p. 20.

and historical standing as the Philippine Independent Church, affiliated with the Episcopalians in 1947. One splinter group, dating from 1955, is the Independent Church of Filipino Christians, which participates in the International Association for Religious Freedom (IARF). Yet another division produced the Philippine Unitarian Church. None of these groups had any ties to Quimada or the Universalists. The Unitarian Universalist Church of the Philippines is the successor to the Universalist congregations that Quimada began, with support from and affiliation with American Universalists. Yet current fundraising for a dormitory has the highest level of giving associated with Aglipay rather than Quimada.

The near constant global warfare that marked the first half of the twentieth century may seem to have generated an interest in pacifism, but international peace was an ideal long associated with Unitarianism and freedom. Representatives from at least seventeen different faiths raised the first known peace flag,[36] dedicated to harmonious living throughout the world in 1894, at Green Acre in Eliot, Maine. Sarah Farmer, Green Acre's founder, had been raised a Transcendentalist, and after meeting with participants in the World Parliament of Religions, she dedicated the camp to peace, which was the message of all the great religions, and could be achieved through open conversation.

In 1900, Farmer cruised to Palestine for health reasons. There, she learned about Baha'i, and returned to Green Acre promoting this faith. Green Acre loyalists felt betrayed by a new form of sectarianism. Over the next ten years, factions battled for control over the site, while Farmer's health deteriorated. Beginning in 1912, her psychiatrist, the Baha'i, and the Transcendentalists vied for custody as her guardian. She was treated with sedatives, electroshock therapy, isolation, and was ultimately stolen away from a psychiatric hospital by the Baha'i in 1915. Abdu'l-Baha (1844–1921), the eldest son of the Baha'i founder and its Head of Faith, visited Green Acre, and declared his hope that it would be the site of the first Baha'i university in the world. The following year, all the programming was Baha'i. The principals who wanted Green Acre to remain non-sectarian filed a lawsuit and lost.

The irony of a new religion growing as a result of a dedication to non-sectarianism is instructive, as is the intense battle over how to live harmoniously. Just as democratic systems awarded the Green Acre site to a specific religion, dispassionate interest in religious ideals awakened a longing for a particular faith. Comparative religion is an academic field,

---

[36] Laurie Maffly-Kipp, Leigh Eric Schmidt and Mark Valeri, eds., *Practicing Protestants: Histories of Christian Life in America, 1630–1965* (Baltimore, MD: Johns Hopkins University Press, 2006), p. 10.

born of a search and an idealism, which transformed Christianity from the inside by inviting science and historicism into religion. World War I became a watershed: An academic faith in all religions as substantially the same justified action in solidarity with those who were threatened. The IARF had been essentially ceremonial, reflecting both an aesthetic interest in worship and in world religions; but after the war, the organization became a forum for discussion and action. Saving religious minorities from persecution was a cause that provided both individual spiritual growth and a corporate purpose. This helped revive Unitarianism in Czechoslovakia, save Unitarianism in Transylvania and create it in the Khasi Hills.

The most numerically significant Unitarian mission developed through the IARF. Tomas Masaryk, who would become the first president of Czechoslovakia, met and then married Charlotte Garrigue, an American Unitarian woman studying in Germany. Active in the IARF, Masaryk introduced his fellow countryman Norbert Capek (1870–1942) to the IARF, and to American Unitarian Association (AUA) officers who were attending the 1910 conference in Berlin. Capek, a liberal Baptist, uncovered the story of the Moravian Brethren and ancient Bohemian liberals, and began to understand the history of his people as rooted in persecution in which doctrine crushed the living faith. Capek tried unsuccessfully to interest the AUA in a Unitarian church in Prague; then left Bohemia in 1914, and served Baptist churches in New York and New Jersey. He left the ministry in 1919 because he could no longer embrace Baptism, and his family joined the Unitarian Church of Orange, NJ. In 1922, with their homeland newly independent, the Capeks returned to Prague and to ministry. The AUA and the British and Foreign Unitarian Association pledged commitment, although Samuel Eliot also supported the Evangelical Church.

Capek founded the largest Unitarian church in the world, initiating a movement that spread across Czechoslovakia and counted 8,000 members by 1941. Capek wrote music and founded what is now a well-established ritual, the Flower Festival. Introduced to Unitarianism through academic connections and the IARF, Capek was a profoundly holistic minister who embraced missionary work because he saw it as a way of offering freedom. Liberty and independence would let people and nations develop in a spirit of truth. Seventeen years after Capek returned to Prague, Nazis took part of Czechoslovakia. Unitarians in America were stunned and sent help that led to the founding of the Service Committee.[37] But, in 1941, Capek was

---

[37] For more information about the founding of the Service Committee, see Susan Elisabeth Subak, *Rescue and Flight: American Relief Workers Who Defied the Nazis* (Lincoln, NE: University of Nebraska Press, 2010).

arrested for treason. He died in 1942 at Dachau, a martyr for the cause of Unitarianism. After the establishment of the Czech Republic and the lifting of the Iron Curtain, international ties among liberal religionists were re-established, as was Czech membership in the IARF.

The IARF was also instrumental in renewing ties among the Unitarians in Transylvania with those in other parts of the world. Contact existed early in the nineteenth century, but Eastern Europe remained fairly isolated from association with Westerners. Leaders of Unitarianism in Transylvania had been part of the IARF since its inception. At the end of World War I, Transylvania was joined to Romania, which caused many Transylvanian Unitarians to flee for Hungary. Both the British General Assembly and the American Unitarian Association (AUA) contributed to building a mission house and a church in Budapest, and a "sister church" program was set up, through which congregations in the United States and individuals in England could send money. Starr King and Meadville Lombard provided scholarships for Transylvanian Unitarians.

But, as had happened in Czechoslovakia, World War II brought Nazi rule to Romania, followed by membership in the Warsaw Pact. In 1948, the state nationalized all church possessions and forced conformity. Within a decade, ministers and professors at the theological schools were political prisoners.[38] One hundred twenty-two congregations and forty fellowships were under government control when Ceaușescu became president in 1963 and developed policies aimed at destroying religion. Churches were demolished and the publishing or import of religious texts, including the Bible, was forbidden. Nevertheless, between six and twelve Unitarians from Eastern Europe managed to attend IARF conferences in the 1960s, forming the primary connection to the larger world.[39]

In 1987, Judit Gellerd, the daughter of a Transylvanian Unitarian minister, was a delegate to the IARF Congress in Palo Alto, California. Dr. Gellerd soon married George Williams in Berkeley, and remained in California, developing IARF relationships. Before Ceaușescu was overthrown, "the UUA began to receive reports of a renewed danger facing the Transylvanian churches."[40] An ethnic-cleansing program, removing Hungarians from their villages and resettling them elsewhere to force assimilation, was

---

[38] Alpar Kiss, "The Transylvanian Unitarian Church: Its Past, Present, and Future," A sermon delivered at the Unitarian Universalist Church in Summit (NJ), April 2, 2000.

[39] Richard Boeke, "The History of the Partner Church Movement," www.uupcc.org/history.html.

[40] Richard Beal, "Partner Church history," First Unitarian Church of Louisville website, www.firstulou.org/groups/pcc.html.

proposed. Their churches would be razed. As soon as travel into Transylvania was allowed in 1989, the Unitarian Universalist Association (UUA) President William Schulz, and Moderator Natalie Gulbrandsen, visited; and the UUA decided to immediately revive the sister church program. The 1990 IARF Congress was planned for Hamburg, with tours in Eastern Europe following. Gellerd, Gulbrandsen, and others established, and re-established, partner church contacts. Under Schulz and Gulbrandsen, the UUA was very interested in international contacts, but in April 1993, the UUA Trustees cut all financial and administrative support. This was presented as a budgetary issue, but it presaged a decade of a rather different philosophy of engagement under the new UUA President, John Buehrens, and his successor, William Sinkford. The Partner Church Council, a completely independent organization with its own bylaws, was formally established in June 1993, with a volunteer board. Currently, approximately 200 North American congregations are partnered with Unitarian and Unitarian Universalist churches in Transylvania and Hungary, as well as the Czech Republic, the Khasi Hills, the Philippines, and Poland.

The need to preserve Unitarianism as a specific religion, despite its wide affinities, was a topic of interest to Jabez Sunderland (1842–1936), who was responsible for bringing the Unitarians of the Khasi Hills into the fold. Sunderland had a vision of Christianity that included Asian spirituality as well as science and evolution, which made him the perfect missionary to Calcutta, where he reunited the Brahmo Samaj. Arrangements were made for Indian men to study at Manchester College, Oxford and for both British and American Unitarians to send books, money, and missionaries.

Sunderland traveled to the Khasi Hills, a remote, sparsely populated region where tribal language and religion flourished without Muslim or Hindu conversion, to meet with Hajom Kissor Singh (1865–1923), with whom he had long been corresponding. The name of this region of India translates to "abode of the clouds," and the religious practice was Shamanistic, featuring ancestor worship, demons, and ritualized customs. Conservative Christian missionaries arrived in Khasi in 1813, built a church and started schools, creating the first written Khasi language by translating a Bible. Khasis were incorporated into the British hierarchy through these schools, which also converted the population to a conservative Christianity. However, Singh, a surveyor, met members of the Brahmo Samaj and was exposed to liberal theology. He read independently and began a church and a school, using materials Sunderland had prepared and translated into Khasi. During his visit, Sunderland ordained a pastor and helped the group write the constitution for their new religion, which had grown to eight congregations and four schools.[41]

The Khasi Unitarians were and are a religious movement that is different from the Unitarianism of any other place. It has helped to preserve a culture that was being destroyed by missionaries and the government. Sunderland's support of Singh helped create a church that could resist Christianity by adopting its model, and then using that model to house the aboriginal myths and concepts that made up the Khasi religion, which is very different from Western faiths. The clan, not the individual, forms the basis for the religion.[42] Tradition is familial, not literate, and the only real use of the Bible is as ammunition against conservative Christians. The Khasi Unitarians have a catechism that does not mention Jesus, but simply defines the religion in terms of service to God, to others, and to the self. The religion preserves their pre-colonial past. This is quite different from Unitarianism in almost every other context, where the goal is reform. There are now more than thirty Unitarian churches and 10,000 members in Meghalaya, while the Brahmo Samaj remains splintered in Bengal. In 2009, the Khasi Unitarians built an orphanage in order to prevent their children from being sent to religiously based orphanages where conversion is typical.

Sunderland was publicly quite critical of Britain and its rule in India, and he returned to the US before World War I to promote self-rule in India. In the Khasi Hills, after Singh died in 1923, a minister was needed. Margaret Barr, an experienced minister and graduate of Manchester College, volunteered for the position in 1932. When officials demurred because of her gender, Barr sought out a teaching job through the Brahmo Samaj in Calcutta, until in 1936 she was appointed as minister to the Khasi Hills Unitarians. British Unitarian women raised funds for her salary, and continued to do so until she was eligible for pension. Barr remained among the Khasi until her death in 1973, and is widely acclaimed as one of the best loved and most respected persons in the twentieth-century British Unitarian church.

Barr took great pride in teaching respect for all religions, and had an intense dislike for missionizing. She wrote, "The job rested on my ability to convince them that my aim was to be . . . a Bridge-Builder and at the same time make a Unitarian contribution to social progress in an area of

---

[41] George Willis Cooke, *Unitarianism in America* (Boston, MA: American Unitarian Association, 1910), p. 303.
[42] John Rex, "Khasi Unitarians of Northeast India," *Unitarian Universalist Ministers Association Selected Essays 2000* (Boston, MA: UUMA, 2000), p. 130.

the world where there happened to be an indigenous Unitarian movement already in existence."[43] Sunderland is completely missing from Barr's story of the Khasi. This preserved her identity as a British Unitarian, who by definition rejected mission work of any kind, and it safely de-politicized her work while allowing her to categorize universal access to a Western concept of education as a ministry of social progress. In 1973, a photograph in the *UU World* had a caption identifying her as a missionary; Barr wrote a letter of protestation, stating that a believer in the essential unity of true religion at its deepest level could never engage in missionary work. Sunderland had consistently been defined as doing precisely that.

The Universalists tried a different approach to the sectarian versus comparative religion dilemma, by syncretizing faith. Harmony could be achieved by understanding the forms of religious practice as particular expressions of something much deeper and universal. This universal faith reconciled differences among believers without critical exploration of how and why religious traditions are embodied and enacted, and embraced the idea of religion instead. The Massachusetts Convention of Universalists acquired the Charles Street Meetinghouse in Boston (1948) and created a "clear alternative to the tradition-bound Unitarian churches."[44] Kenneth Patton (1911–1994) built a center of contemporary worship; a church in the round, walls covered in a variety of religious symbols and a mural featuring Andromeda. World scriptures were placed where an altar might traditionally have been. The Universalism developed at Charles Street was ideological, not interpersonal, and it was delivered through artistic expression rather than arrived at following immersion in the texts or practices of any specific religious tradition. Patton wrote, among other books, *A Religion for One World* (1964), which assembled the symbols necessary for an inclusive, worldwide faith that absorbed and homogenized varied expressions into an essentially Protestant vision, based upon an assumption about sameness at the root of all religions. The institution eradicated difference rather than bridging it, and at some level was at cross-purposes with the ideals of individualism celebrated in liberal religion. Art became a tool of worship rather than a personal expression.

Although the Charles Street Meetinghouse did not live on, Patton's books and worship materials did, and truly shaped the future denomination. The language he used, the recasting of hymns, the world symbols,

[43] Margaret Barr, *A Dream Come True: The story of the Kharang* (London, UK: The Lindsey Press, 1974), p. 83.
[44] David Bumbaugh and Beverly Bumbaugh, "The New Universalism," A sermon preached in Summit, NJ; November 2, 1997.

and the inclusion of science as both central and wondrous gave form to the emerging Unitarian Universalist faith. *Hymns for the Celebration of Life* (1964), the product of a UUA Hymnal Commission that included Patton, helped codify this type of worship and enable its spread. But the growth in Unitarian Universalist churches must be attributed to the institutional developments of Frederick May Eliot, not the liturgical experiment of the Charles Street Meetinghouse. Eliot (1889–1958), the president of the American Unitarian Association (AUA) from 1937–1958, shared the desire for one worldwide liberal church and advanced the faith through decentralized programs, including the New Beacon series in religious education, a commercially competitive Beacon Press, and The Unitarian Service Committee. During the twenty years of Eliot's presidency, the number of Unitarians in the United States and Canada doubled.

The major source for growth was a program initiated in 1948 which fostered the formation of small groups. The Church of the Larger Fellowship (CLF) had begun in 1944 as a way to allow individuals who did not live near a Unitarian Church to have access to liberal religious materials. Sermons and articles were mailed from headquarters to those who requested them, and as families in a geographic area joined, they were encouraged to meet one another. This evolved into a separate Lay Fellowship Plan, in which small groups of lay people formally created Fellowships, certified by the AUA's Fellowship Director, Munroe Husbands. With no building costs or staff needs, it was possible to spread Unitarianism across the continent, in smaller communities, and in a manner responsive to the shifting populations of post-war America.

In the first 10 years, 323 Fellowships and 12,500 people[45] (one third of the growth) affiliated with the AUA through this "do-it-yourself" religious model. Many Fellowships grew to include children, which had never been part of the original concept, and yet in some places became the primary purpose. This challenged the self-start, low-cost model of religion. A religious education program required space and materials, staffing, training, and a curriculum. Neither the AUA nor the seminaries were prepared to support this new form of religious education. In 1958, the high point of the program, with 55 new Fellowships, the denomination hired two ministers-at-large to help the larger Fellowships, and the program shifted from focusing on growth to providing services.

---

[45] Laile Bartlett, *Bright Galaxy* (Boston, MA: Beacon Press, 1960), p. 144; Holly Ulbrich, *The Fellowship Movement* (Boston, MA: House, 2008), p. 21.

In embodying the democratic principles of the faith, the Fellowship movement was a source of tremendous excitement and complicated growth. Many new members did not have knowledge of Unitarianism as a religion rooted in any tradition, and the Fellowships lacked leadership that could inculcate a sense of connection to the past, or to the larger denomination. Yet the Fellowships were dynamic, full of energy and lay leaders, and contributed hugely to the denomination's ability to commit to gender equity, civil rights, and gay rights. Eliot had said, "It is the historic role of Unitarianism to serve as the interpreter of a liberal and spiritual Christianity... to the other high religions of the world; in this, Unitarianism is the servant of Christianity even as it is repudiated by Christendom in the process. Being able to tackle social problems is our vocation. We program to counteract powers destroying human freedoms."[46] The Fellowship movement, organized to help Unitarianism grow, directly counteracted negative social forces.

Under Eliot, the *Christian Register* became an in-house publication, in order to ensure the newspaper reflected the American Unitarian Association (AUA) Board. Because the editor, Stephen Fritchman, had been suspected of Communism, some interpreted his firing as political. Yet when Congress decided in 1954 to insert the phrase "under God" into the Pledge of Allegiance, the AUA vigorously protested. Embracing the principle of separation of church and state in the political climate of the time required the leadership of a religious organization to publicly claim that God was not necessary; a claim that had real consequences in a world where Communism had completely circumscribed relationships with Unitarians in the two countries were the ties had been deepest – Czechoslovakia and Romania. Commitment to that principle was not based on a dismissal of the threat of Communism. It originated with a deep belief that faith has to be free to have any meaning.

Throughout these post-war decades, the Unitarians and Universalists in the US and Canada continued to work towards merger. Despite their joint work in larger associations for over sixty years, the two liberal bodies were separate until May 15, 1961. The birth of the Unitarian Universalist Association (UUA) was the direct result of votes taken in Syracuse, New York, two years earlier, at a joint meeting of the two denominations. That vote, in turn, was the result of six years' work, first with the Council of Liberal Churches, and then the Joint Merger Commission. Dana Greeley

---

[46] David B. Parke, "Liberals and Liberalism Since 1900," *The Proceedings of the Unitarian Historical Society*, Vol. 15, Part 1, 1964, p. 7.

(1908–1986), who had been the AUA president, was elected president of the UUA. Merger commission guidelines stated that neither the AUA President nor the UCA General Superintendent should lead the new denomination; thus, the Trustees did not support Greeley's candidacy. The aim had been for a new organization. The constitution gave policy issues to the Board of Trustees and the Moderator, and charged the president with following policy set by the Board. Greeley resisted this power and claimed both spiritual and administrative authority until the Moderator, Marshall Dimock, resigned. By appointing sympathetic people to the Board, Greeley was able to shape the institution to a greater degree than had been anticipated. This power was the root cause of the serious financial trouble that was obvious by the end of Greeley's term, and which ultimately led to years of eroding membership figures. The Fellowship Program ended, Beacon Press was faltering, and the denomination struggled.

The two major changes initiated during Greeley's tenure reflect his abiding interest in peace as a religious principle: He created a Department of Social Responsibility, headed by Homer Jack, and a Department of Overseas and Interfaith Relations. These offices were in addition to the UU Service Committee (UUSC), an affiliate organization as it had been under the Unitarians. The Universalist Service Committee had functioned within the administration, as an integral part of the core religious identity. The new departments essentially recreated the Universalist model without necessarily co-ordinating the work. Jack was an effective advocate of social justice, but the struggle for racial justice within the denomination became an ugly, politicized battle in 1967. The Black Empowerment Controversy was an extremely unfortunate tangle of administrators coping with the fledgling notion of affirmative action, and the politicized way that funding and affiliation worked within the General Assembly as well as the Board. Greeley had worked against the Moderator and made himself CEO, but was unable to act in this role. Promises of support were made and rescinded more than once, and the process encouraged division. It is estimated that over a thousand black Unitarian Universalists left the church over this issue, and many non-black members lost faith. Greeley left office with this issue not only unresolved, but as a major budgetary, public relations, and identity problem for the next leader.

Although the UUA was founded in 1961, there are ways in which the new religion did not really begin until 1969, when Robert N. West (b. 1929) became president and initiated major changes in administration and services. The financial crisis within the UUA forced West to immediately cut the budget, by 40 percent. He evaluated the necessary core services, determined the minimal staff necessary, and laid off half the UUA personnel and all District staff. In addition, the source of funding for the Black Affairs Council was changed from the UUA to voluntary donations, leading to intensified emotions about the relationship of race to money and leadership. Clear goals about the purpose of the Unitarian Universalist Association (UUA) helped the administration to set priorities, and formally establish policies that made the institution less vulnerable to personal agendas, or a tendency to recapitulate the inner workings of the former American Unitarian Association. West tried to bring the UUSC into the UUA as well, but the overture was rejected because of the UUA's finances. West changed how the Board of Trustees was selected, so that a large majority of members were elected by the Districts, rather than appointed. At least one Trustee place would be reserved for a Canadian, since there were no districts in which the Canadians were the majority. West articulated a crisis of identity within the denomination which affected everything: the role expectations of ministers and of congregations regarding their ministers, religious education, the beliefs and motivations of members, extension, worship, social action, advertising, publications, programming by congregations, and ministerial education. Yet West's greatest contribution to the Unitarian Universalist (UU) cause was his financial stewardship. In addition to reorganizing the UUA in order to operate on a vastly reduced budget, West pursued funds from outside sources. The relationship between the UUA and the Veatch Foundation is a legacy of his administration.

West not only inherited problems far beyond the scope of what he had anticipated, or what anyone understood; he also occupied a position which had basically been familial and parochial up until his presidency. Greeley was a gregarious, social figure who embodied what it meant to be a Unitarian leader, and then extended that to mean a Unitarian Universalist leader. He was a beloved figure; even people who supported a rather different vision of the UUA, to some degree, believed him to be the standard against which UU presidents should be measured. Greeley was the last leader with significant hereditary ties to the old Boston Brahmin traditions, and who lived and breathed in those circles of power. Some leaders, Ray Hopkins among them, genuinely believed that if Greeley had simply stayed on as president, or been retained as a fundraiser,[47] there would have been no financial crisis.

[47] Raymond C. Hopkins, "Recollections, 1944–1974: The Creation of the Unitarian Universalist Association and the Administrations of Dana Greeley and Robert West," *The Journal of Unitarian Universalist History*, Vol. 31; 2006–2007, pp. 1–29.

Under West, the budget became subject to realistic income projections, and by 1973 the debt had been erased, even though membership was slightly declining. Personnel policies were instituted to ensure both standards and pay equity. West courted the Plandome congregation and was able to direct their Veatch Foundation resources to help fund many programs that otherwise would have languished, the first of which was the Racial Justice Fund. These administrative issues cannot be overstated: The UUA could easily have gone bankrupt, and the personnel issues were part of the reason. Currently, there are about the same number of congregations, but the UUA staff is four times what it was during West's tenure. This does not imply a shortage of prophetic action or even program growth during the 1970s: West initiated the development of the About Your Sexuality curriculum (now Our Whole Lives) while serving in Rochester, NY, and was President when it was field tested. Beacon Press published the Pentagon Papers in 1971, leading to government harassment of the UUA staff. The Resolution on Women and Religion was passed by the 1973 General Assembly, setting in motion a profound change in expectations around language use. An Office of Gay Affairs was established in 1973. A denominational newspaper was started. Ministerial education and development was evaluated, and recommendations were made to the seminaries. West's tenure contained the issues still most strongly identified with Unitarian Universalism, almost fifty years later: freedom, of the press and for individuals; holistic education, and inclusion.

Yet it must be noted that the "religion for one world" was a casualty of the 1970s. The concept of a global ethic was challenged by more than just finances. The Office of Overseas and Interfaith Work was closed, and its work became the responsibility of the UUA's executive Vice-President. Greeley expressed frustration about the denomination's lack of interest in overseas work and thought it symptomatic of pathetic provincialism. But West was active in the International Association for Religious Freedom (IARF), and facilitated a shift to professionalism in its management. A council oversaw the IARF with representatives from eight countries, and by tradition the UUA president held the seat representing the United States and Canada. West recommended that the UUA Trustees instead have Diether Gehrmann (1929–2006), who had been active internationally and served – as did his father and two of his sons – a Free Religious church in Germany, fill the council position. Two years later, West's proposal to hire a full-time professional to run the organization resulted in Gehrmann's selection as the General Secretary of the IARF. The Veatch Foundation funded this staff change. A second source of funding introduced through

West has also been significant to international relations. The Holdeen funds, established by an eccentric millionaire in an unsuccessful attempt to fund the government of Pennsylvania and thus permanently abolish taxes, were given to the UUA as a charitable trust, and had been generating small amounts of money. The terms of the trust were challenged at West's direction, and ultimately led to a revenue stream of over a million dollars a year, with restrictions as to its use. Reliable outside funding and specialized staff rather than honorary seats on councils removed the appearance of involvement, but represented a shift from pageantry to professionalism and program development in a post-colonial world.

A second national religious organization was founded at the same time as the UUA. The Canadian Unitarian Council (CUC) was voted into existence to operate within the continental Association. Previously, the institutional connection for Canadians had been to the British and Foreign Unitarian Association. Through World War II, services were provided irregularly in the form of circuit riders or field secretaries. Then the Fellowship movement caused the number of Canadian Unitarians to triple between 1946 and 1961, to over 4,000 members, and with a much more distinctly Canadian leadership. Contributions to progressive causes, especially women's rights and prison reform, were significant from the beginning, but the profile of the denomination emerged in the 1950s. The three Universalist churches in Canada were included in the Unitarian Council. Also included in the CUC were the Icelandic Unitarians, who had diminished from their peak of 18 congregations in the 1930s.

Icelandic Unitarianism was founded in 1886 in Winnipeg and represents perhaps the most successful experience of incorporating diversity into the denomination. Leaders in the immigrant Icelandic community discovered Unitarianism through written works, and established a Unitarian Church, conducted in their own language. Poetry was central to their worship, and social responsibility was the key principle of the faith. The Icelandic Unitarian Church spread through Manitoba, and by 1910 had made the area ripe for English-speaking Unitarians. After the Depression, the Unitarians in Winnipeg sent their minister to Iceland in order to learn the language, and maintained two separate congregations, although they shared both a building and a minister. In 1945, with many second- and third-generation Icelandic immigrants assimilated into the Canadian culture, the two congregations merged, and the Icelandic members gave up their language so that those who could only understand English could participate. By the end of the 1950s, the once strong Icelandic Unitarian community had lost its distinct presence in Manitoba.

The financial crisis at the Unitarian Universalist Association (UUA) resulted in an accord which ultimately sent a mixed message: two points of the accord asserted the Canadian Unitarian Council (CUC) as part of a UUA that was at least nominally continental. One guaranteed a Canadian Trustee, and another a fundraising program in which half the proceeds went to the UUA for services. But the two other points of the accord established the CUC as an independent national body, with separate membership in the International Association for Religious Freedom (IARF) and legal authority over the credentials for religious services. As the CUC developed independently, the financial relationship raised questions about Unitarian identity in an international context. These questions were answered early in the administration of William Sinkford (b. 1946), the seventh president of the UUA, with the 2002 dissolution of the relationship and a general policy of limiting international ties at the administrative level. This reversed the original ideals of the association, and much of the work done in the 1980s, and necessitated bylaw changes for both the UUA and the CUC.

During his short term as UUA president, Paul Carnes (1921–1979) asked the Association's Board of Trustees to re-establish the Office of Social Responsibility. It did, and William Schulz became its head, leaving in 1985 to serve as president. He had a keen interest in international connections, and promoted a bylaw change that would admit congregations outside the continent. This was not theoretical; the acceptance of the UU Church of the Philippines as a member congregation was facilitated by the 1988 bylaw. That same year, the Board approved Project India, which was to revitalize the Brahmo Samaj, and provide support to the Unitarians of the Khasi Hills, Madras, and Hyderabad. The bylaw change allowing overseas congregation was voted in by the General Assembly; Project India was advanced through the Department of Extension, and therefore not subject to a vote by member congregations. The next year, the Sister Church program was re-established and congregations in Prague, Warsaw, and Moscow opened. Soon, as churches in New Zealand and in Australia sought to join the UUA, the Board of Trustees was required to address policy on the admittance of international congregations.

The British General Assembly of Unitarian and Free Christian Churches was also interested in relationships with other Unitarians. In 1987, they voted to support a proposal made by David Usher, an Australian Unitarian who has served churches in the United States and in Great Britain. Usher wanted a coalition of people interested in international work, which he amusingly named AEIOU: Advocates for the Establishment of an International Organization of Unitarians. From this group, and from interest resulting from a World Summit convened in Budapest in 1993, emerged the International Council of Unitarians and Universalists (ICUU). In 1995, in Essex, Massachusetts, representatives from 21 member organizations from 16 countries formed the ICUU, which offers international leadership training and aims to foster growth. The ICUU also creates an administrative layer between the UUA and non-US congregations. By providing "appropriate resources" to Unitarians and Unitarian Universalists around the world, congregations need not apply for membership in the UUA, which ceased accepting them during the administration of John Buehrens. Support for the Sister Church program ended, and Project India was abruptly terminated in 1995 with no transition plan for the leaders or congregations. In 1998, financial ties between the Canadian Unitarian Council and the UUA were severed; in 2002, the CUC lost its status as a member of the UUA. In 2008, with Buehrens saying the UUA "had been generous to a fault" and there had not been "measurable benefits in our member groups,"[48] support for the IARF was withdrawn.

The decision to structure international relationships this way has its roots in the 1970s. It reflects the historical trouble with mission work that Unitarians have had, the establishment of the office of president as primarily concerned with money, and the evolution of contemporary religious practices; but it also represents an ability to take advantage of established financial resources while claiming cultural sensitivity. Robert West's securing of the Veatch Foundation money and his breaking of the Holdeen Trust both provided the UUA with the means to serve the faith broadly, with alliances that were international. Unitarians and Unitarian Universalists have access to these dollars only through UUA grants. The Holdeen Funds, in particular, are restricted by Jonathan Holdeen's will and were intended for work in India. It is this money that funded the IARF and Project India, and now helps fund the ICUU. However, ICUU member groups are asked for fair-share contributions to the annual program fund, so that restricted funds are used to generate a new stream of unrestricted funds. This business practice is presented as an anti-imperialist sensitivity. Buehrens, who headed an international advisory council under President Sinkford, stated that the new approach promotes collegiality among Unitarians and Unitarian Universalists across the globe, and upholds the principles of congregational polity. Earlier international work was, he said, oriented around social justice and prophetic action, and therefore not in

[48] Jane Greer, "UUA Shifts International Focus to Congregations", *UU World* (UUA: Boston, June 15, 2009). See: www.uuworld.org/new/articles/143183.shtml. Last accessed February 11, 2011.

keeping with the UUA mission of deepening the spiritual lives of member congregations. By ignoring how congregations might come into being so that they can relate collegially, and by divorcing social justice from spiritual growth, this argument substitutes a governance method for theology, and actually ignores mission entirely. Congregational polity originally represented a challenge to traditional authority: it was empowering. Polity as a belief system relies on a fear of appearing authoritative to justify inhibited action, limiting opportunities for connection and creating a closed group.

The best-documented delineation of the relationship of financial capital to international work lies in the history of the Canadian Unitarian Council (CUC). Initially, the fundraising section of the accord tied the CUC to the Unitarian Universalist Association (UUA); but soon it represented a reason for separation. As what had been a completely voluntary organization professionalized, annual giving rose dramatically. Both the Veatch Program and the Liberal Religious Charities Society matched each dollar raised in Canada; thus, the CUC generated a sizeable income for the UUA. In 1986, the Veatch Program ceased its grants and instead gave the UUA $20 million in a capital fund. This dramatically reduced the revenue provided by the CUC's annual program fund, so the Canadians were asked to create an endowment. Four years later, this endowment had not materialized, and the UUA determined a cost for their services. The CUC agreed to pay this amount, with an annual increase of 3 percent. But, in 1997, Buehrens stated that "Canada was costing too much, and informally offered three officials of the CUC one million dollars for the Canadians to go on their own."[49] Canadians were not interested in separation, but asked for a new agreement that would gradually provide increased delivery of programs for growth and religious education. This was rejected and the CUC was asked to withdraw from the UUA and Districts. In exchange, the UUA would transfer $1.5 million to fund an independent CUC. In the US, this is presented as the CUC withdrawing from the UUA, even though it was done at the request of the UUA itself. Founded as a member of the UUA in 1961, the Canadian Unitarian Council is now part of the ICUU instead.

Although finances were clearly the driving force behind separation, a philosophy of self-determination also played a part. The UUA did not want to appear paternalistic. As Kim Turner, part of the Canadian negotiating team said, the meetings "were frustrating – as it was clear we had no real leverage until all of a sudden the UUA side started to view us as being a

---

[49] Charles Eddis, "The CUC: From Colony to Nation, 1961–2002," an address to the Unitarian Universalist Historical Society, June 24, 2002, Quebec City, Quebec.

marginal group (like blacks, gays, etc.) to the point that they had to be very careful not to impose upon us their standards, language, views."[50] This form of anxiety about power and authority, and the financial implications of relationships, began in the 1970s and, by the twenty-first century, came to dominate discussions about international work and affiliate organizations. Dana Greeley wrote in 1971, "A rather silly controversy arose over whether fellowships should be created beyond the continental boundaries of North America or allowed to affiliate with the AUA. The negative arguments were that it might look like colonialism, and we couldn't tell what services they might some day require."[51]

The positive notion of one world religion began around the time of US military involvement in the Philippines, and faded as withdrawal from Vietnam began. Seven decades of economic and military engagement across Asia repugned the notion of unity both from within and without. An international faith was regarded with suspicion. The "one world" theme evolved away from the shared physical world, and towards something far more personal and individualized. Unitarian Universalism, at least administratively, responded to worldwide encounter by turning inward and protecting assets. In the United States, the denomination was significantly influenced by the variety of new religious movements that proliferated in the US throughout the 1970s. These movements addressed the longing for a universally accessible faith by making peace a personal, not international, goal. All people could participate in this practice; all people could experience this radically individualistic liberation that was not subject to any authority outside the self. This de-politicized religion did not require reasoned study of texts, yet gave a sense of connection to traditions, such as Zen, pagan, or Native American beliefs, without any of the circumscribing characteristics of genuinely belonging to a specific tradition.

From the Bible and world scriptures, to the natural and empirical world, the journey of freedom ended at the inner life. Ecumenicism produced a belief in relational practice and world peace, but encounter led to internal strife and conflicting desires. Unitarian Universalism is asserted both as a specific faith tradition and as something more global, which assures that all faiths are valued and to some degree interchangeable. A century that began with wide affiliations and a broad interest in reason and reform closed with narrowing national boundaries and a preoccupation with language

[50] Eddis, "The CUC."
[51] Dana McLean Greeley, *25 Beacon Street: And other recollections* (Boston, MA: Beacon Press, 1971), p. 50.

promoting reverence, and a continuing fragile, complex relationship with symbols of authority. A religious movement that was historically activist, and engaged in works that joined people in one beloved community to create "a taste of heaven below," became radically individualized and invested in nurturing the inner life. As the Unitarians and the Universalists finally merged in the United States, the tense call for "co-operation, not consolidation" was refracted out, into the world.

CHAPTER 7

Congregational polity

Unitarian and Universalist congregations all over the globe have mostly adopted some variation of congregational polity as their system of ecclesiastical organization. This method of governance reflects a faith in human abilities to not only "think for ourselves in matters of religion but to act for ourselves also," so that no one, "whether of a Civil or Sacred character, [has] any authority to control us, unless it be by gentle methods of argument and persuasion." This right to judge and act independently of any higher authority, as summarized by Jonathan Mayhew in 1749, reveals the central ecclesiastical affirmation of the free-thinking Unitarians.[1]

Religious organizations that follow congregational polity are intended to be a reflection of the primitive Christian churches, which were small cells of independent believers. It was in Puritan New England where congregational polity reached its developmental zenith, and the strengths and weaknesses it revealed in that initial phase continue today. These include strong local and democratic involvement in each congregation, but also a fierce unwillingness to be organized in any authoritative ecclesiastical body. In recent decades, central organizations in many Unitarian and Universalist communities throughout the world have assumed more authority in attempts to provide common procedures, stronger leadership, and ultimately a common vision and mission for the faith, but for some, the system has become too bureaucratized, and there are new efforts to reinvigorate broader participation.

There are various permutations of this free and democratic way of governance. In Great Britain, Presbyterian forms initially characterized dissenting groups who refused to subscribe to creeds, and who eventually became autonomous Unitarian congregations. The Transylvanian Unitarian system includes bishops as the heads of the church organization in present-day

---

[1] Joseph Barth, *Faith and Practice in Unitarian Universalist Churches* (Boston, MA: Beacon Reference Series, 1965), p. 3.

Hungary and Romania, and they assert a considerable amount of authority in a system that has elements of episcopal and presbyterial systems.

Alan Ruston, a British Unitarian, describes the predominant congregational polity as "autonomous groups or churches of relatively like-minded people who voluntarily come together to worship and witness to their faith." Local congregations worldwide are "sovereign" entities that are linked together in loosely associated national representative bodies, especially in the United States and British Commonwealth nations. The larger bodies have little power over the local groups, who are often suspicious of centralized authority. Each of the congregations controls its property and is financially autonomous. This local and independent freedom and individual autonomy is reflected also in the principles of the Unitarian Universalist Association (UUA), where the fifth principle is: "the right of conscience and the use of the democratic process within our congregations and in society at large."[2]

In North America, most of these self-governing tendencies have evolved directly from the church government explicated in the Cambridge Platform of 1648. This defined a Congregational church as a "company of saints by calling, united into one body by a holy covenant, for the public worship of God, and the mutual edification one of another, in the fellowship of the Lord Jesus."[3] While the Cambridge Platform allowed for the independence of the local congregation in a new church order that had not been seen since the time of the earliest Christian churches, it also asserted that congregationalism "was not [merely] the autonomy of the local church, but the community of autonomous churches."[4] Thus, the Platform called for a Communion of Churches in which they would offer "mutual care in taking thought for one another's welfare." This translated into "consultation," "admonition," "participation" and "recommendation," so that the churches would be more united in their practices.[5]

Most aspects of church life were placed under the authority of the local congregation in the final version of the Platform. With respect to the election of church officers, the Platform declared that "A church, being free, cannot become subject to any but by a free election . . . And if the church

---

[2] Alan Ruston, "The State and Unitarianism: Changing Our Polity?" in Clifford M. Reed and Jill K. McAllister, eds., *The Home We Share: Globalization, Post-Modernism and Unitarian / Universalist Theology* (Caerphilly, Wales: ICUU, 2007), pp. 221–222.

[3] Peter Hughes, ed., *The Cambridge Platform* (Boston, MA: Skinner House Books, 2008), p. 17.

[4] Conrad Wright. *Walking Together: Polity and Participation in Unitarian Universalist Churches* (Boston, MA: Skinner House Books, 1989), p. 21.

[5] Hughes, *Cambridge Platform*, pp. 47–50.

have power to choose their officers and ministers . . . they have power also to depose them." In other words, they can elect whom they want, but can also vote them out if they are not satisfied with their performance. This set the pattern for other types of elections in the communities. This process of calling a minister was typically followed by ordination, or the "putting of a man into his place and office in the church whereunto he had right before by election." The final aspect of local control was the admission of members into the church. These requirements for church membership were determined by these freely elected officers, who were "charged with the keeping of the doors of the church." They would judge who would be fit to enter the covenant that governed all their relationships.[6]

In answer to the question of what makes a collection of individuals into a church, the Cambridge Platform was quite clear. This "form is the visible covenant,[7]" or the agreement of the people to live together in community and watch out for each other with respect to their moral duties towards one another. In effect, the basis for the church was founded upon relationships rather than creed, and so the Platform called for a "voluntary agreement," or "consent" among the congregation, placed in plain language, that "puts us in mind of our mutual duty."[8] The Congregational church that was founded in Watertown, Massachusetts on July 30, 1630 had a covenant that was signed by forty initial settlers who acknowledged their gratitude to God for helping them escape "out of the *pollutions* of the world," and consequently they "promise, and *enter into a sure covenant* with the Lord our God, forsaking all *evil ways* . . . to do him faithful service . . . in all matters concerning our *reformation* . . . and in the carriage of ourselves among ourselves and one toward another . . . "[9]

George Phillips, the first minister in Watertown was, according to Cotton Mather, "better acquainted with the true [congregational] *church-discipline* than most of the ministers who came with him into the country." All churches are true churches, Phillips believed, even though they are "corrupted with error and sinful practices," until Christ "come himself, and unchurch them." He asserted that no church could be a "mother church unto others, but all are sister churches." Here we find that all churches are true, independent and autonomous, and more specifically, that no church exists above the locally assembled congregation who are the body of Christ. Phillips declared, "every church is competent to act alone," or

---

[6] Hughes, ibid., pp. 29, 31, 38.   [7] Ibid., pp. 20–21.   [8] Wright, *Walking Together*, pp. 7–8.
[9] Cotton Mather, *Magnalia Christi Americana; or, The Ecclesiastical History of New England* (Hartford, CT: Silas Andrus and Son, 1855), p. 377.

is complete unto itself. Phillips also believed that it was the congregation's right to choose a minister: "The true calling of a minister is not the Bishop's Ordination," but the calling of a man when "they implicitly chuse him."[10]

While churches typically based their institutional authority on biblical or apostolic tradition, the basis for Unitarian authority is the individual, growing from the Puritan understanding that the being and powers of a church rest purely upon the free consent of its members. Cliff Reed, a British Unitarian, writes: "Unitarians believe that the seat of religious authority lies within oneself. All people develop their own belief system, whether they articulate it or not. All people choose what to accept or reject from the propositions on offer. The Unitarian approach is, therefore, to recognize that each person is his or her own final authority in matters of faith. Our liberal religious ethos grants full individual freedom in this regard."[11] Then what authority does the church have? In 1945, the British General Assembly published *A Free Religious Faith*, which stated that the Unitarians had long been "undervaluing the work of the Church, and regarding people as isolated units, and so, being blind to the profound truth that we are members one of another." The report went on to suggest that sometimes it seems enough to have "abandoned old forms of belief," with no regard for entering new ones. The report suggested that the highest development of conscience and soul for individuals only occurs within the human fellowship, which the church can provide. Unfortunately, the history of affirming a radical individual faith "seemed to leave no vital place for the Church. Experience has shown us the disastrous consequences of our mistake."[12]

Radical ideas about ecclesiastical authority and church formation evolved in the nineteenth century, beginning with the Western Unitarian Conference (WUC), which combined church matters with administrative concerns, including publishing, raising funds, and founding new congregations. In 1882 in *Unity*, editor Jenkin Lloyd Jones asked, "What is the Church?" While acknowledging that answers vary, he stated that the chief emphasis must be on "freedom, fellowship and character *in religion*," and

---

[10] Roger Thompson, *Divided We Stand: Watertown, Massachusetts, 1630–1680* (Amherst, MA: University of Massachusetts Press, 2001), p. 65; Henry Wilder Foote, "George Phillips, First Minister of Watertown," in *Massachusetts Historical Society Proceedings*, Vol. 63 (1931), pp. 193, 196–201, 205, 211–212, 223.

[11] Cliff Reed, *Unitarian? What's That?* (London, UK: Lindsey Press, 1999), p. 13.

[12] Commission of the General Assembly, *A Free Religious Faith: A Report Presented to the General Assembly of Unitarian and Free Christian Churches* (London, UK: Lindsey Press, 1945), p. 36.

that it must "plant itself on a practical basis."[13] Did congregational autonomy allow each society the freedom to define the meaning of Christian, God, and religion for itself, and express those in their own way? In the WUC, Eleanor Gordon argued that the organization was treading on dangerous ground if it presumed that it could codify the views of its members, except in very broad terms, so she ended up voting for "Truth, Righteousness, and Love" as the unifying principles for Unitarians. In the twentieth century, minister Paul Beattie (1937–1989) wrote that a free faith is a direct result of congregational polity, noting, "It was our lack of organization that allowed us to continue to liberalize our way in religion."[14]

In Britain, James Martineau, who moved the Unitarians from a belief in biblical authority to that of individual conscience, said that the church is a "Society for realizing harmony or reconciliation between Man and God." He was especially concerned that the church not merely be an association for free inquiry, as that could produce institutional anarchy, which was something he feared about congregationalism. He advocated for a broad Christian national church without prescribed doctrines. This hindered Unitarian organizational identity and development. Even though he wanted a national church, he never believed it should have authority over local congregations, as he thought this would lead to conformity. He preferred a presbyterian form of government where congregations were held together by a covenant, and not doctrines. This organization's elected leaders would provide services and oversight, but no hierarchy.[15] An unwillingness to create a strong, sectarian, central association reflected the view of many Unitarians in America, too, including the great spiritual leader William Ellery Channing, who refused the presidency of the American Unitarian Association (AUA) when it was organized. In his "Remarks on Associations," Channing said, "In truth all great actions are solitary ones. All the great works of genius come from deep, lonely thought . . . That is most valuable which is individual."[16]

Traditionally, congregational polity has meant that each congregation defines its own standards of membership. There were exacting standards of membership during Puritan times, as each aspiring member was required to

---

[13] "Religious Phraseology, " *Unity*, Vol. ix (1882), p. 83.

[14] Paul Beattie, "Democracy, Covenant, and Dissent in the UUA," unpublished paper for the Prairie Group, 1970, p. 6; Cynthia Grant Tucker, *Prophetic Sisterhood: Liberal Women Ministers of the Frontier, 1880–1930* (Boston, MA: Beacon Press 1990), pp. 138–139.

[15] Frank Schulman, *James Martineau: "This Conscience-Intoxicated Unitarian"* (Chicago, IL: Meadville Lombard Press, 2002), pp. 136–139.

[16] William Ellery Channing, *The Works of William Ellery Channing, D.D.* (Boston, MA: AUA, 1898), pp. 149, 147.

prove the experience of the saving grace of God. When the Puritan system began to break down in the 1600s with the Half-Way Covenant, people could choose to join the church without the experiential component, if they agreed to the covenant of the individual church. By the nineteenth century, members were joining a church by making a personal choice to become part of a covenanted community, rather than being examined and approved by church officials to make sure they met an institutional standard. For example, after 1795 in Concord, Massachusetts, candidates for church membership no longer had to be scrutinized in any public way, or confess their sins before the congregation. The minister, Ezra Ripley, interviewed candidates privately and recommended them for membership. All the new member needed to do was affirm the church covenant (which was liberalized three times during Ripley's ministry) during a service. This practice spread to other congregations. In Watertown, Massachusetts, Convers Francis (1795–1863) reported that on May 6, 1821, "Mr. Hall and his wife were received into the church, the covenant being read to the congregation only, – the first time this practice has been introduced here."[17]

Membership standards in the twentieth century often became more undefined, with some congregations merely requiring that the prospective member sign the membership book, and receive automatic approval. Early in the century, the AUA published "The Organization of Parishes and Churches of the Unitarian Congregational Order, and Their Methods of Work." A sample set of bylaws for the organization indicates that all members shall "sign in the record book of the Society an agreement" . . . : "I agree to become a member of the _____Society and to be subject to its bylaws." Generally, new members were voted in at an annual meeting by a majority of the members present rather than merely being affirmed by the "consent of the Parish Committee," which was considered "a loose and dangerous method."[18] In 1966, the Unitarian Universalist Association (UUA) Ad Hoc Committee on Congregational Polity reported that there was a diversity of procedures on receiving members into local congregations. Only one-tenth of the congregations reported that they "require

---

[17] Robert A. Gross, "'Doctor Ripley's Church': Congregational Life in Concord, Massachusetts, 1778–1841," *The Journal of Unitarian Universalist History*, Vol. XXXIII (2009–2010), pp. 10–11; Convers Francis, "The Journals of Convers Francis" (Part I), ed. Guy R. Woodall, *Studies in the American Renaissance*, ed. Joel Myerson (Boston, MA: Twayne Publishers, 1981), p. 303.

[18] American Unitarian Association, *The Organization of Parishes and Churches of the Unitarian Congregational Order* (Boston, MA: AUA, c. 1920).

agreement with some statement to join them." For some this meant ascribing to a covenant, and for others state laws required agreement with By Laws or Acts of Incorporation.[19]

The Free Church in a Changing World, a UUA self-assessment study published in 1963, listed four rights of the local church. Among these were the right to admit members according to their own definition of membership, selection of leadership, control of property, and entering relationships with other churches. Restrictions on the freedom of members have been a modern concern for Unitarians and Universalists. The local right to determine membership standards was challenged in 1963 by a proposed amendment to the UUA bylaws, requiring congregations to be non-discriminatory in their membership standards. Although this was meant to prevent segregation, and most members agreed with its intent, the principle of applying restrictions on a congregation's freedom to set its own standards was objected to, and the proposal failed. Part of the issue was that the proposal empowered the General Assembly to police the congregations, and potentially to discipline or expel them. This was considered alien to the congregational way. The UUA bylaws now "promote" non-discrimination, but they also continue to state that nothing can infringe upon the freedom of the local congregations "without requiring adherence to any particular interpretation of religion or to any particular religious belief or creed."[20]

Membership today is generally defined as the free choice of the individual, and while some congregations require approval of applicants by their governing board, the impetus for membership comes from individual choice rather than from standards required by the community. Some congregations have considered making membership a more difficult process. The hope is that more stringent criteria might result in more zealous commitments, and could include required financial obligations, membership classes, and/or approval by the congregation or its governing board, for in many congregations, the aspiring member need only sign a membership book.

The commissioners of *The Free Church in a Changing World* declared, "The decision is made by the individual, not by the church." While recalling Channing's view that no one can be ex-communicated from the universal

---

[19] Preliminary Report to the UUA Board of Trustees by the Ad Hoc Committee on Congregational Polity and Membership Practices, April 1, 1966.

[20] *The Free Church in a Changing World* (Boston, MA: UUA, 1963), p. 12; Conrad Wright, *Congregational Polity* (Boston, MA: Skinner House Books, 1997), p. 183; The Commission on Appraisal, UUA, *Interdependence: Renewing Congregational Polity* (Boston, MA: UUA, 1997), pp. 25–26. See Bylaws of the UUA, Article II, Section C-2.3 Non-discrimination.

church except "by the death of goodness in his own breast," the study also found that restrictions on membership might be wise if an extremist group tried to subvert the church. A recent study, *Belonging*, by the UUA's Commission on Appraisal, suggests that removing someone from membership who is a physical or verbal threat to parishioners, or who disrupts worship, is sometimes necessary, but because of the emphasis on individual choice in becoming a member rather than adherence to a congregational standard, it is sometimes difficult to reach congregational agreement on this issue. Nevertheless, there has been a subtle shift in recent years away from serving individual needs to a deeper appreciation for the entire congregation's goal of respectful, "right" relationships.[21]

In the late nineteenth century, simple, theologically inclusive covenants became more common in Unitarian churches in the United States. The confluence of affirming a simple covenant and signing the membership book occurred in some congregations. For example, the history of the Lake Region Unitarian Universalist Fellowship in Lakeland, Florida began in 1955, when thirty-five persons signed the membership book and the first service was held. The cover of their membership book included the following: "Love is the Spirit of this Fellowship and Service is its Law. In Freedom of Truth, We Unite for the Worship of God and the Service of Man." Signing the book signified a commitment to this covenant. Yet the idea of covenant as a total bonding principle for the congregations was used infrequently until it was revived in the 1980s within the Unitarian Universalist Association (UUA). The then UUA President, William F. Schulz, wrote, "Covenants refer to the common insights and affirmations, derived from tradition and experience, that bind a religious community together in voluntary loyalty." Covenants reflect the past, but they are built from the shared needs, values, and principles of the present congregation, embodying the promises the members make to one another in the present.[22]

Covenants were often paired with the idea of mission. The covenant may express how the people relate to one another internally, while mission reflects the vision of the church in the world. Many congregations write new mission statements or revisit old ones when they are considering a major undertaking, such as a capital fund drive or building campaign. While

---

[21] *The Free Church in a Changing World*; Commission on Appraisal, UUA, *Belonging: The Meaning of Membership* (Boston, MA: UUA, 2001), pp. 57, 60, 70.

[22] Tom Chulak and John Morgan, *Mission-Covenant, Prelude to the Growing Series* (Boston, MA: UUA, 1987), p. 5; For the history of the Unitarian Universalist Congregation of Lakeland, Florida, see: mysite.verizon.net/vzno5ylk/History.htm.

the democratic structure and non-creedal faith help facilitate a sense of freedom and diversity of belief, mission and covenant help Unitarians and Universalists find common identity in their religious community. Rather than a strict hierarchy of power relationships, the covenant is based on the mutual consent of the people. Each congregation elects its own officers and committees to manage the property and plan the programs of the church. The membership meets at least annually to approve budgets and make decisions about the life of the congregation.

Unitarian and Universalist congregations have historically been organized with a power-sharing, co-operative model between minister and congregation. If anything, congregations are cautious of vesting too much authority in a minister or congregational leader. When Unitarian churches were being organized in the American South, historian John Allen Macauley found that "what was exceptional . . . was the extent to which Unitarian ministers were aided in the process by the educated professionals in their own congregations." The Rev. Samuel Gilman in Charleston, South Carolina reported that it was not enough to "contemplate his relations and duties from his own point of view. He must naturally be very much assisted in the task by borrowing . . . sentiments [from] enlightened and conscientious laymen." The active leadership also proved vital when congregations were without ministers. After fourteen English Unitarians established the First Unitarian Church in Philadelphia, Joseph Priestley moved to Northumberland, PA, and members continued to conduct services. Its next minister, William Christie, left the congregation because "he feared that the members had more power than the minister." The congregation continued to worship with lay preaching for another twenty-nine years before a minister was called.[23]

With a structure that calls for congregational leadership to exert authority in matters of church government, and with the authority for the call and ordination of the ministry seated within the congregation, the minister must attain influence and authority through relationships of trust rather than through actual structures of power. The democratic structure and dispersed authority means that a layperson can do most anything a minister can do. This was realized in the United States in the 1950s with the advent of the Fellowship Movement, which developed specifically lay-led groups. *The Free Church in a Changing World* study suggested that the "church is the value-celebrating and value-demanding institution in society." These

[23] John Allen Macaulay, *Unitarianism in the Antebellum South: The Other Invisible Institution* (Tuscaloosa, AL: University of Alabama Press, 2001), pp. 23, 71–72.

values, the UUA's Commission on Appraisal said, are expressed in public worship on the local level, and are discovered and articulated by the membership. "For this reason the ministry of a free church is the task of the whole church. It is a mutual ministry, involving each member of the religious community with every other member and with the community at large. All members of the church are ministers in a sense."[24]

Central to congregational polity is the right of the congregations to call, elect, ordain, and install their own ministers. Clergy are asked to fill a variety of needs, and professional training qualifies them to be leaders of worship, pastoral counselors, teachers, group facilitators and planners, and representatives of the faith community in society. After the Civil War, women began to enter both the Unitarian and Universalist ministries in increasing numbers, but by the early twentieth century, most were being discouraged. In 1914, Florence Ellen Kollock Crocker (1848–1925) argued that the reasons for women to be ministers were the same as those for men: "to spread the gospel; to give religious instruction; to train the young in the ways of virtue and righteousness – in brief to help the world . . . in the great uplift of humanity." Furthermore, Crocker suggested that women had special abilities to understand the domestic and social life of parishioners and would thus have considerable "sympathy" for others, and young people would "recognize her as a friend and counselor."[25]

While the Unitarians in America came from a Puritan tradition of highly educated clergy, who wore the black robes as a sign of their scholarly attainments, the Universalists were more suspicious of highly educated ministers. For one thing, they worried that learning about faith from books would stifle the passion for God ignited in the heart of each person who was converted to Universalism. They also feared that a uniform education would lead to a standardized clergyperson who would not be able to preach the gospel to all types and classes of people. Their impromptu enthusiasm is exemplified by the ordination of Hosea Ballou in 1794, when Elhanan Winchester, in concluding his sermon, grasped the Bible and pressed it against Ballou's chest, declaring, "I press to your heart the written Jehovah!"[26] By the middle of the nineteenth century, Universalists supported an educated clergy, but their credentialing and

---

[24] *The Free Church in a Changing World*, ibid., p. 6.

[25] Dorothy May Emerson, ed., *Standing Before Us: Unitarian Universalist Women and Social Reform, 1776–1936* (Boston, MA: Skinner House Books, 2000), pp. 454, 456.

[26] Mark W. Harris, *Historical Dictionary of Unitarian Universalism* (Lanham, MD: Scarecrow Press, 2004), p. 332; Ernest Cassara, *Hosea Ballou: The Challenge to Orthodoxy* (Boston, MA: Beacon Press, 1961), p. 23.

ordination process continued to be administered by each separate State Convention.

By the beginning of the twentieth century, exacting standards to determine what qualified an individual for the Unitarian ministry were still in a fledgling state, following the establishment of a Committee on Fellowship by the National Conference in 1878. It remained difficult to determine an accurate list of who was a qualified minister, what the standards were, and how someone could be removed from fellowship. In 1909, the Worcester Association (Massachusetts) suggested that a Fellowship Committee be formed to "pass upon the moral and mental qualifications of such ministers as it might be requested to recommend" to Unitarian churches. The American Unitarian Association (AUA) pushed for even higher standards after Dan Fenn wrote an essay for the study, *Unitarians Face a New Age*, in which he argued that ministers were still granted credentials based purely upon their service to a Unitarian church, and thus the holding of the position was more important than the qualifications of the person.[27] After the Unitarians and Universalists in North America merged in 1961, the new association created a national Ministerial Fellowship Committee that has increasingly centralized and standardized the process, so that the act of receiving fellowship has become more important in attaining the designation of minister than the call to a church or ordination.

In recent decades in the United States, the significance of ordination has been eroded by the increased authority of the Unitarian Universalist Association (UUA) bureaucracy in determining who can be given the title of minister. Conrad Wright has suggested that in the ordination service, "the distinctiveness of our pattern of congregational government is most clearly revealed."[28] The ordination process is symbolic of congregational polity because it reflects an expression of each congregation's right to assert its authority to choose its own leadership. Behind this is the principle that no hierarchy of bishops or bureaucrats charged to approve of ministerial qualifications has the power to tell a congregation whom they can and cannot ordain. This principle was reaffirmed at the time of Unitarian Universalist merger, as the new bylaws of the UUA in 1961 affirmed, "that member churches alone have the right to call and ordain ministers."

Minister Earl Holt says that the UUA credentialing processes, "have made *de facto* encroachments upon this . . . crucial aspect of our radical

---

[27] Frederick Lewis Weis, *A Short History of the Worcester Conference and of the Worcester Association* (Hudson, MA: Worcester Conference, 1947), p. 28. Commission of Appraisal, *Unitarians Face a New Age* (Boston, MA: AUA, 1936), pp. 128–129.

[28] Wright, *Walking Together*, p. 63.

congregationalism." Much of this change has been instituted as standardized UUA policies and procedures to ensure that highly qualified, professional clergy are leading the congregations. By tradition, ordination made a person a minister; this has been transformed so that, today, ordination has been made subordinate to approved fellowship status for all ministerial candidates. The UUA's Commission on Appraisal has recently stated, "ordination has...become a mere ceremony."[29] While ordination was once frequently combined with installation to signify the importance of the relationship with one congregation, students today are frequently ordained by their home church or by the congregation where they perform an internship, and only after they achieve fellowship status.

Slowly, professional schools for the training of ministers were established. Historically, Harvard Divinity School has been the East Coast center for liberal clergy. This was especially true after Andover Seminary was established in 1807 to train Calvinist ministers. Both these schools have evolved to become modern seminaries that attract large numbers of aspiring Unitarian Universalist students. The primary Universalist seminaries were at what are now Tufts University (Massachusetts) and St. Lawrence University (New York), but these were both closed at the time of the merger, leaving only Unitarian schools open, and causing resentment among the Universalists. The Unitarian schools were considered more geographically favorable to a nationwide faith. One of these was originally Meadville Theological Seminary (1844) in Pennsylvania, but it merged with Lombard College to become Meadville Lombard Theological School, and relocated to Chicago. A West Coast center was established in the early twentieth century in Berkeley, California. The Starr King School for the Ministry (1904) became an innovative educational institution, and has managed to survive despite an institutional history often marked by financial hardship. Many seminaries across denominational lines are now finding it hard to survive in an era of dwindling resources. Still, there is an abundance of candidates in the United States. Unitarian Universalist clergy increased by 46 percent between 1961 and 1991, despite declines of 3 percent in membership and 2 percent in number of congregations.[30]

Some of this increase in the number of clergy can be accounted for by the addition of two classifications of ministry to the previously general

---

[29] *Interdependence*, p. 47; Earl K. Holt, III, "Congregational Ordination and the Call to Ministry," unpublished sermon at the ordination of Cynthia Johnson (Dallas, TX, 1991), pp. 1–3.

[30] Paula D. Nesbitt, *Feminization of the Clergy in America: Occupational and Organizational Perspective* (New York: Oxford University Press, 1997), pp. 140, 150, 165.

understanding. As a result, the Ministry was divided into Parish Ministry, the Ministry of Religious Education, and Community Ministry; each requiring, for a number of years, separate certification. Yet the "tracking" of Ministry cannot fully explain the increase, which has persisted despite the increasingly bureaucratic procedures and more rigorous fellowship requirements that have been put in place. By the end of the twentieth century, clergy began voicing concern that the role of Minister had become overly professionalized. Some expressed the feeling that religious leadership rooted in study and reflection had been replaced by social organizing. In 1966, Robert Haney told the Massachusetts Convention of Congregational Ministers that emphasis on clerical training was being shifted from a "ministry learned in the languages, holy books, history, and lyric languages," to a "class of professional technicians skilled in making people work well," or "masters of group dynamics."[31] Another major change occurred when women became the majority of those ordained to the Unitarian Universalist ministry in 1999, which also apparently resulted in leadership style changes to more shared concepts of ministry dependent upon interpersonal relationships rather than traditional lines of authority.

In Great Britain, the Unitarians have struggled with dwindling church life in general, and have had only a handful of ministerial candidates in the last generation. Ordination there is not an issue, as there is no recent tradition of ordination among the clergy. Governance was originally drawn from the English Presbyterian tradition where the ministers had the power to ordain rather than the congregations. Once the Presbyterians had to accept that the national church would be episcopal in its polity, they had to form churches like the Congregationalists. As we have seen, in this tradition, a person could not usually be a minister except in relationship to a congregation. Historian Andrew Hill has suggested several reasons for the decline of the tradition of ordination in England and Wales. In the newly emerging, democratically-led Unitarian congregations, there was no reason to set clergy apart as having any special powers that lay people did not possess. Furthermore, it appeared undemocratic because it limited access to the profession, and these ceremonies with accompanying dinners were expensive and elaborate, and not compatible with simple traditions. Most important of all, the Rational Dissenters believed this kind of sacrament was too superstitious in form, reflecting high church Episcopacy. One former Unitarian minister, William Johns, commented, "With the decline

---

[31] Robert W. Haney, "The Goals Report," An Address to the Massachusetts Convention of Congregational Ministers, May 24, 1966, p. 6.

of priestly usurpation and ghostly pretensions among the sect of Protestant dissenters . . . entitled Rational, the ceremony of ordination fell by degrees into deserved disrepute and general disuse."[32]

New ministers began to assume the special clerical functions such as serving communion, and so ordination slowly became superfluous. At their graduation from seminary, ministers have a valediction service, and this presently serves as the equivalent of ordination. When ministers are called (elected) to a parish, there is a service of induction (called installation in the US), which is a ceremony to affirm the new relationship between pastor and people.

The democratically-led faith has de-emphasized any special authority or power being delegated to the ministry. Neither the British nor American ecclesiastical headquarters upholds the idea of calling, but many of the aspiring clergy do. The UUA website reads: "Unitarian Universalism believes in learned rather than called clergy. What separates ministers from lay members within Unitarian Universalism is the graduate-level training that constitutes the ordination process, rather than a summons from God. Because of this, lay leaders are also highly respected within our congregations."[33] Lay pastors or leaders serve some of the congregations in Britain. There is a more formal training process for lay leaders in Britain, with some of this training occurring at the established seminaries at The Unitarian College at Manchester, and Harris Manchester College at Oxford. Lay people often fill former ministerial roles, and then undergo training, leading to full ministerial status.

Granting authority to any hierarchy has been accomplished with great difficulty in the history of Unitarian and Universalist institutions throughout the world. In the United States the Unitarians organized themselves in 1825 as the American Unitarian Association (AUA). This was an association based on individual membership, and there was no means for congregations to be part of a larger community of churches. The first delegate body to be established was the National Conference of Unitarian Churches, which formed in 1865. This national body, later called the General Conference, was a programmatic and policy-recommending body that had no specific administrative or executive function. In 1923, the AUA Commission on Polity advocated a number of administrative changes. Prior to this, churches had begun to join the AUA (this was permitted after

---

[32] Andrew M. Hill, "The Death of Ordination in the Unitarian Tradition," Address delivered before the Annual Meeting of the Unitarian Historical Society, London, 1970, p. 9.

[33] See: www.uua.org/visitors/worship/ministers/index.shtml.

1884), and send delegates to its annual meetings (known as May Meetings). A new constitution provided that the AUA become a federation of churches, and although individual membership was retained, effective power was removed from individuals and given to congregations in 1925. This Commission also proposed the merger of the AUA and the General Conference, and that the president's term of office cover four years instead of one.[34]

The Universalists first organized in 1793, and also had a long history of fear of centralized authority and organization, claiming that under congregational polity each congregation and minister needed a large degree of independence and freedom. They began to organize State Conventions after 1825, and eventually established a system of state superintendents and ministerial fellowshipping, thus developing a mixture of congregational and presbyterian polity. The office of General Superintendent was formed in 1898 after Willard C. Selleck pleaded with the Universalists to develop "The Organized Church" during a speech he gave in 1896. Selleck argued that the churches needed more central oversight, and the General Convention meeting in Chicago in 1897 passed a resolution calling for greater unity and continuity in the work of the parishes. Many Universalists feared the creation of an executive position, and rejected the title of bishop. Robert Cummins assumed the office of General Superintendent in 1939 and tried to change the "alphabetical assortments and geographical provincialisms" of disparate affiliate groups, and small, struggling, and subsidized congregations. Cummins declared that the Universalist Church of America could be transformed into a "unified church." In 1955, he reiterated that the Universalists had "rendered our own elective officials almost powerless," and let "independent and freedom-loving individuals and groups" be "irresponsible." Unfortunately, continued skepticism about giving authority to a central body led to the inability of the Universalist Church to function effectively.[35]

Harry Scholefield, long-time minister in San Francisco, once wrote, "it has been a chronic problem for both Unitarians and Universalists to reconcile their love of individual freedom and autonomy with necessary church structures. There has been a strong bias against any kind of

---

[34] Arthur Cushman McGiffert, Jr. *Pilot of a Liberal Faith: Samuel Atkins Eliot, 1862–1950* (Boston, MA: Skinner House Books, 1976), pp. 115–116.

[35] Russell E. Miller, *The Larger Hope, The Second Century of the Universalist Church in America, 1870–1970* (Boston, MA: UUA, 1985), pp. 31–35; Robert Cummins, "A United Church, Address at the Convention in Washington," *The Christian Leader* (November 4, 1939), p. 1053; Robert Cummins, "Freedom for What," *Introduction to Universalism* (Boston, MA: Universalist Church of America, 1955), p. 4.

organizational – particularly denominational – structure..." This problem is inherent in a structure where the local unit is the most significant
entity. The UUA has been described as an organization whose "primary
purpose is to serve its member congregations, organize new congregations,
extend and strengthen Unitarian Universalist institutions, and implement
its principles." A national Board of Trustees governs the UUA, many
of whom are representatives from geographic areas called districts. Professional district executives serve in regional offices and help to provide
services at the local level. The recent UUA study, *Interdependence*, suggests
that the UUA serves these purposes in a variety of ways. The Board has
its own independent existence beyond its service to the congregations, and
thus can raise funds, and carry out the broad mission of serving "religious,
educational and humanitarian purposes."[36]

In *Interdependence*, the Commission on Appraisal suggests that the USA
congregations have much to learn from their Canadian neighbors. In
Canada, the basic political unit is the collective, not the individual, so
the primary goal of government is not to ensure rights, but rather to provide for the citizens. This is reflected in congregational life, too. The basic
unit is not the individual members, but rather the congregation itself. The
Commission report says that the Canadian ethos and identity could have
ramifications for congregations throughout North America, as a stimulus
to helping "the building of a community of autonomous churches," as the
congregations in the United States have much to learn about the strengths
that can be found in "collectivity."[37]

Yet, a greater sense of collective will would probably not change the ethos
of anti-authoritarianism that seems inherent in Unitarianism. The British
are organized in the General Assembly of Unitarian and Free Christian
Churches (1928), the successor of the British and Foreign Unitarian Association (1825) and the National Conference (1881). Like the UUA headquarters in Boston, Massachusetts, although much smaller, the General
Assembly headquarters in London has various administrative arms dealing
with ministry, religious education, youth, social action, worship, development, international matters, and finance. There is also a Welsh department,
as most of the 22 congregations in Wales use the Welsh language. Christine Hayhurst, a former Deputy Secretary of the British Unitarians and
active member of the International Council of Unitarians and Universalists,

---

[36] Harry B. Scholefield, ed., *The Unitarian Universalist Pocket Guide* (Boston, MA: UUA, 1981), p. 28;
Interdependence, p. 46,
[37] *Interdependence*, pp. 58–59.

points out that, "The General Assembly has no control over its constituent congregations and fellowships. There may be shared values, but there is no uniform product or service . . . for that would be contrary to the Unitarian ethos." While some hail the strength of this local independence, others, such as George Chryssides, a Research fellow in Contemporary Religion at the University of Birmingham, feel that congregational democracy leads to "a lot of intransigence in the movement." He says we should be thinking of the label "Unitarian" as a "franchise . . . that presupposes a number of key recognizable elements."[38]

The "franchise" congregations in Transylvania are the most tradition bound of any in the world. Both the Unitarian Churches in Romania, and the smaller group in Hungary, are governed by bishops. This form of church government dates to the time of the church's founding under Francis Dávid, who held this title. Authority comes from a Consistory that is made up of clergy and lay persons who hail from different church districts, with the lay members elected by the churches. The Consistory has a presbyterian structure. The bishop, who has always been a male clergyman, carries a considerable amount of power, although that has been modified. He once served a life term, and had absolute control over all property. He still controls the high schools and colleges, and supervises the deans, who are the executive ministers in the church districts. Church membership is not the free choice that is typical of the Western world, where new members often are people who are dissatisfied with the church of their childhood. In Transylvania, church membership is dependent upon parentage and is determined at birth (boys to father's church and girls to mother's church), and thus changing churches would be considered unusual. Locally, the individual congregation has a lay board, but the ministers have a great deal of power. Often the only educated professionals in a village, clergy are generally deferred to, and expected to be fully in charge. During the Communist era, the Unitarian Theological School in Kolozsvár (Cluj-Napoca in Romanian) was allowed only one new ministerial student per year. In recent years, this number has expanded, and now includes women. The appointment of ministers, similar to an episcopal system, comes through the bishop.

Power on the local level is limited by the bishop, the districts, and even the state, and so the polity features we associate with the rest of the Western world – including local ownership of property, selection of clergy, and open

---

[38] Stephen Lingwood, ed., *The Unitarian Life: Voices from the Past and Present* (London: Lindsey Press, 2008), p. 49.

membership affiliations – are not present, except for the election of local officers. The center of religious life in Transylvania is the village, and most Unitarians there are ethnic Hungarians. Today, many of the congregations in Transylvania are partnered with congregations in the United States who provide material and emotional support. This relationship, which first flourished in the 1920s in a joint effort with the British, was revived during William Schulz's presidency of the UUA in the late 1980s.[39]

What is the future of Unitarian Universalist systems of governance? In the United States, a system known as "policy governance" has received positive attention and adoption, especially from many regional districts, and the UUA Board. This empowers a stronger executive with increased administrative abilities to carry out the goals of the district or national Board of Trustees. Presently, the UUA is considering "bold changes" in several areas. Wanting to involve congregations more in the electoral process, candidates for president and moderator will no longer be self-selected, but will be part of a committee-nominated slate of candidates. The UUA Board declared that its system of governance was "too big, too complex, and too expensive." A comprehensive plan to transform governance on the General Assembly (GA) or annual meeting, board and district levels has been proposed. These changes include holding the GA every other year, and making it more representative of the congregations by reducing the number of delegates, and making them more accountable to the congregations. The proposal also reduces the size of the UUA Board. Involving congregations more in the business of the UUA will satisfy some critics. In 1999, David Bumbaugh wrote that the GA had become more of a "pep-rally rather than a governing body." This followed a legal ruling that actions of the GA were only advisory, not mandatory.[40]

The British General Assembly (BGA) has also considered proposals for stronger and more responsive executive leadership at the national level. In 2003, the annual meeting of the BGA passed a resolution to appoint a task force to develop a proposal to "change the system of governance to have a nationally elected leadership." In 2005, a plan for a new Executive Committee of nine persons was passed by the annual meeting, and has been implemented since. This Executive Committee, similar to the UUA's Board

---

[39] *Interdependence*, pp. 37–38; Mike Young, "The Latest News from Vlad Dracul's Home Town," unpublished sermon, First Unitarian Church of Honolulu, Hawaii, September 14, 2003.

[40] Jane Greer, "UUA contemplates bold changes," *UU World*, Vol. xxiv, No. 2 (Summer 2010), pp. 42–44; David E. Bumbaugh, "Why Anti-Racism Will Fail: A Response," archive.uua.org/ga/ga99/238bumbaugh.html.

of Trustees, works with an executive, the Chief Officer, at the Unitarian headquarters in London. Another issue in the UK is the greater demands the government places upon having a more organized national faith. While the national government claims it does not wish to interfere with free voluntary associations, such as the churches, there have been attempts at more "monitoring and control techniques, often for financial reasons." Historically, the Unitarians have welcomed as little involvement as possible, but since the 1990s the British government has increasingly sought to control the activities of religious groups. As a result of new laws, it seemed that the central bodies of churches would need to officially monitor each registered congregation as a charitable group. This proved controversial among those Unitarians who are uncomfortable with local control by a national body. If implemented, "The GA would become the authority to which each local congregation would have to defer." Charitable status for Unitarian churches in Britain has also been called into question because it was argued that "few believe in God," as was required by the BGA rules of 1928. Terrorist threats all over the world have also prompted the British government to want clearer authority structures in place. Registrations and adherence to government regulations may challenge the freedom-loving Unitarians in the decades ahead.[41]

With stricter ministerial fellowship guidelines, and the change to policy governance, there is some concern that individuals and congregations no longer have the kind of personal and democratic authority they once had, but that this is concentrated in more formal systems, as the denomination becomes more systematized with added rules and guidelines. At the same time, there is a desire to move beyond the kind of personalism and individualism that has characterized liberal religion and congregational polity since its inception. Congregations often speak of nurturing "right relationships" among their members in the context of community development rather than simply affirming individual rights. New ways to connect autonomous congregations, especially through technological means and by campaigns that solidify their sense of mission, may help the Unitarians grow in number. There is a new emphasis on finding connections and building interdependence throughout the liberal religious world. Perhaps the advent of the International Council of Unitarians and Universalists (ICUU) in 1995 will help facilitate a new era in polity where liberals from all over the world

---

[41] See: www.unitarian.org.uk/info/ga-resolutions2005.shtml for the text of the resolution; see Ruston, "The State and Unitarianism," pp. 223, 227–235.

have a voice in articulating a common faith for the twenty-first century, and help develop emergent groups in many new places, especially developing countries. Presently, there are about 500,000 Unitarians and Universalists worldwide. It is the hope of the ICUU that part of their mission "will be to build relationships through communication and collaboration."[42]

[42] See: www.icuu.org for the latest information on international developments.

CHAPTER 8

Worship

Worship is a necessary response to human life. Among Unitarians and Universalists, that response is unusual among the Western religious traditions because it is never presumed that the worshipper is paying homage to a deity, and so worship does not need to be oriented towards the supernatural. Unitarians often focus on the root of the old Anglo-Saxon word "worship" (weorthscipe) or "worth ship," which means to reflect upon or celebrate things of worth in the natural world – an idea, a value, or a vision of how the world could be.[1]

At a conference for the Unitarian Association for Lay Ministry in 2008, Martin Gienke of Bury St. Edmunds, England asked how Unitarian worship was different from other forms. He suggested that, "At best, our worship is unpredictable, varied and diffuse – it takes place in congregations free to choose their own patterns." He also wondered, "Is our worship too word-centered, do we lack symbols, do we contain enough emotion?"[2] These are questions that concern Unitarians and Universalists all over the world. The liberal religious movement generally does not follow prescribed liturgical patterns, but rather celebrates a "free" tradition when it comes to orders of worship, with each congregation choosing its own forms. This means that generally no established prayer book is followed, but services are "open" to include a variety of materials that the minister or service leader chooses. While Unitarian services in Transylvania follow an exclusively Christian format, many Unitarians elsewhere have services with readings that are not biblical, but may come from literary or humanist sources, or other world religious scriptures. The question of whether the services

---

[1] Frederick E. Gillis, "Common Worship – Why and How?" Commission on Common Worship (Boston, MA: UUA 1981), p. 1.; Congregation of Abraxas, "Worship" (Overland Park, KS: Congregation of Abraxas, 1979).

[2] Jim Corrigall, "Unitarian lay leaders 'surprise and inspire,'" Unitarian Association for Lay Ministry (December, 2008), ualm.org.uk/news_archives.htm.

have too little emotion has been around ever since Ralph Waldo Emerson accused the rational Unitarians of being "corpse-cold."[3]

Unitarian and Universalist worship services are conducted in the context of a long history of rebellion against more orthodox forms of worship. In Transylvania, the early leaders defied the religious and political leaders who wanted them to worship Jesus, and thus they refused to address him in prayer as if he were a deity. In Great Britain, two competing types of Unitarianism existed side by side: one eschewed sectarianism in favor of ecumenism, and the other was more militantly Unitarian. The ecumenical version led by James Martineau supported more structured styles of worship, frequently producing their own Unitarian versions of the Book of Common Prayer that their dissenting ancestors had rebelled against in 1662. Like the British, much of the American form of Unitarian Universalist worship comes from the Puritan tradition, and thus it has a heritage that is pulpit centered and anti-ritualistic. Just as many adult members in America, and to some extent in Britain, come to a Unitarian church rejecting the forms and words of worship they experienced as children, so too, the Puritan service had a sincere emphasis on simplicity in rebellion against the more elaborate and sacramental forms of worship found in Anglican and Catholic liturgies.

The central focus of Puritan worship, like most Protestant faiths, was not the altar where Christ's sacrifice was re-enacted, but rather the pulpit where the words of the Bible were filtered through the mouths of preachers. Following this tradition, Unitarian services have always been filled with words, more than ritual, with the sermon as the sacramental equivalent of the Mass. The meaning and value of words as each person understood them from the written page superseded the traditions and the interpretations of the church, and its priests. The central part of the service, the sermon, was meant to be the explication and application of a scripture passage to the people's lives. In New England, this was followed by a period of questions from the congregation to clarify and understand the sermon's meaning in their own lives; what might be called the sermon talk-back today.[4]

Over the centuries, this pattern has evolved in Unitarian and Universalist congregations. Much of the time is still spent on proclaiming the word, but the words today have become what are sometimes referred to as a

[3] Ralph Waldo Emerson, *The Heart of Emerson's Journals*, ed. Bliss Perry (Boston, MA: Houghton, Mifflin and Co., 1926), p. 218. This reference is from May 1, 1846.

[4] John von Rohr, "Worship in the Puritan Tradition: An Historical Statement," Occasional Paper, Pacific School of Religion (Berkeley, October 1976).

loose-leaf Bible, where all literature has the potential to be scripture, if it is deemed worthy of ethical and spiritual instruction, and especially if it can be used as a source of teaching and inspiration. Because words also have a time and place, most Unitarians do not wish to mouth words that they do not believe are true or relevant. Historically, members did not wish to sing hymns that had references to damnation or sinfulness, or to the Trinity. The tunes were often the same as those used in other Protestant faiths, but the words had to reflect their beliefs. This liberal faith teaches that all people need to be included, and that all faiths need to be respected and reverenced equally. A generation ago, women wanted to be affirmed equally to men, so they began to question the references to mankind and God the Father, and then substituted inclusive language.[5]

Despite the common history of rebellion and the primary focus on the sermon, the British and the American styles of worship throughout much of their history have, until recently, been quite different. In his "The Hymn Sandwich: A Brief History of Unitarian Worship," Duncan McGuffie says that although most Unitarian congregations in Britain once used a set liturgy, by 1981 only one eighth of the churches used a publication such as *Orders of Worship* (1932), and that number was declining. The hope of having a "reformed" Book of Common Prayer was evident throughout much of the nineteenth century, especially among the more ecumenically minded Unitarians. The Presbyterian Dissenters who once wanted the national church to follow their form of polity continued to express "a nostalgia for a unified national church sharing a common worship." They also wanted their rational faith to show care and preparation in worship, rather than an enthusiastic or impulsive style that an extemporaneous prayer might incite. The first avowed Unitarian congregation founded in London in 1774 used *The Book of Common Prayer reformed according to the Plan of the late Dr. Samuel Clarke*. Clarke was an Arian who insisted that prayers only be addressed to God the Father.[6]

The Anglican traditions and influence became prominent in the nineteenth century when James Martineau had a marked influence on all Unitarian worship. He helped Unitarianism move away from a biblical

---

[5] Christopher Raible, "Our Ways of Worship," in *The Unitarian Universalist Pocket Guide*, ed. Harry Scholefield (Boston, MA: Skinner House Books, 1981), pp. 35–37.

[6] Duncan McGuffie "The Hymn Sandwich: A Brief History of Unitarian Worship", a lecture given at the General Assembly of Unitarian and Free Christian Churches, (1981). See www.vary.freeuk.com/learning/relthink/unihisliturgies.html; "Unitarian Worship" by A.J. Long in The *New Westminster Dictionary of Liturgy and Worship*, ed. J.G. Davies (Philadelphia, PA: Westminster Press, 1986), p. 514.

rationalism to a more pietistic approach to faith, but he also feared the impulsiveness of evangelicalism. His worship theory reflected an attempt to balance the "free spirit of Dissent and the dignity of the Established Church." The result of Martineau's theory that a prayer book could success-fully blend high liturgy with Unitarian theological simplicity was *Common Prayer for Christian Worship* (1862), compiled with Thomas Sadler. His later prayer book (1879) showed his increasing unwillingness to invoke Jesus' name, and so he eventually removed every instance of praying "through Jesus Christ our Lord."[7] In the latter half of the twentieth century, British Unitarians increasingly turned from the old Anglican-inspired prayer-book format to freer and more diverse patterns of worship. This was reflected by such publications as *Unitarian Orders of Worship* in 1976 by Upper Chapel in Sheffield, England. In the introduction, the Rev. Peter Godfrey said his Chapel trustees had concluded that any "liturgy used should represent the thoughts and feelings of the living congregation."[8]

W. D. Davies has suggested that the "warmth of Unitarian devotion" is especially reflected in hymnology. Martineau followed the eighteenth-century lead of Isaac Watts, and expanded congregational singing to use more secular and poetic materials to reflect his elevation of "Reason" above scripture in discerning spiritual truths. He produced what became the most popular Unitarian hymnal of the day, *Hymns for the Christian Church and Home* (1840).[9] Important influences upon him included the writer Anna Barbauld (1743–1825), who wrote hymns for children, and advocated the need for more emotion in worship. Martineau's catholic taste in his use of materials is emblematic of his dream of a national Presbyterian church that would become free in spirit. He wrote: "Unitarianism . . . must discover more variety in its resources, must avail itself of more flexibility of appeal, must wield in its turn its critical, its philosophical, its social, its poetical, its devotional powers, before it gain its destined ascendancy over the mind of Christendom."[10] The most famous contributor to all hymnody in Britain was Sarah Flower Adams (1805–1848), the composer of "Nearer my God to Thee." The irony of this composition is that although it is a popular hymn in Christendom, it is not sung much in Unitarian circles, due to its devout

---

[7] Frank Schulman, *James Martineau: "This Conscience-Intoxicated Unitarian"* (Chicago, IL: Meadville Lombard Press 2002), p. 25; *New Westminster Dictionary*, ibid., p. 514.

[8] Peter B. Godfrey, and Upper Chapel members, *Unitarian Orders of Worship* (Sheffield, UK: Upper Chapel, 1976), Introduction.

[9] Schulman, *Martineau*, p. 36.

[10] Andrew Brown, "Martineau's Hymn Books: His Evolving Thought and Their Influence on the Unitarian Movement," *Transactions of the Unitarian Historical Society*, Vol. XXII (No. 4), April 2002, p. 405.

and pietistic language. The hymn is legendary due to its association with the sinking of the Titanic, as some say the band was playing it as the ship sank.[11]

The British continued to be active in hymnal publications in the twentieth century. The primary hymnbook for well over a half-century was *Hymns of Worship* (1927). More recently, new hymnals have changed with the times, reflecting contemporary themes and principles, including a popular selection that introduced inclusive language, *Hymns for Living* (1985), edited by Sydney Knight.

The Americans replicate the British in emphasizing the sermon and the importance of hymnody in their worship services, but their history generally follows more open patterns of worship with less set liturgies. Theological differences from mainstream Christianity resulted in Unitarians and Universalists composing their own hymn texts, beginning in the late eighteenth century, while using familiar hymn tunes. In colonial America, congregational singing was restricted to psalm singing only, but this tradition faded in the eighteenth century, as the introduction of hymn singing (biblical texts other than psalms) and the placement of organs in churches increased. The congregation at King's Chapel in Boston, Massachusetts, published the first avowedly Unitarian hymnal, *A Collection of Psalms and Hymns for Public Worship* in 1799. Right from the start, Unitarians and Universalists resisted singing what they did not believe. Francis W. P. Greenwood of King's Chapel gathered the most popular Unitarian collection, *A Collection of Psalms and Hymns for Sacred Worship* (1830), in the first part of the nineteenth century. It appeared in fifty different editions, and was recommended by Emerson in a sermon in 1831 while he was still a minister, and even after he had long since left the ministry, he remarked in his journal in 1847 that it was "still the best."[12] By the mid-nineteenth century, Unitarians showed a particular proficiency for becoming outstanding hymn writers.

Hymns gave theological and liturgical context to Unitarian and Universalist worship, and provided a common expression of faith, especially for the Universalists, to respond to their orthodox opponents. When John Murray founded the first Universalist church in Gloucester, Massachusetts in 1779, he had already published James Relly's Universalist hymnal from England (1776). Universalists produced many hymnals, including *Hymns Composed by Different Authors* (1810), at the request of the General Convention. In the

---

[11] Frank Schulman, *A Manual of Worship* (Boston, MA: UUA, 2006), pp. 39–40.
[12] Eugene B. Navias, *Singing Our History* (Boston, MA: UUA, 1975), p. 8.

preface, the authors, including Hosea Ballou, stated that the Convention had expressed the view that Dr. Isaac Watts had "extended the idea of the punishment of sin, infinitely beyond the design of the inspired authors; and has thereby sorely wounded the divine theme of devotional psalmody." The authors felt that Watts' book reversed the theme of God's "Universal Joy," and this was sufficient reason to "disuse" his material and write their own. Perhaps owing to their radical theology, Universalist hymns generally did not receive a wider audience beyond denominational bounds.[13]

The golden era of Unitarian hymn writing was the second half of the nineteenth century. Prior to this, several of the Transcendentalist poets had texts set to music, including Frederic Henry Hedge, who translated Luther's "A Mighty Fortress is Our God" from the original German, and also wrote his own texts. Hymn writing knew no bounds as to its choice of theme, and included an increasing interest in social causes. Unitarian minister Edmund Hamilton Sears (1810–76) wrote one of the most popular Christmas carols, "It Came upon the Midnight Clear," but its underlying theme was anti-war. Eliza Lee Cabot Follen (1787–1860) wrote hymns for children, but also counseled parishioners to "Remember the Slave." Julia Ward Howe (1819–1910) took up the theme of freedom during the Civil War when her "Battle Hymn of the Republic" was set to the popular tune "Glory, Glory, Hallelujah." Howe's minister, James Freeman Clarke, asked her to compose something more uplifting than "John Brown's Body," which the troops sang was "a-mould'ring in the grave." The Battle Hymn asked that we "die to make men free."[14]

Later in the century, such prolific writers as Samuel Johnson (1822–1882) and Samuel Longfellow (1819–1892, poet Henry Wadsworth Longfellow's brother) wrote many hymns and together compiled *Hymns of the Spirit* (1864). William Channing Gannett and Frederick Lucian Hosmer (1840–1929) also composed many original hymns and, along with James Vila Blake, gathered *Unity Hymns and Chorals* (1880). In 1868, the American Unitarian Association (AUA) produced its first denominational hymnal, *Hymn and Tune Book*, which was marked by the appearance of hymns and tunes on the same page; prior to this, the church musicians chose the tune from among a small group that each congregation knew well. Lyrics began to express a theological diversity fomented by liberalism. Gannett's

---

[13] Navias, *Singing Our History*, pp. 7, 27; *Hymns, Composed by Different Authors, at the Request of the General Convention of Universalists* (Charlestown, MA: Samuel T. Armstrong, 1810), Preface, p. 42.

[14] Several hymn texts are included in *An American Reformation, A Documentary History of Unitarian Christianity*, eds. Sidney E. Ahlstrom and Jonathan S. Carey (Middletown, CT: Wesleyan University Press, 1985), pp. 311–319; Navias, ibid., p. 62.

"Things Commonly Believed Among Us," which provided the basis for the theological compromise of 1894, was embodied in such hymns as "It Sounds Along the Ages," which is still popular today. Gannett said spiritual inspiration comes from varied sources, including "Sinai's cliffs," "Buddha's tree," "every Bible scroll," and even the "oracles of Concord." Another development during this period of increased theological inclusiveness was the use of unison congregational affirmations or covenants during the service, often twinned with a Unitarian doxology, a song of affirmation that is sung to the tune of the Old Hundredth. In 1894, James Vila Blake wrote the most popular affirmation, still commonly used today, for the Unitarian church in Evanston, Illinois. It reads: "Love is the spirit of this church, and service is its law. This is our great covenant: To dwell together in peace, To seek the truth in love, And to help one another."[15]

This kind of religious diversity was reflected in worship by drawing upon multiple religious sources, which generally became the Unitarian and Universalist orientation as they both increasingly began to pull away from their Christian roots, especially after 1930. In the 1936 Commission of Appraisal report, *Unitarians Face a New Age*, Aurelia Henry Reinhardt (1877–1948), a lay person and the first woman moderator of the AUA, gave a report on "Worship: Its Fundamental Place in Liberal Religion." Here, she said liberals must "face the charge that the dynamic of worship has largely been lost in liberal churches." While acknowledging the important role of historical material, Reinhardt said modern worship had to contain content from the "new science, the visions of integrated humanity, and wider concepts of deity." With this essay, Reinhardt helped set in motion a denomination-wide effort "reviving adequate public worship." The Unitarians and Universalists had already been working together on a joint hymnal, and the result was the 1937 edition of *Hymns of the Spirit* (unrelated to the 1864 volume of the same name), which drew on music from diverse sources, and also made a special attempt to appeal to humanists as well as theists. The material was gathered from "extra-biblical sources," as well as from the "treasury of liturgical literature." The hymnal included sixteen set liturgies and responsive readings for use in worship, and two forms of communion, which by this time was only celebrated in a small minority of congregations. The increasing tendency not to use set liturgies among the American Unitarians and Universalists meant that the appeal

---

[15] *Singing the Living Tradition* (Boston, MA: UUA, 1993), "It Sounds Along the Ages" is hymn number 187. See "Hymnody" in Mark Harris, *Historical Dictionary of Unitarian Universalism* (Lanham, MD: Scarecrow Press, 2004), pp. 263–266, 309.

of set services was limited, even though the use of the hymnal for singing was widespread.[16]

This heavy emphasis on liturgy was primarily the influence of Von Ogden Vogt (1879–1964), who had inspired Reinhardt to realize that liberal worship needed more creative imagination: "the religious moment is not the moment of thinking, nor of action, but of joy." Vogt was called a "master liturgist" by his student, the Rev. John Hayward. In his *Art and Religion*, Vogt suggested that a worship service was an art form. He saw a promising trend when free churches replicated Gothic architecture, and arranged a chancel area with the communion table at the head of the building, with the pulpit on one side, rather than the traditional Protestant central pulpit. He wanted to emphasize other aspects of the service besides the sermon, and found the chancel arrangement "tends to minimize the personality of the minister and to merge him into the background as a voice and messenger of the historic church and the communal faith." This suited Vogt's hope of interjecting "Gothic passion" into worship, as he felt most liberal worship had too little appeal to the senses. He wanted to improve the art of worship, and seemed to feel that the "desire for liturgical worship" increases in proportion to the "level of culture." Vogt did not want to restrict the liberal religious value of freedom, but he believed that it was best found through the use of more form, not less.[17]

While Vogt's set liturgies did not ultimately prove popular, his definition of worship as the "celebration of life" became the title of the subsequent Unitarian Universalist hymnal. Although he was not the chairman of the Hymnbook Commission, Kenneth Patton, the minister at the innovative Universalist Charles Street Meetinghouse in Boston, became the driving force behind its production. In the congregation's newsletter, "The Meetinghouse Messenger," Patton called the meetinghouse a "laboratory" for experimental worship services. He created an auditorium with seating in the round. In December 1965, the newsletter editor wrote that they had created a new "ritual" which "involves the lighting of the atom, the galaxy, and the lamp . . . [which] sets the 'cosmic dimensions' of the service." Patton wanted more diversity in liberal worship services, and used representative

---

[16] *Hymns of the Spirit*. Boston, MA: UUA, 1937, 19th printing 1981, v–vi.; Aurelia Henry Reinhardt in, "Worship: Its Fundamental Place in Liberal Religion," in *Unitarians Face a New Age* (Boston, MA: AUA, 1936), pp. 70, 77–78.

[17] Von Ogden Vogt, quoted in Reinhardt, "Worship: Its Fundamental Place in Liberal Religion," p. 76; John F. Hayward, "Von Ogden Vogt: Exemplar of Religion and Art, 1879–1964 www.harvardsquarelibrary.org/unitarians/vogt.html.; Von Ogden Vogt, *Art and Religion* (New Haven, CT: Yale University Press, 1921), pp. 119, 216; Gillis, "Common Worship," pp. 5–7.

readings from such sources as Chinese traditions, Hindu or Jewish faiths or modern writers, and these became fodder for his contributions to the new hymnal. Patton was building upon the foundations of a Universalist group called the Humiliati, a cadre of Universalist ministers who sought liturgical renewal, and championed what they called "Emergent Universalism," an understanding of the faith that carried it beyond Christianity to a synthesis of all religious knowledge.[18]

In his Berry Street Essay, "Hymnbook Reminiscences and Reflections," hymn writer and minister Vincent B. Silliman (1894–1979) says that *Hymns for the Celebration of Life* (1964) includes 124 hymns or stanzas that are fresh contributions to Unitarian Universalist hymnody. Patton had prepared 219 texts on thin sheets of paper, which the Commission dubbed "Ken Patton's Flimsies," to be considered for inclusion in the hymnal. The final hymnal also includes 13 hymns and 23 readings exclusively composed by Patton. His humanistic and universalistic theology was reflected in the meetinghouse's decoration with the first use, in any sanctuary, of symbols of all the world's religions. Silliman calls the hymnal "essentially a compendium of this-worldly religion." There is no real mention of personal immortality, and it also includes a celebration of death as a meaningful part of life. There is also a celebration of the earth as our human home. Silliman calls these topics unique to Unitarian Universalist hymnody. In addition, he says that liberal religious hymnody includes recognition that each of the world's religious traditions must be "evaluated on its own merits," and that "freedom" is a "religious value." In some ways the new hymnal was an antidote to the set liturgies and primarily Christian materials that were found in its predecessor. With humanism the dominant theological position in the movement, the hymnal reflected the need to celebrate the human condition in the here and now. It also suggested an increased focus on worship that would be especially emphasized in the next generation. In conclusion, Silliman said that this hymnal gave the movement "a widening sense that something called worship is the central business of churches."[19] However, as Mark Morrison-Reed has pointed out, *Hymns for the Celebration of Life* has no representation from any African Americans, despite the *bona fides* of several of the Commission's members.

---

[18] "The Meetinghouse Messenger," Charles Street Universalist Meeting House (Boston), December 1965, pdf file of newsletters at Andover Harvard Theological Library, Harvard Divinity School. See Russell Miller, *The Larger Hope; The Second Century of the Universalist Church in America, 1870–1970* (Boston, MA: UUA, 1985), pp. 636–643 for a history of the Humiliati.

[19] Vincent B. Silliman, "Hymnbook Reminiscences and Reflections," See www.uuma.org/berrystreet/ Essays/BSE1977.html; *Hymns for the Celebration of Life* (Boston, MA: UUA, 1964).

Unitarians have taken to heart the Protestant notion of freedom from outgrown forms and words in developing worship services. While the first half of the twentieth century brought a diversity of materials and perspectives to challenge liberal Christian origins, the latter part of the century transformed worship even further, with more religiously diverse materials, inclusive language for both hymns and readings, a new emphasis on ritual and sensory experience, and, perhaps most obviously, a majority presence of women clergy leading the worship services. The 1977 General Assembly of the Unitarian Universalist Association (UUA) passed a Resolution on Women and Religion, which called upon every Unitarian Universalist to "make every effort to put traditional assumptions and language in perspective, and to avoid sexist assumptions and language in the future." The UUA responded to this directive in 1979 with *25 Familiar Hymns in New Form.* In practice, this meant that the exclusive word "man" was often changed to the inclusive "human," while pronouns naming God with the exclusive patriarchal references "He" or "His" were altered to be impersonal. The UUA's Commission on Common Worship concluded that just as "our forebears changed and adapted the religious language," (especially by removing references to Hell and the Trinity) "as an act of conscience and theological affirmation; we also would move beyond gender to affirm the inherent worth and dignity of every person."[20]

In an article called "The Changing Face of Worship: How Women Ministers Are Influencing UU Worship," Susan Manker-Seale suggests that much stereotyping has occurred about women clergy. There are those who believe that women clergy are inherently more spiritual and less intellectual than their male counterparts. Changes, such as personal sharing of joys and sorrows, the inclusion of stories specifically for children, the lighting of candles and of the chalice, and even repetitive singing at certain points in the service, have all at times been attributed to the presence of women in leadership roles.[21] Nevertheless, the traditional Protestant hymn "sandwich" of readings and prayers alternating with hymns remains the prevalent form of worship.

The current generation of Unitarian Universalist worshippers has witnessed a renewed interest in what has sometimes been called "spirituality."

[20] UUA Commission on Common Worship, *Moving Beyond Gender in Worship* (pamphlet) (Boston, MA: UUA, 1985); UUA Women and Religion Committee, *Avoiding Sexist Language* (pamphlet) (Boston, MA: UUA 1980); *25 Familiar Hymns in New Form* (Boston, MA: UUA, 1979).

[21] Susan Manker-Seale, "The Changing Face of Worship: How Women Ministers Are Influencing UU Worship," in *Leaping From Our Spheres – The Impact of Women on Unitarian Universalist Ministry,* ed. Gretchen Woods (Boston, MA: Unitarian Universalist Ministers Association, 1998), pp. 127–128.

In practice, this means more ritual, more interest in meditation, and even shorter sermons that "are more personal and accessible." It would be difficult to quantify where this impulse has emerged from, and it most certainly is not entirely from the presence of women. There have been important demographic changes among Unitarian Universalists in the last generation, such that those raised Roman Catholic, especially in New England, became a significant group of converts to the faith, increasing from 6.2 percent to 15 percent from 1967 to 1979. Former Catholics are perhaps more comfortable with liturgy and ritual than the previously predominant groups who were mostly "come-outers" from a variety of liberal Protestant groups. Many of the new religions also had a profound impact on Unitarian Universalism. With the advent of the women's movement, pagan and new-age groups began to proliferate, and their nature-worshipping, ritualistic formats that sang and re-enacted a reverence towards the earth and her seasons won broad acceptance. This earth-centered worship often included interest in female images for God (or goddesses), which was further stimulated by a popular adult education curriculum, *Cakes for the Queen of Heaven*.[22]

Manker-Seale concurs that it is difficult to determine which aspects of worship were especially influenced or introduced by women. She cites examples from her father's ministry in the 1950s, when having a children's story in the church he was serving in Wayland, Massachusetts was the norm. Women were sometimes credited with introducing new rituals, such as the Water Communion service, a popular innovation where participants pour water they have gathered from a summer excursion into a common community bowl. Others have argued that this service was initiated by youth. More lay participation in worship, which Manker-Seale claims was instigated by Mary Safford in the late nineteenth century, was also implemented by James Freeman Clarke in Boston (see Chapter 5). So, it is difficult to pinpoint specific innovations, but what is certain is that women's presence in worship has helped to uplift the experience of a population that has been historically degraded. In turn, this has meant that worship services are now more of a partnership between minister and congregation, reflecting the need for a stronger sense of community solidarity. Surveys of what Unitarian Universalists value in a worship service show that while intellectual stimulation remained high in studies from 1967, 1979, and 1989, three categories showed a significant increase of more

---

[22] "Report of the Committee on Goals" (Boston, MA: UUA, 1967), p. 40; Commission on Appraisal, UUA, *The Quality of Religious Life in Unitarian Universalist Congregations* (Boston, MA: UUA, 1989), p. 48.

than 20 percent of respondents. These values were "celebrating common values," "group experience of participation," and "fellowship," making it clear that many more worshippers value the joint community experience in what has heretofore been described as an individualistic faith. Increasingly throughout the United States, worship has become more participatory and engaging, featuring new worship associate programs in many congregations where lay members take leadership roles in conducting worship, and a wider variety of musical choices has become possible.[23]

This impetus to make worship more spiritual reached fruition in the most recent UUA hymnal, *Singing the Living Tradition* (1993). The Hymnbook Resources Commission, which first met in 1986, was committed to the embodiment of the revised Principles and Purposes in the new book. As was often the case in the past, there was agitation for change to make the "words equal to our intentions." This meant a language of faith that expressed justice by extending beyond feminism to include anti-racism. The Commission looked at ways in which color was used to express moral values, such as light for good and dark for bad. It made recommendations that light and dark not be paired as opposing ideas, that darkness can be redemptive, and that white can be demonic, such as "blinding light." The new hymnal included such efforts as the hymn "Dark of Winter," where darkness gives "quiet calm." The new hymnbook continued to be sensitive to inclusive language issues, but the radical degenderizing – which had a tendency to remove all pronouns – is broadened here, so that there is more use of both "he" and "she." Nevertheless, the popular "Morning has Broken" continues to make a strange reference to "God's feet" rather than "his feet." The feet in the original hymn belonged to Jesus. The effort to avoid the masculine pronoun gave us instead a God with feet. Nevertheless, this hymnal expresses "a full range of spiritual imagery," including "feminine imagery for the divine." The hymnbook is organized to reflect the pluralism of the present-day faith, which means not only hymns and readings that speak to humanists, Christians, and other world faiths, but other Unitarian and Universalist traditions worldwide including works from Nigeria, the Philippines, India, England, Transylvania, and the Czech Republic, featuring five texts from the founder of the Czech church, Norbert Capek.[24]

Capek has given Unitarians and Universalists throughout the world an important modern ritual, the Flower Communion. When he started the

---

[23] Manker-Seale, "Changing Face," p. 131; *Quality of Religious Life*, p. 19.
[24] W. Frederick Wooden, "Is There No Beauty in Darkness? Faith Language and Racism" (Boston, MA: UUA, 1988), pp. 1, 7; *Singing the Living Tradition* (Boston, MA: UUA, 1993). "Dark of Winter" is #55 and "Morning has Broken" is #138.

Czech church, his services were extremely simple, with a lecture sermon and no hymn singing. He felt the need for more "symbolic ritual" as an emotional outlet to bind people together, but he did not want to alienate either former Catholics or Jews. He developed what he called the Flower Festival service, wanting to avoid the word "communion," and it became the last service before the summer break, as it still is in many congregations in the United States. Capek asked the parishioners to bring a flower of their own choosing to the service, where they placed it in a common vase. After the service, people were asked to come forward to a central table where the vase had been placed, and take a flower other than the one they had brought, representing their community need for one another. The first Flower Communion service in Czechoslovakia was held in 1923, and the tradition was introduced to America in 1940.[25]

The free tradition in Unitarian and Universalist congregations means that a variety of rituals is celebrated, but none are universal. The two sacraments in Protestantism are the Lord's Supper or communion, and baptism. Liberals have struggled with the significance of communion, especially since Ralph Waldo Emerson decided that it was outmoded and never intended to be a permanent ritual, and he quit the ministry in 1832, refusing to administer it. Even before then, it was controversial. Shortly after Convers Francis was called to the church in Watertown, Massachusetts, the congregation voted to hold communion once every other month. Francis noted in his journal that this proposal provoked "some opposition and some indication of bad feelings." He thought this was evidence "of that spirit who loves to oppose for the sake of seeming more wise or pious than others." While some Unitarian and Universalist churches in America continue to celebrate communion as a kind of memorial to Jesus, few congregations are habitual, with many having communion once a year on a day such as Maundy Thursday, when Jesus is said to have celebrated Passover. In the few places where the service continues to be held, the Unitarians may interpret it "as an act of consecration, exemplifying the power of sacrificial love and the triumph of good over evil, and as a symbol of the spiritual unity of the household of faith and of the continuity of the life of the spirit in all ages."[26] While the British generally celebrated communion until recently, it has mostly died out there too. The symbolic value of sharing

[25] Reginald Zottoli, *The Flower Communion Service* (pamphlet) (Boston, MA: UUA, c. 1961).

[26] Convers Francis, "The Journals of Convers Francis," Part I, July 18, 1819, ed. Guy R. Woodall, *Studies in the American Renaissance*, ed. Joel Myerson (Boston, MA: Twayne Publishers, 1981), p. 288; Carl Seaburg, ed., *The Communion Book* (Boston, MA: Unitarian Universalist Ministers Association, 1993), pp. 6–7.

food and drink means a wide diversity of communion services has been developed. In America, cider and corn bread are sometimes substituted for the traditional bread and wine, especially for a meal that commemorates the first Thanksgiving. The variations are endless. One tradition, created by Richard Boeke, celebrates a Salt Communion, which commemorates Mohandas K. Gandhi's famous Salt March of 1930.

One congregation that has remained faithful to its Christian tradition, and the celebration of communion, is King's Chapel in Boston, Massachusetts. It is an anomaly among Unitarian Universalist congregations, with its Anglican liturgy. The congregation initially followed Samuel Clarke's revised prayer book, which launched the Unitarian movement in London. In the communion, James Freeman, King's Chapel's first Unitarian minister, changed the word "sacrament" to "ordinance," and removed any references to eating "flesh and blood." While many of the British Unitarian congregations continued to revise Clarke even further over the years, King's Chapel made fewer substantial revisions. The most comprehensive changes were begun in 1981 when the minister, Carl Scovel, was asked to proceed with revisions. After adding several services and private devotionals, and even altering the language slightly, a new book was published in 1985. King's Chapel has followed a conservative path in its revisions over the centuries. In 1918, a Chapel revision committee declared their intention to "bring the language of the service into closer agreement with what is to be taken to be the thought and feeling of enlightened religion at the present day." Yet Scovel later commented, "Those are perilous words, for nothing is dated more quickly than that which seems most obvious and agreeable to the spirit of the age," and so King's Chapel has remained mostly out of step with the Unitarian Universalist tendency to reject traditions.[27]

While King's Chapel has upheld what many believe is the timeless language of the prayer book, other Unitarian Universalists have tried to incorporate new rituals, and at the same time reflect a pluralistic approach to faith journeying, rather than an exclusively Christian perspective. This was true of the Universalist liturgical renewal group Humiliati, and a later group, Abraxas, established in 1975. Mark Belletini, a member of Abraxas, became chair of the hymnbook commission that produced *Singing the Living Tradition*. Belletini is the author of "Worship in Unitarian Universalist Congregations," in which he says, "we choose to worship

[27] Carl Scovel, "The History of the King's Chapel Prayerbooks," *The Unitarian Universalist Christian*, Fall/Winter 1992 (Vol. 47, Nos. 3–4) pp. 31, 36.

together for the strength of many hearts beating in the spirit of shared wisdom," even though the range of worship styles spans the formal to the radically informal. The sermon remains central, addressing issues such as the existence of God, or a personal or ethical struggle, issues of justice, or a historical topic. The minister's "personal testimony" is meant "to help members of the congregation reflect honestly on their own lives." Worship should both challenge and comfort the parishioner. Traditionally, Unitarian Universalists have asked how they could inform themselves of those issues that cloud the human condition, and then use that knowledge to make the world a better place. Increasingly, liberals have wanted to balance this need to make a difference in the world with a faith that helps heal human wounds with love and compassion. The public sharing of joys and sorrows helps facilitate this, along with an increased desire for more silence in worship, so that there is an experience of quiet time to reflect and pray, and an opportunity to express gratitude for life and creation. Minister Lynn Ungar writes, "During the moment of silence in our Sunday service I close my eyes and sing silently, inside my head, 'Guide my feet while I run this race for I don't want to run this race in vain.' As I sing in silence, I imagine myself and the congregation enfolded in the arms of love."[28]

Lay participation and increased longing for ritual signal that some of the wordiness informing an individualistic and rational Unitarianism is being balanced with community support and silent reverence. In the wake of World War II, ex-Navy Chaplain, John Ruskin Clark, a Unitarian minister, reported how difficult it was for Protestants to serve the emotional needs of servicemen, when their Catholic counterparts seemed to have a rite for every occasion that they could enact. Clark wrote, "I had no religious ministrations that I could confidently use to ease the emotional tension of the Protestant wounded. The priest, on the other hand, administered the appropriate rite to all Catholic wounded." Clarke concluded that he could not accept Catholic authoritarianism, but that he needed a "liturgy to minister to human needs." One common ritual that has been adopted by Unitarians and Universalists throughout the world is the lighting of the chalice, providing the common symbolic bond that a cross cannot provide, as so few Unitarians are professing Christians. The chalice was developed as a symbol for the Unitarian Service Committee (USC) during World War II, when it was founded to assist Jews and others who were being persecuted

---

[28] Mark Belletini, *Worship in Unitarian Universalist Congregations* (pamphlet) (Boston, MA: UUA, c. 1990); Lynn Ungar quoted in Catherine Bowers, ed., *Unitarian Universalist Views of Prayer* (pamphlet) (Boston, MA: UUA, 1999). See also "Our Worship" by Mark Belletini in *The Unitarian Universalist Pocket Guide*, ed. John A. Buehrens (Boston, MA: UUA, 1999), pp. 15–25.

by the Nazis. The USC needed some brand to "symbolize the spirit of our work." This is what then director, Charles Joy, asked of the chalice's designer, Hans Deutsch, who wrote how impressed he was with this work, saying that, "if your kind of life is the profession of your faith, ... then religion, ceasing to be magic and mysticism, becomes ... active, really useful social work ... to which even a 'godless' fellow like myself can say wholeheartedly, Yes!" The flaming chalice became a symbol for a life of service to others, or even the light of hope in difficult times. It has become a focal point for worship, and a common ritual that many liberals find both inspiring and comforting.[29]

Unitarians have gained some degree of notoriety by the personal nature of their rites-of-passage ceremonies. Liberals approach weddings, memorial services (or funerals), and child dedications with extreme flexibility. Even more so than with Sunday services, these rites are personalized for the users, often giving them a hand in the design. Child dedications usually occur as part of a Sunday service, embodying both the dedication of the parents to the child's welfare, and the congregation to watch over the child's development. Among liberals, this service replaces baptism, and is grounded in the "refusal to believe in a permanent defect in human character." Rather than washing away sin, the water symbolically represents purity and life. Unitarian churches may use the terms "christening," "dedication," or "naming." Service books, especially in Britain, have often recommended alternate formulas including the use of the term "baptize" for scriptural authenticity, not theology.[30]

Weddings in the tradition usually follow a Protestant pattern, but like the Sunday worship services, a wide variety of readings is possible, and couples may participate in writing portions of the service, but at the very least, the materials are compiled to reflect the personal nature of the couple's relationship. In America, ministers and congregations have been actively involved in the campaigns to enact same-sex marriage into law, where the emphasis is placed on the enduring quality of love. Memorial services or funerals (where the body is present) in the Unitarian traditions are also highly personalized. An emphasis is placed upon the life of the deceased, with the eulogy being the central element of the service, and with an increased involvement of the mourners participating in the service,

---

[29] "Religion: The Act & the Word," *Time Magazine*, December 9, 1946; Daniel D. Hotchkiss, *The Flaming Chalice* (pamphlet) (Boston, MA: UUA, 1993).

[30] Mark W. Harris, *How We Welcome Our Children* (pamphlet) (Boston, MA: UUA, 1992); Kenneth Twinn, ed. *In Life and Death: A Book of Occasional Services* (London, UK: Lindsey Press, 1968), p. 13.

especially by sharing reflections about the deceased.[31] Without theological or religious restrictions on confession or membership, Unitarian ministers are usually willing to perform such ceremonies for any person who seeks their services. Every one of these rites-of-passage ceremonies is designed to be personally significant, reflecting an individualistic and free faith. While the content of these services is freely chosen by the participants, and can include materials and rituals from many faiths, the services reflect the Protestant Christian tradition. This is true of all Unitarian worship. While liberals have painstakingly constructed a theological orientation that denies primary affiliation with Christianity, the forms and structure of almost all of its worship, including its rites of passage, still reflect its roots in a Protestant and Christian tradition.

This is especially so in both Hungary and Romania where the worship services draw on the Christian heritage more than most Unitarian churches elsewhere, and special ceremonial rites are especially important. Former Romanian Bishop Lajos Kovacs stated that "worship is the reality, the act of being religious, and we consider worship to be the most important part of our religious life." In 1990, Unitarian Universalist Association (UUA) moderator Natalie Gulbrandsen reported that in worship services in Transylvania, men sat on one side and women on the other, and "the pulpits give the appearance of being hung on the wall." If we think of Dissenters playing a strong role in the development of the hymn, this seems to be true in Transylvania as well, where Gulbrandsen said the service started with the men singing, and "It was beautiful."[32] Four hymns are sung during the Sunday service. Botond Koppandi, writing about "The Theological Foundations of Our Liturgy," calls the hymns "sung prayers," which must be as "Unitarian as possible!" Some of the hymns go back centuries, but others are modern, and folk songs are used on special occasions. The older hymns sometimes raise theological concerns, as they remind the Transylvanians of a time when they were "forced to state the opposite of what we believed."[33] Typical of village life, Unitarians are called to worship

[31] Polly Laughland Guild, *Celebrating Birth, Marriage, Death and Other Occasions* (pamphlet) (Boston, MA: UUA, 1987).

[32] Melinda Sayavedra and Marilyn Walker, "Curriculum: The Garden of Unitarian Universalism." Unit 2 – Transylvania: The Oak Tree, p. 11. International Council of Unitarians and Universalists, 2005. See www.icuu.net/resources; Natalie Gulbrandsen, Excerpt from Annual Report of the Moderator to the 1990 General Assembly. See: www.uupcc.org/re/materials/trans-roots-gulbrandsen-schultz-visit.doc.

[33] Botond Koppandi, "Theological Foundations of Our Liturgy," in *The Home We Share: Globalization, Post-Modernism and Unitarian/Universalist Theology* ed. Clifford M. Reed and Jill K. McAllister (Caerphilly, Wales: ICUU, 2007), p. 187.

by the ringing of church bells, and, in smaller towns especially, the role of bell ringer is an important position.

One common thread among all Unitarians is the importance of the sermon, including in Transylvania, where the sermon, because of "the rationalist and humanist heritage," Bishop Kovacs says, "remains the main part of our worship, pointing us toward the divine and transcendent." Most of the prayers and readings are led by the minister, but there has been an increasing effort, "being Unitarians," to involve more parishioners in worship. Every service includes the Lord's Prayer and a Bible reading. Leaders are concerned that young people feel that the service is "too cold, too sober for them." Koppandi asks the question, what makes the liturgy Unitarian? It has a simple theology, reflected by the belief that is inscribed on every church steeple, "God is one." The liturgy also has the traditional Unitarian teaching element that addresses the mind as well as the heart. Koppandi says, "it [the Unitarian faith] needs thinking" on the part of its adherents, and that thought in turn "requires action." Unitarian worship emphasizes human responsibility and work in the world, and thus it focuses on new challenges that must be faced, and the thought is always open to reformation.[34]

Special services are an important part of a life of worship. Other than church holidays, these include baptisms, confirmation and the Lord's Supper (communion), in addition to weddings and funerals. Baptism has a particular Unitarian focus in Transylvania, more so than in Britain or America. Here, parents express their devotion to the Unitarian faith, and confirm that they expect their children to grow up in that faith. While Unitarians elsewhere often offer their children a choice of adult faiths, here the children more commonly inherit their faith. This is made manifest by the service of confirmation that is typically conducted for youth aged 14 to 16. This process can take up to two years, and the youth learn the church catechism as part of this process; again, a more traditional Christian approach to indoctrination. A short credo that is typically recited summarizes the faith well in a liberal Christian context, and it is sometimes used on other occasions, even at funerals: "I believe in One God, the creator of life, our caring Father. I believe in Jesus, the best child of God, our true teacher. I believe in the holy spirit. I believe in the vocation of the Unitarian church. I believe in forgiveness and in eternal life." Each congregation typically celebrates communion four times a year at special church holidays. It is a memorial service to Jesus, and is not considered a sacrament. The elements – the

---

[34] Sayavedra and Walker, "Curriculum," p. 11; Koppandi, "Theological Foundations," p. 196.

bread and wine – are distributed in order of seniority, and traditionally begin with the men forming a semi-circle around the communion table, followed by the women. Of personal significance is that members consider that the communion offers a symbol of how each member belongs to the congregation, and to each other. Like the message of the congregational unity found in the communion, Unitarians throughout the world use their worship services as a vehicle to inspire them to live lives full of compassion and love, and to express that faith in everyday acts towards their fellow members and others. Bishop Lajos Kovacs wrote, "worship is a unique opportunity for everyone to find himself, to find the 'other' person, to find the divine, and through the divine to find the spirit of life."[35]

---

[35] Sayavedra and Walker, ibid., pp. 11–12. For the complete catechism see: www.unitarius.hu/english/liturgy.html. See also Imre Gellerd, "Holy Communion in European Eyes: The Lord's Supper in Tranyslvanian Unitarianism," *Unitarian Universalist Christian*, Spring/Summer 1993 (Vol. 48), Nos. 1–2, pp. 47–55; George Chryssides, *The Elements of Unitarianism* (Boston, MA: Element Books Limited, 1998), p. 61.

CHAPTER 9

Sources of faith

On the eve of the gathering of the General Assembly of the Unitarian Universalist Association (UUA) in Boston in 2003, *Boston Globe* writer Michael Paulson declared, "Words of 'reverence' roil a church," that is "not sure how it feels about God." The President of the UUA, William Sinkford, had provoked a debate by suggesting that the Association needed to reverse its drift away from the "language of reverence," and begin to "name the holy." Events were precipitated when David Bumbaugh, a professor at the Meadville Lombard Theological School in Chicago, wrote an article in *Religious Humanism*, called "Toward a Humanist Vocabulary of Reverence." Bumbaugh sensed that the time had come for religious liberals to lay down their defenses against mainstream religion: "We have manned the ramparts of reason and are prepared to defend the citadel of the mind... But in the process of defending, we have lost the vocabulary of reverence, the ability to speak of that which is sacred, holy, of ultimate importance to us." When Sinkford spoke of his own conversion from atheism to theism, some members felt like he was suggesting that the denomination should begin to use traditional language as an expectation of membership, and it was even erroneously reported that Sinkford had proposed the word "God" be added to the denomination's Principles. Humanists and atheists panicked that the denomination would lose its eclectic theology. Furthermore, there were others who feared that Sinkford was suggesting the use of this language for public relations purposes, so that Unitarian Universalism would appeal to more mainstream believers.[1]

Freedom of belief and controversies about belief in God has sometimes led Unitarians to feel a prevailing sense of confusion about their religious

[1] Michael Paulson, "Words of 'reverence' roil a church," *Boston Globe*, June 28, 2003, Section A, pp. 1, 4; David Bumbaugh, "Toward a Humanist Vocabulary of Reverence." *Religious Humanism*, Volume xxxv, No. 1 and 2 (Winter/Spring 2001), pp. 49–50, 58–59; "The Language of Faith," A sermon by Rev. William G. Sinkford at First Jefferson Unitarian Universalist Church, Forth Worth, Texas, January 12, 2003, pp. 1–4. www.uua.org/president/030112.html.

identity. Paul Rasor, a theologian and Unitarian Universalist, says that the need for identity is a crucial issue for Unitarians, as some feel that a theological center needs to be clarified or the group's diversity will make it fall apart, while others feel a defined center would be the equivalent of adopting a creed. A recent UUA Commission on Appraisal study, *Engaging Our Theological Diversity*, has attempted to discover this theological center of Unitarian Universalism, but beyond raising the importance of studying theology in greater depth, no central unifying theology could be succinctly stated. At an International Council of Unitarians and Universalists (ICUU) theological symposium in 2006, Rasor suggested that he could identity three core values in Unitarianism that might fill the identity void: spiritual freedom, social justice, and interdependence.

Spiritual freedom summarizes the most basic principle of Unitarianism. It is a non-creedal faith, in which individual members are free to pursue religious truth from any source. There is tremendous religious diversity among members. Ken Oliff, a Unitarian Universalist minister, has stated, "the strength of the contemporary liberal church lies in its openness, its respect for difference, and in the value that the church places on the sanctity of individual conscience."[2] Yet this central affirmation of freedom means that the church cannot articulate a theological vision for its constituency.

Perhaps the real problem lies with trying to define the faith in traditional terms. Philip Hewett, long-time minister in Vancouver, British Columbia says, "The real reason why it is so difficult to define Unitarianism in a few words is that its distinguishing characteristics are not to be found in the realm of beliefs and doctrines at all ... Unitarianism represents a wholly different approach to the question of authority in religion, by which an individual's beliefs and lifestyle are to be justified. Within traditional Christianity, this authority is found in the Bible, or in the Church, or in the recorded sayings of the founding fathers. Unitarians find it in the reason and conscience of the individual."[3] Thus, there cannot be theological unity when the emphasis is on the process of finding truth, with individual experience as the main guide.

This desire to have some common articulation of faith that will clarify religious identity has led to the recent popularity of the Principles and

---

[2] Paul Rasor, "Postmodernity, Globalization and the Challenge of Identity in Liberal Theology," in *The Home We Share: Globalization, Post-Modernism and Unitarian/Universalist Theology*, Clifford M. Reed and Jill L. McAllister, eds. (Caerphilly, Wales: International Council of Unitarians and Universalists, 2007); Olliff, as quoted in Commission on Appraisal, *Engaging Our Theological Diversity* (Boston, MA: UUA, 2005), p. 138.

[3] Phillip Hewett, *Unitarians in Canada* (Don Mills, ON: Fitzhenry and Whiteside, 1978), p. 2.

Purposes, a covenant of shared assumptions that was passed by the UUA General Assembly in 1985. The process for developing these Principles also led to theological controversy. On June 27, 1983, *Time Magazine*, in an article called "Deleted Deity," reported: "How does a Unitarian begin his prayer? Answer: 'To whom it may concern . . . ' That dog-eared ecclesiastical joke became a real possibility last week, as the Unitarian Universalist Association opened debate on a rather radical proposal: to delete any mention of God from its founding statement of principles."[4] When the final Principles were adopted, they included religious values such as the inherent worth and dignity of every person, the use of the democratic process, the goal of world community, and respect for the interdependent web of all existence. These Principles were supported by a pluralistic smorgasbord of faith sources including direct experience, Jewish and Christian teachings, world religions, and humanism. Members have sometimes embraced these principles as a kind of substitute creed, as the Principles and Purposes represent the only common articulation of faith passed by the General Assembly.

The Principles have proven to be an important statement to those Americans who hungered for a sense of identity. They have been able to articulate common values, and impart those to their children, which is important since Unitarians have always been hesitant about indoctrinating children into the faith. This quest for identity even seems to have affected the British, who "have partially overcome a centuries-old suspicion of denominational self-definition," to have passed an Object of the General Assembly of Unitarian and Free Christian Churches in 2001. This upholds a free faith that worships God, serves humanity, and respects all of creation. Until World War I, Unitarian belief in Britain was centered upon the five precepts that came from the American, James Freeman Clarke: the Fatherhood of God, the Brotherhood of Man, the Leadership of Jesus, Salvation by Character, and the Progress of Mankind, onward and upward forever. Yet the events of 1914 and thereafter shook the basic optimism of this faith, and it had "almost disappeared from Unitarian churches by the 1950s." Jaume de Marcos Andreu, a Unitarian Universalist in Spain, says that the Transylvanians are the only Unitarian group with "no major problems with identity." This group has remained predominantly liberal Christian, while being grounded in a solid foundation of 400 years of history with a near veneration for their founder, Francis Dávid.[5]

---

[4] "Deleted Deity," *Time Magazine*, June 27, 1983.
[5] Alan Ruston, "Unitarianism . . . the continuing story . . . " (London, UK: The General Assembly of Unitarian and Free Christian Churches, c. 2000); Jaume de Marcos Andreu, "Liberating the Self,

In its formative years in America, the emerging liberal faith's image of God changed from a powerful being who rewarded the worthy few and harshly punished the many sinners, to a belief in a benevolent deity who desired the happiness of all his children. God evolved even further with the advent of the radical philosophy of the Transcendentalists. The implications of experiencing God directly through nature threatened the traditional Christian idea that God was revealed through the Bible. This was especially apparent in the response to Ralph Waldo Emerson's *Divinity School Address* in 1838. Henry Ware, Jr., in his address, *The Personality of the Deity*, stated that a person could not add up a series of laws or principles such as righteousness, truth, and love, and say that it constitutes God. "It is in vain to hope by so doing to escape the charge of atheism," he noted. "There is a personal God, or there is none."[6]

Early in their history, Universalists were attracted to the idea of common affirmations of faith, and while the notion of "gospel liberty" kept them non-creedal, they still found a basic religious identity in the Winchester Profession of Faith (1803). Here, they expressed their fundamental belief in a God "whose nature is Love," and who would restore humanity to both "holiness and happiness." Partly in response to the threats of Transcendentalism and Darwin's theories, Universalists had a thirty-year period at the end of the nineteenth century during which the Profession was a required creed. Even after this, they continued to be more inclined to compose denomination-wide statements of faith than did their Unitarian counterparts. Universalists passed two subsequent statements: the Boston Declaration in 1899, and the Washington Avowal of Faith in 1935. The Universalists remained closer to their Christian origins than the Unitarians, who, despite their own battles over Christian revelation, mostly managed to accommodate those who advocated required creeds, and evolved more quickly towards a humanistic approach to faith, while steadfastly opposing any threats to their freedom of belief.

As the decades passed, Unitarians such as Francis Ellingwood Abbot (1836–1903) accepted Darwin's theories, and began to argue that ultimate answers to religious questions would come from science, and were not written on the human heart from the beginning of time. God's palpable absence from the world led to the development of humanism in the early twentieth century. Humanism became the dominant philosophy

---

Saving the World: A Study of Unitarian & Universalist Identity in Global Society," in *The Home We Share*, pp. 108–109.

[6] Henry Ware, Jr., "The Personality of the Deity," in *Sermons by Henry Ware, Jr. D.D.*, Vol. 1 (Boston, MA: James Munroe and Company, 1847), pp. 27, 32.

among Unitarians. Its leaders in America were John H. Dietrich (1878–1957), Curtis Reese (1887–1961) and Charles Francis Potter (1885–1962). The Reformed Church defrocked Dietrich in 1911, when it was discovered that he denied the infallibility of the Bible, and the deity of Christ. He sparked the ongoing Humanist–Theist controversy within Unitarian ranks when he delivered an address before the Unitarians' General Conference in 1921. Although humanism is sometimes defined as a religion without God, it was never Dietrich's intention to reject God. In his sermon, "Unitarianism and Humanism," he wrote, "'By religion I mean the knowledge of man and our duties toward him'... It does not deny the right to believe in God... but it places faith in man, a knowledge of man, and our duties toward one another first." In summary, Dietrich said, "the task of Humanism is to unfold the personality of men and women, to fit and qualify them for the best use of their natural powers, and the fullest enjoyment of the natural world and the human society around them."[7] Humanism was codified in 1933 with the publication of *The Humanist Manifesto.*

By 1967, many Unitarians and Universalists agreed that the term "God" did not designate a tangible supernatural being. The Committee on Goals report indicates that 28 percent of the denomination in America considered the concept of God "irrelevant," with an additional 2 percent calling it "harmful." That same year, the UUA published, "Unitarian Universalist Views of God," where Robert Storer said that, "for more than a century this personified God has been declared inadequate by the... churches." One author, Harry Meserve, stated: "God is not a person who knows us and loves us. He is that power within us and within all life by virtue of which it is possible for man to love."[8] Others preferred not to use the term at all. As indicated by the statistics above, this included a sizeable number of atheists. Although atheists have historically been subject to a good deal of prejudice, many liberals find, as Brad Greeley asserts in "The Faith of an Atheist": "One does not have to believe in a Supreme Being to find comfort, support, courage and insight in a worship service. One does not have to affirm a belief in deity to feel awe, inspiration or mystery in life... One does not have to worship God to be able to lead a life motivated by the good, the true and the beautiful."[9]

---

[7] William R. Hutchison, *The Modernist Impulse in American Protestantism.* (New York: Oxford University Press, 1976), p. 31. John. H. Dietrich, "Unitarianism and Humanism," *Humanist Sermons,* Curtis W. Reese, ed. (Chicago, IL: The Open Court Publishing Company, 1927), p. 96.

[8] Robert A. Storer, ed., "Unitarian Universalist Views of God" (Boston, MA: UUA, 1967), pp. 7, 11.

[9] W. Bradford Greeley, "The Faith of an Atheist," (Boston, MA: UUA, 1983).

Recently, there has been renewed interest in God, perhaps born from the ability to conceive of God in other than supernatural terms, coupled with a growing humility that people do not have the answers to all problems. From 1967 to 1987, the percentage of members who thought that God was an irrelevant concept dropped from 28 percent to 18 percent. Moreover, during that same period, the percentage of people who were willing to give credence to some concept of God increased from 70 percent to 81 percent. It is difficult to know precisely how well this reflects a more theistically-centered faith, but it does show a renewed interest in considering the possibility. Forrest Church (1948–2009), long-time minister at All Souls Church in New York, told the 2003 General Assembly: "When people tell me proudly that they don't believe in God, I ask them to tell me a little about the God they don't believe in, for I probably don't believe in him either. God is not God's name. God is our name for that which is greater than all, and yet present in each."[10]

Henry Nelson Wieman (1884–1975) and Charles Hartshorne (1897–2000), two major theologians associated with Process thought, helped lead a resurgence of liberal theology and "God" talk. A Unitarian Universalist Association (UUA) meditation manual, *Outstretched Wings of the Spirit*, by Donald S. Harrington, based on the thoughts of Wieman, was published in 1980. Harrington told how Wieman introduced him to a God that harmonized with his use of reason and a scientific worldview at a time in his life when he had come to "reject both the idea of God and more traditional theological concepts." This God was identified with the natural processes of creation in the universe, or what Wieman called "creative interchange." Wieman said that one of the important functions of worship is to "call to mind the vast and unimaginable possibilities for good which are inherent in this integrating process called God."[11] Hartshorne, like Wieman, was heavily influenced by the thoughts of Alfred North Whitehead. Hartshorne coined the term "process theology," by which he meant that everything in the world is experienced by God, but nothing in the world *is* God. He said that God is always calling us, in our human freedom, towards greater fulfillment, and that God changes and grows as a result of human life. He found a historic Unitarian parallel for his beliefs with Polish founder Faustus

[10] Commission on Appraisal, *The Quality of Life In Unitarian Universalist Congregations* (Boston, MA: UUA, 1989), p. 34; Forrest Church, "Born Again Unitarian Universalism," General Assembly Address, June 29, 2003. See: www.allsoulsnyc.org/publications/sermons/fcsermons/bornagainuuism.html.

[11] Donald S. Harrington, *Outstretched Wings of the Spirit* (Boston, MA: UUA, 1980), Introduction, p. 66; Mark Harris, *Historical Dictionary of Unitarian Universalism* (Lanham, MD: Scarecrow Press, 2004), pp. 516–517.

Socinus, whom Hartshorne says rejected the traditional idea of God as an unmoved mover, an immutable and all-determining power. Following a belief that humans have genuine freedom, Socinus denied "that God either determines or eternally knows our free acts." If God only knows human acts after they occur, this implies, Hartshorne believed, that humans can "create novelty in the divine consciousness," and "cause changes in God."[12]

Even as the American theologians were revitalizing liberal thought, leading Unitarians in Britain were at once heartened that a liberal Christian theism based on reason and experience was influencing many, but worried that as liberal "ideas became intellectually respectable, the more difficult it becomes for us to justify our separate existence as a small floundering sect." Arthur Long, who expressed this skepticism about the future of the church in Britain in *Fifty Years of Theology, 1928–1978 – The Vindication of Liberalism*, refuted the notion that "theism and humanism are mutually exclusive. Unitarian theism arises directly from that true Christian humanism of the Renaissance."[13] Yet it is also clear that a non-theistic humanism never had much impact on the churches in Britain, as humanism was never as predominant there as it was for the Americans. This is also evident in the passage of the Object of the General Assembly in 2001. It directly states that the purpose of the church is to: 'Promote a free and enquiring religion through the worship of God and the celebration of life . . . and the upholding of the liberal Christian tradition." The UUA could never make such a sweeping statement about God and Christianity. Nevertheless, Unitarians worldwide seem to recognize that a deeper spirituality and reverence for the mysterious forces that uphold life is necessary for the church to flourish in the new millennium.

While a renewed interest in things spiritual swept through the American movement in the late twentieth century, there was also increased interest in scripture and sources of religious inspiration. In early nineteenth-century Unitarianism and Universalism, scriptures were held as the fundamental authority for believers, but they insisted on the use of reason in scripture interpretation. The method of interpreting scriptures was to study them like any other book, and to uncover corruptions in the texts. There was also a larger purpose, which was to subordinate dogma to ethics, so that the object of scriptural study is how to lead people to a holy end of moral and spiritual

---

[12] Charles Hartshorne, "A New World and a New World View," in *The Life of Choice: Some Liberal Religious Perspectives on Morality*, ed. Clark Kucheman (Boston, MA: Skinner House Books, 1978), p. 43; Harris, *Dictionary*, pp. 235–237.

[13] Arthur Long, *Fifty Years of Theology, 1928–1978 – The Vindication of Liberalism* (London, UK: The Lindsey Press, 1978), pp. 15, 16.

improvement.[14] Joseph Stevens Buckminster was the earliest Unitarian scholar advocating the use of the latest in biblical criticism. Buckminster said that not all scripture is equally authoritative, and must be read in historical context. He also believed that the Bible was not God's direct word, but rather a vehicle by which the word comes to us. Yet, the historicity and the authority of the Bible were still central, along with the historical validity of the miracles.[15] The Transcendentalists shook the foundations even further with the rejection of the revealed truth of biblical miracle stories, in favor of affirming immediate truth found through intuitive experience. They also began reading scriptures that were not Christian, and began the journey of Unitarianism towards accepting truth from many religious sources.

While this was still the era where Christian supremacy was taught, the two basic approaches to a Unitarian Universalist understanding of scripture today were beginning to be present. One of these approaches is a belief in an open canon, where spiritual truths are found in different types of writing, they inspire humans only when they lead to a deeper understanding of human life, and they must be in concert with scientific truths. Second, the progressive revelation points to a belief that religious truth does not end with the Bible, but that truth is found in all the world's great faiths, as taught by Buddha, Jesus, or Mohammed; and that humans draw meaning as scriptural truth is discovered in each individual life. By 1950, the primary value of the Bible was in its literary and historical context, rather than its inspirational or religious qualities. In his "Religious Education in the Liberal Church," Norman Dowd wrote, "Somewhere in the course of training there should be an opportunity to learn something of the Bible as a collection of Hebrew and Early Christian Literature ... [the child] should be encouraged to appreciate its literary value, and learn something of the history of it.[16]

In subsequent years, some wondered if the Bible was relevant at all. In *Challenge of a Liberal Faith*, the standard introduction to Unitarian Universalism for decades, George Marshall wrote, "The Bible abounds in gory incidents. We shall skip over ... all manner of uncouth conduct and unworthy ethics presented in the Bible. The Religious liberal cannot

---

[14] Daniel Walker Howe, *The Unitarian Conscience: Harvard Moral Philosophy, 1805–1861* (Cambridge, MA: Harvard University Press, 1970), pp. 91, 100.

[15] Conrad Wright, ed., *A Stream of Light* (Boston, MA: UUA, 1975), pp. 13–16.

[16] Norman Dowd, "Religious Education in the Liberal Church," *The Unitarian Register*, Vol. 114, 1935, p. 174.

look upon the Bible as a sacred book."[17] Sometimes, the Bible was edited and watered down to present only positive stories where there was no violence. Despite a theological history of avoiding suffering and evil in favor of progress and human potential, there was renewed interest in the Bible in late twentieth-century Unitarian Universalism. Today, Unitarian Universalists see the power of myth and story in revealing certain deep truths about human life. In "Unitarian Universalist Views of the Bible," minister Ed Lane says that he "rejected the Bible because I could not accept it literally. Now the liberation from literalism allows me to put new wine into old wineskins, to understand the biblical concepts of God, Christ... etc., as a human effort to find meaning and rapprochement in this world."[18]

Doctrines of Unitarianism and Universalism were first promulgated based upon an interpretation of the Bible. "The concern of the early Unitarians was a clearer, simpler, and more accurate interpretation of what the Bible taught, which would, they believed, result in a purified and more ethical Christianity."[19] For some religious liberals today, the Bible is only literature, or history, but for others there is a way in which "God speaks through the Bible," at least metaphorically. This means that for the reader who wrestles with the stories about Jesus, "you confront your own life in their light, you can begin to see things you've never seen before, you can understand and feel and know something of who Jesus was and is. And you can be changed."[20]

The traditional affirmation of the use of reason in the interpretation of scriptures has meant that Unitarians have usually followed the latest methods of Biblical criticism, coupled with a great interest in uncovering the historical Jesus. Curiously, while the Unitarian movements in Transylvania and Great Britain have remained more faithful to Christian traditions than their American counterpart, both groups held more liberal or human views of Jesus in the early period of their development than was true of the Americans, especially in New England, where an Arian view – one where Jesus is characterized as an intermediate being who is neither fully human nor fully divine – held sway.[21] The Transcendentalist movement

---

[17] George Marshall, *Challenge of a Liberal Faith* (Boston, MA: Skinner House Books, 1988), p. 129.
[18] Edwin A. Lane, "The Human Quest for Spiritual Insight and Understanding," in *Unitarian Universalist Views of the Bible* (pamphlet), ed. Daniel G. Higgins (Boston, MA: UUA, c. 1985).
[19] Harry C. Meserve, "We Compile Our Own Bible," in Higgins, *Unitarian Universalist Views*.
[20] Thomas D. Wintle, "There are Bible Thumpers and Bible Bashers – We Are Neither" (Boston, MA: Unitarian Universalist Christian Fellowship, 1987).
[21] Conrad Wright, *The Beginnings of Unitarianism in America* (Boston, MA: Starr King Press, 1955), p. 202.

challenged the Arian position that Jesus was more than a man. This was found in Emerson's *Divinity School Address*, where he says that Jesus was "one man" who was "true to what is in you and me." This completely human Jesus, who understood the divine nature of his own being, made Jesus the teaching standard for judging the achievement of human perfection. Emerson went on to say that historical Christianity had "fallen into the error that corrupts all attempts to communicate religion," especially with its "noxious exaggeration about the *person* of Jesus."[22]

Over the centuries, Unitarians around the world have struggled with the question of the role of Jesus in their faith. Despite its origins in Christianity, many people refuse to characterize Unitarianism as a Christian faith because Unitarians do not adhere to the Christian standard of accepting Jesus Christ as Lord and Savior. Judith Walker-Riggs captures some of this dilemma when she reflects, "One day, as I was separating bottles and paper for recycling . . . I was struck by the thought that, as a Unitarian, I do something similar in my religious life as I seek to separate what is truly worth preserving and of permanent value in the Christian tradition from what has been damaging and limiting." For some, Jesus is one of many religious teachers, part of a pantheon of heroes that includes Buddha and Mohammed. For those who reject the Christian faith of their childhood, Jesus may only be an important historical figure, who provided the inspiration for what became the Christian faith, and the subsequent culture it created, which some continue to see as misogynist and destructive. Because of Unitarianism's historical roots in Christianity, many Unitarians still prefer to be considered Christian, and there are organized groups to affirm this faith stance, especially among the very pluralistic Americans. Many still affirm Francis Dávid's sixteenth-century view that Unitarians follow Jesus rather than worship him. Betty Smith, a British Unitarian, writes: "Jesus to me means following his teaching as an example to live by, something to strive for . . . For me, the supreme affirmation of Christian discipleship is not 'I believe' but 'I follow.'" This confirms Unitarianism as an ethical rather than a creedal faith, and makes Jesus the human embodiment or symbol for the potential of every life.[23]

Unitarian Christianity includes individuals who not only believe that Jesus was the greatest religious teacher who ever lived, but may also affirm that in "the life, teachings, death and resurrection of Jesus, we see the

---

[22] Ralph Waldo Emerson, *The Complete Works of Ralph Waldo Emerson*, Vol. 1 (Boston, MA: Houghton, Mifflin and Co., 1876), pp. 128, 130.

[23] Walker-Riggs and Smith are quoted in "Unitarian Views of Jesus," Matthew Smith, ed. (London, UK: Unitarian Headquarters, no date).

revelation of what the God/human and the human-to-human relationship is meant to be." For these Unitarians, Jesus is the supreme guide to a faithful life. Wendy Fitting says a conversation about Christianity must include "resurrection," and that it is not enough to call it a metaphor. She says, "The resurrection represents the living presence of Jesus, an ongoing and unsealed revelation of God's compelling love." Jesus is conceived of as "risen," not literally in heaven, but "into my life and alive everywhere that evil is persistently resisted and everywhere that a revolution for goodness is thoughtfully engaged."[24] In a recent book, Scotty McLennan, the Dean for Religious Life at Stanford University, declares *Jesus was a Liberal.* In this work, he says, "What matters most is love and community, including a commitment to social justice and careful stewardship of the earth's resources." Following Jesus' words, McLennan says we cannot serve both God and wealth, but must find "freedom from material desires and material anxieties." McLennan believes there is hope through a renewed proclamation of liberal Christianity, and its firm commitment to the "essential goodness of humanity, tolerance, and freedom. Jesus came that we might have life, and have it abundantly."[25]

While some Unitarians might blanch at the reaffirmation of liberal Christianity as an affront to their focus on freedom of belief, few liberals would deny the second of Rasor's core values, social justice, in determining a Unitarian center. The social implications of faith, and how people act in the world as a result of their religious orientation, has long motivated Unitarians and Universalists to action. In the early twentieth century, the Social Gospel movement reconceived Christianity as being less about faith and salvation, and more about "ushering in the Kingdom of God on earth through social reform and service." Using the new social science methodology, this effort to improve the human race found its leading Unitarian proponent in Francis Greenwood Peabody, who brought the implication of Jesus' message to bear with *Jesus Christ and the Social Question* (1900). Peabody felt that the test of salvation is the individual's contribution to social service. He believed that, "A part of good citizenship lies in bearing others' burdens."[26]

---

[24] Judith L. Hoehler, quoted in *Unitarian Universalist Views of Jesus* (pamphlet), Daniel G. Higgins, Jr., ed. (Boston, MA: UUA, 1982); Wendy Fitting, *A Unitarian Universalist Perspective on Christianity* (pamphlet) (Boston, MA: UUA, 1995).

[25] Scotty McLennan, *Jesus Was a Liberal* (New York: Palgrave Macmillan, 2009), p. 225.

[26] Barton J. Bernstein, "Francis Greenwood Peabody: Conservative Social Reformer," *The New England Quarterly*, Vol. 36, No. 3 (September, 1963), pp. 320, 326; Francis Greenwood Peabody, *Reminiscences of Present-day Saints* (Boston, MA: Houghton, Mifflin and Co., 1927), p. 151.

Involvement in social and political change has also given Unitarianism a broader voice in society than its meager numbers would usually allow by the mere circumstances of cultural influence. Unitarian congregations often exist on the margins of society. The fact that highly educated, liberal, and cultural minorities are historically attracted to this rational and free-thinking faith means that finding a voice to influence society requires a greater degree of participation in public and private institutions seeking to effect political, economic, or legal changes in society. One example of the need to exert a strong influence from the margins of a culture occurs with the Unitarian movement in Australia and New Zealand. Unlike most Unitarians in Britain, America, or Transylvania, these adherents represent a pure transplanted movement rather than a mostly indigenous one. Unitarians who migrated from Great Britain to Australia first founded congregations in Adelaide, Melbourne, and Sydney in the 1850s. These groups have always been small, reaching their numerical peak around 1890.[27]

Despite insignificant numbers, the Unitarian ethos of achieving equal opportunity and justice for all has given the faith an influence far out of proportion to its numbers. This is seen with Catherine Helen Spence (1825–1910), who appears on the Australian five dollar bill. Spence emigrated from Scotland to Adelaide with her family in 1839. She became a novelist, and then a journalist. Particularly concerned with "pure democracy," she began to advocate demographic and geographic fairness in the electoral process. Her interest in reform, education, and freedom of religion led her to the Unitarian Church. Her major political concern became the legal status of women and children. Her newspaper article, "Marriage and Wrongs," (1878) helped bring political change, including the legal right for women to divorce. At the same time, she helped establish a foster-care system in Australia. Her greatest political achievement occurred when the right to vote was extended to the women of South Australia in 1894. This work made her "the best known woman in public affairs in South Australia."[28]

The historical legacy of Spence is a reminder that ongoing work for justice and equality are central to a faith that aspires to build "a community of freedom and mutuality." Following the inspiration of James Luther Adams (1901–1994), Paul Rasor suggests that liberation lies at the heart

---

[27] Philip Hewett, "A Faith Transplanted: The Unitarian Experience in Canada, Australia and New Zealand," *Transactions of the Unitarian Historical Society*, Vol. xxii, No. 1 (April 1999), p. 3.

[28] Diana Samson, "The Influence of Catherine Helen Spence on Social and Political Reform in South Australia, 1860–1910," Occasional Paper #14 (Medford, ma: Unitarian Universalist Women's Heritage Society, 1996).

of liberal religion. The word "liberal" derives from the Latin *liber*, which means, "free." Liberals believe there is a fundamental faith commitment to liberate themselves, and, by implication, others who are denied some form of freedom. Adams, the most prominent Unitarian social ethicist of the twentieth century, has said, "human beings... should liberate themselves from the shackles that impede religious, political and economic freedom and which impede the appearance of a rational and voluntary piety and of equality and justice for all... "[29] In his "Faith for Free Men," Adams said that God is that reality "which works in nature and history... creating human good in human community." Central to his "The Five Smooth Stones of Liberalism" are beliefs that each person must work "toward the establishment of a just and loving community," and that liberal faith "must express itself in societal forms." This means the work of the church must be to shape the social, economic, and political institutions to end abuses of power so that people can achieve "freedom in history."[30]

The passion for liberation can be associated with three social justice movements within Unitarian Universalism (UU) over the past fifty years: African Americans, women, and bisexual/gay/lesbian/transgender people. All of these movements have had a profound impact on UU in the last generation. During the era of Civil Rights, most UUs in America believed in a society where equal rights and justice could be enjoyed by all black Americans. After a promising start, the hope of more justice for blacks and a more fully racially integrated church was squandered in the Black Empowerment Controversy (1968–1969), where some have suggested that the withdrawal of funds from black-controlled programs was precipitated by battles over white, middle-class leadership and fears of "Black Power." This led to long-standing resentments and resignations of many black members. More recently, the Unitarian Universalist Association (UUA) has committed itself to achieving greater racial and cultural diversity in a predominately white, upper-middle-class, highly educated denomination. The most "definitive leap forward in terms of racial progress" occurred with the election of the first African American UUA president, William Sinkford, in 2001.[31]

---

[29] James Luther Adams, *On Being Human Religiously*, ed. Max L. Stackhouse (Boston, MA: Beacon Press, 1976), p. 101; Adams, as quoted in Rasor, "Postmodernity," p. 68.

[30] James Luther Adams, quoted in David B. Parke, ed. *The Epic of Unitarianism* (Boston, MA: Skinner House Books, 1985), pp. 151, 152; Adams, *On Being Human*, pp. 12–21.

[31] Juan H. Floyd-Thomas, *The Origins of Black Humanism in America: Reverend Ethelred Brown and the Unitarian Church* (New York: Palgrave Macmillan, 2008), pp. 199–200; *Engaging Our Theological Diversity*, p. 115.

Dr. William R. Jones, now emeritus professor at Florida State University, declared in 1975 that there is no "inevitable historical development, sponsored by ultimate reality, that ensures the liberation of the oppressed or a more humane society." Two years before this, Jones, an African American, had asked the question in a book titled, *Is God a White Racist?* He wrote, "The issue of divine racism surfaces whenever a specific type of suffering, which I identify as ethnic suffering, is joined with particular interpretations of God's sovereignty over human history, and His activity within human history or both." Jones says black theology must be re-evaluated so that the normative framework that permits the imposition of, and the acceptance of, such suffering must be seen as a fatal flaw. He believes that African Americans must reject oppressive theologies and choose "humanocentric theism," where they are active participants in their own salvation, and not continuing victims of violence."[32]

In 2000, at the UUA General Assembly, Dr. Rebecca Parker, President of the Starr King School, spoke about Jones' concept of "white-ianity," the idea that white racism is at the heart of Christianity, where the sacrifice of human life has been depicted as redemptive. Parker notes that the construction of identity as a white person is to become more ignorant, rather than seeing and understanding the world we actually live in. Knowledge, she says, allows us to disrupt injustice: "To know is to love." Personal growth through knowledge reaffirms the traditional Unitarian Universalist (UU) understanding of salvation by means of continuous education. The Rev. Dr. Thandeka, a UU theologian, wants whites to feel what it is like to take on a racial identity in America, to "give voice to . . . whiteness as the racial unsaid." In her book, *Learning to Be White: Money, Race and God in America*, she says that racism is built upon white guilt and shame. In response to an address Thandeka gave in 1999, David Bumbaugh stated that UU anti-racism programs can compound the issue of guilt and shame, but moreover, they also personalize the issue with this guilt while ignoring the larger issue of who has the money and the power. An anti-racist Unitarian Universalist Association (UUA) means that liberal guilt can be assuaged with an inward-directed agenda, while power and wealth are concentrated in fewer and fewer hands.[33] As a result, the affirmation and liberation of

[32] William R. Jones, "Theism and Religious Humanism: The Chasm Narrows," *The Christian Century*, May 21, 1975, pp. 520–525. See: religion-online.org/showarticle.asp?title=1874; William R. Jones, *Is God a White Racist?* (Boston, MA: Beacon Press, 1973, 1998), xxiii.

[33] "Racism, Theology, and the Institutional Church," archive.uua.org/ga/ga00/243.html; "Why Anti-Racism Will Fail: A Response" by David E. Bumbaugh, archive.uua.org/ga/ga99/238bumbaugh.html; Thandeka, *Learning to Be White* (New York: Continuum, 2007), p. 3.

certain groups may give those members who have a particular racial, gender, or sexual orientation a sense of individual freedom from oppression about their identity, but may cloud the larger issues of inequality in society.

The second liberation movement, that of feminism, had a long history within Unitarianism and Universalism. Groundbreaking women's rights' advocates, such as Catherine Spence, have argued for marital and educational rights, and these initial forays into equality eventually led to economic and political rights as well. The 1970s began a wave of change where the women's liberation movement led to concrete changes in worship services, and increasing numbers of women filled the pulpits, surpassing the percentage of male clergy in 1999. The UUA study, *Engaging Our Theological Diversity*, shows that while many cultural changes have shaped the movement in recent decades, "the impact of the changing role of women in the past thirty years has been especially dramatic." The study suggests that many values became central as the result of feminism, including: "relationship, equity, and justice, inclusiveness, open process, compassion, and focus on family and children."[34] The UUA's Beacon Press became known during the 1970s as a publisher that specialized in feminist theological works, including *Beyond God the Father* (1973), by the radical Catholic theologian, Mary Daly, who proposed that God had been used to legitimize the existing social order, and keep women and other victimized groups subordinate.

The exposure of patriarchal patterns in the history of the church was only the beginning of more fundamental changes within the entire church structure, so that the authority of women and women's experiences were ultimately affirmed. In the pamphlet, "The Faith of a Feminist," Unitarian Universalist minister Judith Meyer said, "the religious values of Unitarian Universalism and the spirit of feminism are inseparable." She wrote, "Feminist religion is concerned with justice – not just for women, but for all humanity – and with an ethic that recognizes the interdependent web of all creatures and the ecological system in which we live." Like the Americans, British Unitarians have also witnessed changes in worship patterns, in leadership positions, and in values. Vina Curren, a lay leader of a Unitarian chapel, says, "In every area of Unitarianism, women's spirituality is evident, encouraged, and accepted naturally. Unitarianism leads in equal opportunities." This freedom and equality has a theological voice in Sharon Welch, who now teaches at Meadville Lombard Theological School. In her *A Feminist Ethic of Risk*, Welch focused on power in relationships, so that the love

---

[34] *Engaging Our Theological Diversity*, pp. 37–38.

extended to others, and the love people receive from others, empowers them to work for justice. She sees liberation as an "expanding understanding of human possibilities, individually and structurally. The specific possibilities include a vision of a world free of racial discrimination, sexual violence, and economic exploitation." Welch believes that God or the divine is our human relational power, and that the human ability to show compassion and care for one another is divine in and of itself. Feminism draws some of its strength from earth-centered or pagan beliefs, which are found in the UUA Sources as "the teaching of Earth-centered traditions." Richard Lee suggests that this reflects a "theology of *interdependence and immanence* – the view that reality is an interconnected whole whose essence is divine... [and] each person is divine." Some Unitarian Universalists have reformulated a religious humanism that is less person centered and named it "religious naturalism."[35]

The third key liberation movement within Unitarian Universalism is the support for bisexual, gay, lesbian and transgender (BGLT) issues. BGLT programs and denominational support, like the feminist movement, began in earnest in an era of political and social turbulence, but the history of gay and lesbian support was neither public nor generally acceptable prior to 1970. Some of the first women who entered the ministry, such as Florence Buck (1860–1925) and Marion Murdoch (1848–1943), had formed "special friendships" as early as 1890, combining their call to ministry with their enduring affection for each other, and were "considered a couple." Yet most gay or lesbian clergy have lived their lives in the closet. One such minister, Charles Vickery (1920–1972), endured, as Carl Seaburg later wrote, a life of "pain and doubt... loneliness and vulnerability... What kind of integrity was it to conceal your basic nature?" As early as 1971, Vickery was running a Gay Awareness group in Mexico City, where he served. Vickery "invented a ministry to fit his gayness," and, by this effort, showed that he wanted "to reform and reshape society in more human ways."[36] Echoing the relationship of Buck and Murdock, British minister Ann Peart has written about theologies of friendship: "Queer people do not find acceptance in their original families, so they have to make friendships and

[35] Judith Meyer, "The Faith of a Feminist," (Boston, MA: UUA, c. 1990); Vina Curren, as quoted in "Women in the Unitarian Movement," ed. Celia Kerr (London: Information Department, Unitarian Headquarters, c. 1995); Sharon D. Welch, *A Feminist Ethic of Risk* (Minneapolis, MN: Fortress Press, 1990), pp. 157, 173; Richard Wayne Lee, "Strained Bedfellows: Pagans, New Agers, and 'Starchy Humanists' in Unitarian Universalism," *Sociology of Religion*, Vol. 56, No. 4 (1995), p. 387.

[36] Cynthia Grant Tucker, *Prophetic Sisterhood* (Boston, MA: Beacon Press, 1990), p. 83; Carl Seaburg, *Inventing a Ministry: Four Reflections on the Life of a Colleague, Charles Vickery, 1920–1972* (Boston, MA: Minns Lectureship Committee, 1992), pp. 66, 70, 72.

support networks in order to survive . . . justice-making friendship . . . This friendship is available to everyone . . . The Church is seen as a coalition of justice-seeking friends."[37]

After this history of silence and prejudice, a remarkable shift in attitudes took place in Unitarian Universalist congregations. The UUA Goals report of 1967 had indicated that 88 percent of Unitarian Universalists felt that homosexuality should be discouraged. In 1970, the first General Assembly resolution calling for an end to discrimination against homosexuals and bisexuals was passed. In 1989, the General Assembly created the Welcoming Congregation program, a hugely successful effort to identify homophobia institutionally.[38] The program has renewed commitments in the congregations to build "right relationships," and empowered them to act on a vision for social justice and equality in the world, resulting in congregations being at the forefront of working to legalize same-sex marriage in several US states. For many Unitarian Universalists, this commitment to affirm loving relationships fulfills the vision of a theology that begins with the equal worth of all people, and discovers the divine within the historical context of the relationships humans may freely enter.

At one time, Unitarians believed that "our encounters with other religions confirm the view that essential themes of love and peace are embodied in them all."[39] Unitarianism has sometimes been described as an amalgamation of all the world's faiths, whose goal is to merge all religious expressions into a new universal faith. Gertrude von Petzold (1876–1952), the first woman ordained to the Unitarian ministry in Britain, wrote: "Study the religions of the world, hearken devotedly to the psalms of the East, and to the songs of the West, kneel silently in the temple of the Buddhist, join the worship of the Jewish synagogue, or listen to the prayers of the Christian Church; in its essence all worship is one, for all religion is one; for all religion leads to God."[40] In the post-modern world, this view is now regarded with suspicion, and can result in the cultural or historical misappropriation of religious practices. It may even be a way to say that all religions are really the same, when what is central to one faith may be peripheral to another. Still, members are encouraged to discover the religious values

---

[37] Peart, as quoted in *The Unitarian Life: Voices From the Past and Present*, ed. Stephen Lingwood (London, UK: Lindsey Press, 2008), p. 154.

[38] *Engaging Our Theological Diversity*, p. 115. See www.uua.org/leaders/idbm/bglt/welcomingcongregation/index.shtml.

[39] Wendy Fitting, ed., *Religions of the World, A Unitarian Universalist Perspective* (Boston, MA: UUA, c. 1990).

[40] Gertrude von Petzold, as quoted in Lingwood, ed., *The Unitarian Life*, p. 58.

and beliefs they find most meaningful among all the world's faiths, and thus an individual Unitarian might call him/herself multi-religious. Forrest Church invokes a type of universalism by describing one divine light as seen through many windows. Unitarians believe that "all world religions possess the power of meaning-making and validity for human lives," therefore "all are worthy of our respectful attention."[41] The openness to many religious perspectives means that opportunities for education and dialogue are possible, including the adoption of principles and practices that liberals find present in other faiths. This has been true of the increasing popularity of Buddhism among Unitarians.

James Ford, a Unitarian Universalist minister who is also a Zen Buddhist teacher, believes that Unitarian Universalism has evolved to "be a religion that more resembles East Asian religions than classical Western religions."[42] Humanists began to be interested in Buddhism as a faith that was not directly concerned with questions of God or gods. Western Buddhism has given Unitarian Universalists a new tradition of spiritual discipline encouraging many practitioners of meditation. Many Unitarian Universalists also believe that Buddhism is helpful in giving insight to the problem of human suffering. Ford says there is a "middle way" of meditation, morality, and wisdom. Meditation is the examination of every emotion without judgment. Morality is a way of achieving harmony with all creatures in the universe. And "wisdom is what emerges out of these practices of presence and harmony." This perspective affirms interdependence as a core value, and so ecological concerns and justice issues are central for Unitarian Universalist Buddhists. Ford suggests that Buddhism and feminism are the two spiritual currents that could transform Western religious thought and Unitarian Universalism into something more focused on compassion and healing than either have traditionally been.[43]

Paul Rasor sees interdependence, his third core value, as a theological claim about the nature of reality, or an "affirmation that the world is an organic whole." Historian Charles Howe agrees that a broad theological consensus might be evolving around the principle of the "interdependent web of existence of which we are all part." Whether it is through choosing Buddhism or feminism, Christianity or humanism, Unitarians aspire

---

[41] Fitting, *Religions of the World*.

[42] James Ford, as quoted in "Unitarian Universalists on the Eightfold Path" by Rick Heller, *UU World* Vol. XXI, No. 2 (Summer, 2007), p. 28.

[43] James Ishmael Ford, "What is Unitarian Universalist Buddhism?" *UU World* (Summer, 2007), pp. 30–32; James Ishmael Ford, *The Faith of a Unitarian Universalist Buddhist* (Boston, MA: UUA, 2000); Rasor, "Postmodernity," pp. 70–71.

to express their religious pluralism through personal relationships, local communities, and a global ecological consciousness that will lead to the realization of this third core value of interdependence. This theological assertion keeps the historical understanding of the word "Unitarian" relevant to the present. In their quest for the truth, Unitarians once asserted that God was indivisible; interdependence now asserts that the same is true of creation. In the identification of God with the earth and its unfolding history, Unitarians have asserted a principle that also embodies the traditional Christian theology in Transylvania – Egy az Isten or God is One. Arpad Szabo concurs that the traditional Transylvanian theological foundations are in concert with worldwide Unitarian values. He says human experience is the ultimate authority, and that Unitarianism, in his view, has no creeds or systemic beliefs, but rather is "an attitude of mind." God (or the spirit of love), according to Szabo, is incarnate in all people, and there are no specific miracles, but "we revere the great miracle of creation and all of life." This faith in the oneness of creation is an embodiment of "interdependence," when the Transylvanians assert that God is revealed as a living presence throughout the universe. Transylvanians join with all Unitarians worldwide who are seeking, in these times of ecological crisis, to embody a theology of global oneness, and to actualize their capacity for love through divine living.[44]

[44] Charles Howe, *For Faith and Freedom* (Boston, MA: Skinner House Press, 1997), p. 187; Rasor, "Postmodernity," pp. 68–70; Arpad Szabo, "Theological Foundations of the Transylvanian Unitarian Faith," in *The Home We Share*, pp. 19–20.

CHAPTER 10

Science and ecology

Early this century, a new form of flaming chalice appeared on the newsletters of Unitarian Universalists. A rippled bowl holds a single-lobed leaf, stem down. Bowl and leaf are always green, and yet the symbol is recognized as a flaming chalice. This new design is the imprint of the Green Sanctuary movement, which, over the past twenty years, has blended religious celebration with environmental education and community action. Between 2002 and 2010, more than 10 percent of the Unitarian Universalist Association's (UUA's) member congregations have completed the program and achieved accreditation as Green Sanctuaries. This program represents the degree to which science, theology, and religious practice are entwined for Unitarian Universalists.

Administered by the UUA since 2008, the Green Sanctuary program is in many ways a direct result of the 1985 delineation of new Principles and Purposes. The Seventh Principle, "Respect for the interdependent web of all existence," immediately attracted practical interest. How could congregations embody this principle? A handbook was developed in 1991, and led to the 2002 incorporation of the Seventh Principle Project, focusing on climate change and critical environmental issues. This group, now known as the Unitarian Universalist Ministry for the Earth, originated congregational certification as Green Sanctuaries.

Ministry for the Earth was one of the groups deemed to be serving UUA needs when a 2008 policy change reduced the number of affiliate organizations from forty-six to five. The primary advantage of affiliate status is the right to workshop slots during the annual General Assembly. Up until very recently, the forty-six affiliate groups had a presence at General Assembly based upon their status; this presence, in turn, gave them a way to offer programming and attract interest in their work. Now, each of these groups must compete for a workshop slot through an application process. The Ministry for the Earth newsletter notes that their status as an independent affiliate means that their mission is core to the UUA's, and that the "care and celebration of the earth are moving into the mainstream of Unitarian Universalism."[1]

This statement reveals an expectation of outsider status. Although the Ministry for the Earth group was originally called the Seventh Principle Project, it is equally tied to the Sixth Source, "Spiritual teachings of earth-centered traditions which celebrate the sacred circle of life and instruct us to live in harmony with the rhythms of nature." This source, added in 1995, was widely acknowledged to be the result of changes in the composition of Unitarian Universalist congregations. Neo-pagans and practitioners of pantheistic spiritualities, including Native Americans and Zen Buddhists, were being explicitly included. This shift in status, from marginal to central in a 25-year-period, represents the power that science has had, and continues to have, for Unitarian Universalists. Eclectic approaches to reverence for nature can be housed within the science of ecology, which also provides lines of connection among disparate species, theological or otherwise. A principle designed as a spiritual counterpoint to rational, humanistic theology evolved into a practical, evidence-based program in which personal growth and change is linked to justice. Although not everyone would accept as corollary that "restoring Earth renews Spirit," most Unitarian Universalists accept the validity of engaging in activities that limit environmental degradation.

Some would trace the denominational interest in nature back to Emerson, with his *Divinity School Address* definition of miracles as something that happen within the known world, as observable phenomena, such as the "blowing clover and the falling rain."[2] This form of reason

---

[1] "Unanimous Vote! UUMFE Retains Affiliate Status," *Newsletter.* Winter 2008, Vol. 7, Issue 2, p. 1.
[2] Ralph Waldo Emerson, "Divinity School Address (1838)," in *Emerson: Essays and Lectures* (New York: Literary Classics of the United States), p. 80.

is well known to Unitarian Universalists; it is poetic, natural, and, to some degree, mythic. It is daily life and experience made into a pattern that takes advantage of powerful symbols, and places them to provide uplift, consolation, and meaning; and also to instigate change. In the years after the American Civil War, this methodology became a critical way of binding Unitarians together. William Channing Gannett's 1887 essay, "Things Commonly Believed," described an unfolding universe, where all grow in nobility. The external landscape symbolized both an indwelling and personally accessible God, and natural law, which refuted Calvinistic determinism, making it possible to go beyond rejecting the negative and to assert a positive belief. Among the readings designed to be read aloud in church services, and included in current hymnals, is one written by Kenneth Patton over fifty years ago. It describes a "house . . . for the ingathering of nature and human nature . . . (A) house of truth seeking, where scientists can encourage devotion to their quest, where mystics can abide in a community of searchers . . . This house is a cradle for our dreams, the workshop of our common endeavor." Trustworthy experiences and workplace values are patterned to create an interpretive framework with transcendent, yet not supernatural, meaning. The words being used to designate religious feeling are drawn from nature, the scientific quest, and the processes associated with human development. Religion is universalized by science, which destroys any claim of special status for one revealed truth. We are all bound by the same laws of nature.

For Unitarian Universalists, there is one universe, one creation, and all knowledge is religious. This faith must be compatible with scientific method. But if nature becomes a way of talking about what is good, it becomes difficult to acknowledge the power of nature to destroy. Death can be recognized as natural and necessary, but the experience of suffering becomes distant from the religion if science is posited as the only reasonable method with which to represent meaning. Religion needs to recognize that information can be gathered via different channels. Empiricism provides a reliable framework for interpreting our individual experiences in the world. What is seen, tasted and touched is a concrete source of our knowledge. Morality, which develops from values rather than sensory perception, is part of a communal tradition. The most interesting issues occur where these domains clash, often in issues of medical ethics, where human decision-making relies both on an understanding of what is natural and what is just, and where issues of individual liberty and social welfare combine. Unitarians represent a long tradition that flourished in border countries where Jews, Muslims, and Christians encountered, and were transformed by, one another. This analogy of border countries provides a rich image. Living in the interstices between objective and subjective experience can prod our general faith in science to be informed by biblical injunctions to love one's neighbor as oneself.

Historically, Unitarianism interpreted "scientific" to mean "truthful." Science and religion went hand in hand. A rational approach to the Bible would rid the church of doctrines that resulted from human error. The equation of observable phenomena with truth grants scientific disciplines a status outside the realm of human value; they are presumed to be neutral systems that simply represent the workings of the world. One effect of this presumption is that intellectual achievement becomes the mark of understanding. Wisdom is the result of study and discipline instead of the common experiences of loneliness, agony, beauty, terror, and joy. Many Universalist and Unitarian clergy were early adopters of Darwin's theory of evolution, and understood it to mean that progress was inevitable, because it was in accordance with the design of nature. But this belief in reason above all else created an optimistic faith that was vulnerable to literalism and sometimes failed to speak to human needs for a community of warmth, for comfort as companionship, not a product derived from knowledge. Since truth was the provenance of God, it was assumed that arriving at the truth would inevitably mean participation in a divine community. Salvation became linked to intelligence, or achievement.

This achievement could be socially redeeming. In nineteenth-century Europe, scientific principles drastically improved survival rates for the war injured. Impersonal statistical analyses determined where interventions would be most effective and transformed the perception of the "natural course of events." Women at the Church of the Divine Unity (now All Souls) in New York City used this information to change conditions in the Civil War camps. Their minister, Henry Whitney Bellows (1814–1882), centralized and co-ordinated services and care, resulting in the United States Sanitary Commission. Clara Barton (1821–1914) organized field hospitals to treat the wounded during the Civil War, and later dedicated herself to forming an American branch (established 1881) of the Red Cross, offering humanitarian care to all victims of war, regardless of nationality. The Red Cross soon broadened its mission, both by serving in the wake of all disasters – floods, fires, and earthquakes in addition to war – and through programs designed to maintain a level of preparedness. The Red Cross certifies programs for water safety; organizes blood drives regularly to proactively supply hospitals; and receives donations of clothing and household goods to have at the ready. Originally devoted to compassionate response to traumatizing events beyond human control, the Red Cross was transformed by scientific principles which suggested that suffering might be prevented through planning, rather than ameliorated by human care.

Certainly, these programs do help, and promote common welfare. They also communicate an assumption that a rational, systemic process will be just. The eugenics movement provides a counterpoint: Understanding natural processes as opportunities to elevate the human condition, both mentally and physically, skips over the steps which depend upon human intervention. Noble aims are not a guarantee of good outcomes, nor are they scientific.

The eugenics movement originated as a desire to create a better society, and used the emerging science of genetics to select for superior abilities. In the United States, the science became a method of eradicating and preventing problems. The selective genetics practiced on plants and animals was applied to humans. Psychiatric illness, physical disabilities, and cognitive impairments could all be eliminated, while desirable traits could be preserved. The amount of suffering in the world would be drastically reduced. Eugenics, for believers, was a harbinger of world peace. Although "most basic scientists . . . shunned eugenics as vulgar and an unproductive field for research,"[3] by the middle of the 1920s, there were widespread efforts to prevent those deemed unfit from having children. Among the Universalist and Unitarian lawyers, scientists, educators, and clergy involved in policy-making and popularization of this "scientific" method of achieving perfection were Oliver Wendell Holmes, David Starr Jordan, and John Haynes Holmes.

The notion of segregating people considered unfit to reproduce dates back to antiquity. The Hebrew Bible describes a depraved group that God supposedly condemned to death. But a biblical narrative in which blotting out the memory of the enemy of Israel is attributed to God is not a scientific task to be carried out by human hands. Among the problems with eugenics as a public health policy was that the traits targeted for removal, such as criminality, feeble-mindedness, alcoholism, epilepsy, and bipolar disorder, are either not transmitted genetically at all, or are the result of something far more complex than a direct genetic link. Environmental factors had not been considered, even though by the time eugenics policies were forming,

---

[3] Elof Carlson, "Scientific Origins of Eugenics," Dolan DNA Learning Center, Cold Spring Harbor Laboratory. Image Archive on American Eugenics Movement, see: www.eugenicsarchive.org/eugenics/.

practicing scientists had long known that toxins and social inequities, poverty, poor nutrition, or a lack of access to education, among other things, were implicated in degeneracy. This information could have led to a different kind of reform; one based on environmental awareness and economic justice, or one that addressed the anxiety caused by immigration patterns after a global war. The eugenicist's vision of community was built on sacrificing people, but the retreating into science allowed believers to turn a blind eye: the truth of science had already ex-communicated these people. They were not capable of achievements that would allow them to possess the qualities associated with a God of Truth. The problems of injustice were removed without being addressed. This vision created a theology in which compassion was abstract. Instead of gaining personal solace, through direct contact with fellow human beings, consolation was derived from the belief that actions taken would build a better society in the future.

Science is related to literacy for Unitarians, and to word-for-word translations of the Bible, which led to the application of the historical–critical method in Bible studies, and then to a demythologizing of the texts. Removing the miracles in order to preserve the authority of the Bible ended up promoting the authority of reason in its most rigid form. Metaphors were taken literally. David Starr Jordan stated that the "blood of a nation determines its history" and "the history of a nation determines its blood," reducing justice to a communal blood bank, vulnerable to contamination. This concern with blood is biblical. Ritual slaughter and sacrifice laws are based upon the injunctions in Leviticus and Deuteronomy, which stem from Genesis 9:3–4: "Every moving thing that lives shall be meat for you; even as the green herb have I given you all things. But flesh with the life thereof, which is the blood thereof, shall ye not eat." This argument is the basis of many who do not believe in abortion: Life begins at the moment the blood of a new life is created. Breath keeps an individual alive, but the life of God is in the blood, not the breath.

In his 1945 *History of Unitarianism*, Earl Morse Wilbur wrote of a scientific analogy dating back to the sixteenth century: Miguel Servetus explained that examining how the body works to oxygenate blood would help us understand how the divine spirit is communicated to people. "The human spirit, complement of the divine, is seated in the blood," he wrote. It is produced "by a mixture in the lungs of inspired air with blood which the right ventricle of the heart communicates to the left, but this communication does not take place through the middle partition of the heart, as is commonly believed, but the blood is driven, by a long course, through the lungs."[4] Wilbur proceeded to discuss this as a revolutionary step in understanding human anatomy and to entertain a debate as to who owned the discovery of pulmonary circulation, but his literal history of the facts came at the expense of the metaphor: Human beings are imbued with the spirit of divinity in the same manner that breath circuitously enters blood.

This interest in knowledge itself, in the discovery of how life in this world works, and in the wonders of creation, led many to believe that science was somehow a religion: a process of truth-seeking which was inherently meaningful. Wilbur's epic was published before the atomic bomb was dropped on Hiroshima, and before the Nazi concentration camps were liberated. Ironically, or perhaps inevitably, it was the eugenic vision carried out to its logical extreme that provided a challenge to the idea of science as the key to a better community: The Nuremberg trials resulted in guidelines for research which preserve society by protecting individuals, acknowledging that science does not intrinsically serve the good. Community rests on safeguarding the most vulnerable, not on advancing the scientific agenda of possibilities. The tension between these poles exists today in issues of abortion, euthanasia, stem-cell research, and access to health care. Science does not dictate beliefs about the validity of any of these practices: defining who is vulnerable does.

Between World War II and the Unitarian Universalist Association's adoption of the Principles and Purposes in 1985, science was a very complicated topic for liberal religionists. Post-war denominational growth in the United States and Canada came primarily through fellowships, many of which were intentionally planted in newly formed research centers, and in small college towns. Large numbers of these new Unitarians were attracted to the religion because it offered community without creeds or submission to an authority beyond reason. Fellowships were largely lay led, which meant that often the scientific expertise and orientation in the group was not counterbalanced by the presence of a religious professional or trained minister. Peace was a topic of enormous interest, and drove a new perspective on science. "If the new astronomy makes a first-century God unthinkable, then let's have a God who is thinkable in terms of the twentieth century. If modern chemistry, physics, and biology make old ideas about creation and destiny impossible for the modern mind, let us discard them. We want truth, wherever it comes from and wherever it leads us," wrote Clarence

---

[4] Earl Morse Wilbur, *A History of Unitarianism: Socinianism and its Antecedents* (Boston, MA: Beacon Press, 1945), pp. 146–147.

Skinner. But science "can only deal with quantitative phenomena . . . and the deep questions concerning the nature of reality, purpose, destiny, and the ultimate relation of good and evil cannot be measured."[5] Skinner proposed a truth made good by religious faith, and goodness made true by scientific objectivity.

The American Unitarian Association's (AUA's) religious education curricula already reflected this philosophy. The New Beacon series, beginning in 1937 and developed under the auspices of an education team that included Sophia Lyon Fahs (1876–1978), designed child-centered, experiential curricula, which were rooted in the natural world. The curricula in this series, which included "Animal Babies," "Experiences with Living Things," "Beginnings: Life and Death," and "How Miracles Abound," promoted science, and approached the Bible in a new way. Moses, Joseph, and Jesus were explored biographically, as human beings, so that children could understand the trajectory of a life and compare themselves with these characters. The goal was personal growth and development, rather than teaching the historical role Moses played for the Hebrews. Many Unitarian congregations were less than satisfied with these curricula, and felt that the approach used by the AUA did not help children navigate the culture they were living in, which was based on a different, much more mainstream, understanding of the Bible.[6]

But, by 1950, the world had dramatically changed, and in a period of unprecedented growth and lay leadership for Unitarians, the New Beacon series suddenly had enormous appeal. The liberal church had a role to play, as the popular culture struggled to incorporate scientific understandings into a moral framework condemning inhumane uses of technology without rejecting science itself. The problem was the decision to use an atomic bomb, not the existence of the bomb itself. The Universalists and Unitarians were working together, and created programs for use in other liberal congregations and in private school settings where evolution was not controversial. The curricula were aimed at helping children "see the awe and wonder of the immensity of the universe of which they are a part, and yet sense an equal awe and wonder about the majesty of man. Man who has struggled against odds, and reached his present position, and who can, we have faith, go on to make his planet a better place than ever it has been before . . . We do not need to worry . . . if we have faith,

---

[5] Clarence R. Skinner, *A Religion for Greatness* (Boston, MA: Universalist Publishing House, 1945), pp. 105, 109, 111.

[6] Edith Hunter, "Sophia Lyon Fahs: Liberal Religious Educator," see: harvardsquarelibrary.org.

and the strength to implement that faith in action – faith in man, in the world, in the universe, in the everlasting potential of the future."[7] This positivist statement does not specifically mention science, but it does clearly avoid delineating anything remotely like a traditional religious faith.

In 1964, two years after the Seattle World's Fair with its "Sermons from Science" pavilion, featuring children dressed as Pilgrims and astronauts, science was made explicit as a cornerstone of religious education. "A Possible Partnership Between Science and Religion" listed five tenets necessary in Religious Education. Four were scientific: observation and experimentation; reading scripture scientifically, as documents of human experience; developmental psychology; and a morality based upon relationship with the living universe. But, by the time this call was made, the denominational support for religious education had vanished. The New Beacon team dispersed in 1964. The Charles Street Meetinghouse, which represented a philosophy very much in accord with Fahs' program, downscaled that same year. Over the next decade, very few curricula were developed, and they were rooted more in the social sciences: "Man the Culture Builder," "The Haunting House," and "About Your Sexuality." The Theological School at St. Lawrence University closed in 1965, and Crane Theological School at Tufts University closed in 1968. In addition to being historically Universalist, these were the schools most associated with religious education. The denominational energy was directed towards social problems both within and without: racism, war, and finances.

Underlying this shift from "hard science" to social science was a consistent concern with authority, and with individualism. What can objectively be relied upon? In the popular culture, science had generally been understood as common sense, not theoretical or speculative. The understanding of science as objective and experiential had been seen as a path to reverence and wonder, as a direct way to participate in the glory of creation by the earlier curriculum teams. By the 1960s, professional science operated on different terms. It was more abstract, less available to lay people, and a bit defensive or intimidating, depending upon where one stood. As the field of "pure science" emerged, there was general confusion about what "science" meant. Professionals who wanted to maintain moral integrity by disassociating themselves from practical applications of science, instead opened themselves up to charges of elitism. Liberal religious scientists, such

---

[7] Charles Howe, "Dorothy Spoerl," *Dictionary of Unitarian Universalist Biography*, see www25. uua.org/uuhs/duub/.

as Ralph Burhoe (1911–1997), found themselves valued in a small academic circle, but the denomination did not particularly engage with the work. Burhoe founded the Institute on Religion in an Age of Science (IRAS) in 1954, and later organized the Center for Advanced Study in Religion and Science at Meadville. Together, members of both the Center and IRAS began *Zygon: Journal of Religion & Science*, in 1966. *Zygon* is the only peer-reviewed academic journal in the field of religion and science, and it is well known as a valuable interdisciplinary publication. Yet Burhoe's science is not often genuinely explored in Unitarian Universalism. When attention is paid, it tends to take note of "mysticism;" for example, "Ralph Burhoe and Teilhard de Chardin share a vision of mystical unity with God."[8] Burhoe believed, echoing Clarence Skinner, that the confusion and anomie so many people suffer from was the result of the separation of religion and science, of meaning and knowledge. He outlined an evolutionary theory of religion, and in 1980 was honored with the Templeton Prize for Progress in Religion. He was called a "missionary for a new reformation, a reformation which may be far more profound and revolutionary than the reformation led by Martin Luther."[9] This seems to have been based on optimism more than reason.

A British Unitarian scientist, and also a winner of the Templeton Prize (1985), shares a similar fate. Alister Hardy (1896–1985) was a marine biologist and Oxford professor who established the Religious Experience Research Centre in 1969 in Manchester College, Oxford University. Hardy's accomplishments as a scientist were many, and earned him a knighthood in 1957, after which he went public with a theory of evolution in which human characteristics unique among land mammals could be traced back to marine mammals, indicating that human evolution had its origins in the ocean. Hardy's interest in evolution extended to religion as well, which he believed had biological origins. However, the Religious Experience Research Centre, now based at the University of Wales, functions more to collect descriptions of spiritual phenomena than to relate these experiences to any scientific framework.

Instead of scientific discipline or its objective truths gaining authority, the individualism of practice was embraced. The New Beacon series sacrificed the historical culture of religion as intrinsically meaningful by making the figures in these stories subservient to an agenda of personal growth,

[8] J.S. Nelson, "Ralph Burhoe and Teilhard de Chardin: An affinity in mysticism?" *Zygon*, Vol. 35, No. 3, Spring 2000, pp. 687–698.
[9] Philip Hefner, "Remembering Ralph Burhoe," *Zygon*, Vol. 33, Issue 1, March 1998, p. 168.

which could preserve faith for individuals, but prevented a communal understanding of the past. Religion, like science, could encourage each person onward, but did not communicate a shared story of meaning. Gene Navias (b. 1928), staff member at the UUA Department of Religious Education from 1963 until 1992, said the science curriculum "failed because few understood – either teachers, parents, or children – what was religious about it. And further . . . it did not produce children who knew what they believed – in any terms that met their expectations or that of the culture around them."[10]

The goal in Unitarian Universalism had been to explicitly link morality to natural science. Whether or not the curricula met that goal during the 1950s and 1960s, later educators did not perceive the connection. Scientific theologians were relegated to the realm of mysticism, thus Unitarian Universalists missed an opportunity to foster a communal understanding of what it meant to be human; to have a view of personal development that was intrinsically collaborative, relational, and contingent. Morality as a biological function of humanity could have given a corporate identity to Unitarian Universalism quite different from one valuing personal growth, derived through natural experiences. Making mystics of scientists substitutes nature for the natural world. The objective universe becomes metaphorical, and nature takes on the characteristics of a being separate from humanity. This invites the opposite conclusion of what was once hoped: Rather than scientific method demonstrating the evolving nature of truth itself, nature becomes divine, and human beings adore, celebrate, and preserve nature through ritual and action. Nature is a poetic source of meaning, either in addition to or instead of simply the environment in which we live, and move, and have our being.

This process of reinterpreting the literal world as emblematic of divinity did provide unity, if not commonality, among Unitarian Universalists. Scientists, like mystics, could simply be understood as seekers, and the method of seeking need not be relevant. It was enough to recognize in science the unseen forces, both very big (the cosmos) and very small (genetic material), which shape us, without needing to understand why or how; but to accept those who did practice science as questing after some sort of divinity in the same way as another person might practice meditation. Interest in science as a discipline necessary in religion waned dramatically through the 1970s and 1980s, while interest in earth-centered traditions, which led

[10] Maureen Killoran, "And Light of Science in their Eyes," *Unitarian Universalism 1989: Selected Essays* (East Greenwich, RI: Unitarian Universalist Ministers Association/Minuteman Press, 1990), p. 82.

to the Sixth Source (1995) grew dramatically. Most of this growth originated with the Covenant of Unitarian Universalist Pagans, which formed in 1985 and affiliated with the Unitarian Universalist Association in 1987. Christa Heiden Landon, one of the founders and currently the director of the Pagan Institute, went to Meadville Lombard to study Unitarian Universalism specifically because of authority issues within the pagan community, for which she thought congregational polity would provide useful redress.[11] Landon's task has been to re-form the pagan belief community by empowering members rather than venerating the priests and priestesses. The content of the faith remains completely centered on relationships with nature, which is explicitly understood as sacred, and the practice is ritualistic. Although the Covenant of Unitarian Universalist Pagans was one of the many groups that lost affiliate status in 2008, the effect of this group has been profound.

Scientific literalism, such as that employed by Earl Morse Wilbur in his description of Servetus' work as an anatomist, illustrated the ability of a rigorous, observing, exploring Unitarianism to comprehend the truth. This is very much an individual pursuit, which can also be seen in curricula where biblical figures are treated separately, as distinct characters that may be an inspiration for personal growth. This individualized, personalized understanding of truth is precisely what made the faith hospitable to mysticism, especially mysticism that used the language of nature. Reason and natural law were employed as a path to discovery, with an assumption that the objective, universally accessible nature of the method would create a bond. Instead, as definitions and interpretations of "reason" and "natural" evolved, religious truth grew privatized. Servetus described the "inspirited blood" in one person's heart, knowing that all human bodies functioned the same way: After a long journey, the blood on the right side of the heart arrives on the left side, full of oxygen. This was a descriptive metaphor, based on observations of nature. David Starr Jordan used "blood" communally, to define humanity by observable traits. This was used literally, as a reason to believe in divisions, and prescriptively to promote a vision. Science can be used metaphorically to simplify concepts and to create emotional resonance, but it ceases to be science when meaning is ascribed. The circle of life and the Sacred Circle may both be describing a natural process that we respect and participate in, but they are not exactly the same. When the words are capitalized, an empirical

---

[11] Christa Heiden Landon, "Encountering A Sacred Cosmos," *Liberal Religious Education – Nature as Teacher: Science and Theology.* No. 7, Fall 1991 (Boston, MA: LREDA), pp. 27–28.

truth becomes ritualized and conveys a meaning beyond the observable facts.

Married couple Connie Barlow and Mike Dowd, a science writer and former fundamentalist preacher respectively, are "evangelical evolutionists": itinerant preachers of "The Great Story." In this story, an inspiring narrative is formed around the facts of evolution, in order to help people change their behavior, and so change human destiny. Although the Great Story does not anthropomorphize nature, it does describe the natural universe as God. The image used is that of Russian dolls, with layers of "nested creativity: subatomic particles within atoms, within molecules, within cells, within organisms, and so on. Each level is uniquely creative, that is, has the power to bring something new into existence. Stars create atoms; atoms create substances like the oxygen we breathe; human cultures create art, religions, and technology. The largest nesting doll is God, or Allah, Adonai, Source of Life, Ultimate Reality, Nature, the Universe – whatever name describes the divine whole for you, the ultimate creative reality that includes and transcends all other levels of reality."[12] Although this story is seen as a theological bridge for Unitarian Universalists, using both scientific facts and reverential language, it is a narrative that imposes meaning and direction onto the template of evolution. It is a conversion story for scientists.

The Great Story has its roots in a version of evolution that changes the process of natural selection from randomness to design. It is rooted in the work of a Jesuit priest, Teilhard de Chardin, and of Julian Huxley, who worked with Alister Hardy and believed that there was an evolutionary basis to ethics. Huxley, a eugenicist, believed the way humanity participated in evolution could be direct; that people could use scientific information to "better" the world. Spirituality and ecology are woven into a story aimed at change. The Great Story does represent democratic values, it does empower people to act, and it does speak to pagans and humanists as well as theists, who can see God in the organizing principle of the narrative. But it is a metaphor that is drawing together people who actually have rather different beliefs about the world.

Action can elide these differences in theology, and create unity in and across congregations through programs for action. Interest in nature derived from contemplative study, scientific discipline, and ritual practice all lead to environmental ethics; and to bonds among those who believe

---

[12] Amy Hassinger, "Welcome to the Ecozoic Era," *UU World*, Spring 2006 (Boston, MA: UUA), p. 28.

that nature is divine, those who understand creation as a divine gift with humanity as its stewards, and those for whom the environment is the product of evolutionary processes. In the end, it is Unitarian Universalist polity more than any special status for science that fosters a commitment to the Ministry for the Earth. Democratic values of respect for diversity and empowered laity have pragmatic results.

The use of the words "democracy," "pragmatism," and "environment" bring to mind John Dewey, the philosopher, educator, and signatory of the 1933 Humanist Manifesto. Dewey was a profound influence on the team which developed the New Beacon series: Dorothy Spoerl and Sophia Fahs wrote from a conviction that "experience," as Dewey used the term – an integrated understanding of the self and the environment – was the starting point for religious growth. Kenneth Patton's description of the church as "an ingathering for nature, and human nature" echoes Dewey: "Experience denotes the planted field, the sowed seeds, the reaped harvests . . . [I]t also denotes the one who plants and reaps, who works and rejoices, hopes, fears, plans, invokes magic or chemistry to aid him, who is downcast or triumphant. It is double-barreled in that it recognizes . . . no division between act and material, subject and object, but contains them both in an unanalyzed totality."[13] This totality, or unity of experience, is what ecology provides for Unitarian Universalists. It is a counterpoint to the individualism, creating a web of connections relating organisms that appear to be very different, and yet do have an effect on one another. Individuals can be simultaneously irrelevant, and yet agents of enormous change.

Ecology provides a house for Unitarian Universalist theology and practice because it has rooms for the disciplines of physics, chemistry, biology, geology, marine and earth sciences, and for free will. The inclusion of free will means that ecology is a scientific field that explicitly acknowledges that the power of science to create change rests in human hands, but that nature has its own patterns, within which we must live. Understanding based on observable phenomenon may help people accept the facts of limited resources, and then motivate new behaviors, and new inventions. Ecology is civic environmentalism; it externalizes the system and interchange metaphor of Servetus' oxygenated blood, makes it visible and communal, and promises a kind of universal salvation in which the destiny of each is related to the destiny of all. An example can be found in the current programs supporting the practice of "ethical eating," which was

---

[13] John Dewey, *Experience and Nature* (Whitefish, MT: Kessinger Publishing, 2003), p. 8.

chosen as an issue for congregational study and action, beginning in 2008. These programs link food and environmental justice, and ask congregants to consider the manner in which food is produced and transported, and the impact on workers and the environment, as part of how they plan food purchases.

Unitarian Universalists have had a scholar of ethics and ecology for several decades. J. Ronald Engel (b. 1936) has been a strong voice for inter-faith environmental justice programs, both in an urban environment and in nature preserves. Echoing Burhoe and Hardy, Engel has said that religious experiences happen in the real world; that ecology is a physical approach to faith development, centered in the body and its relationship to the land. Engel has worked on biosphere reserves, which include a central wilderness area, so that evolution untouched by human technology can proceed, surrounded by a layer of land that is used for sustainable food and craft production, and a buffer zone, in which new technology and economic systems are introduced. The landscape has a direct spiritual function for Engel: spaces become sacred as they are set "apart from human will and purpose," and reflect a world "still centered on ultimate beginnings and endings."

Engel embraces an environmental pluralism. There are those who champion wilderness, those who would save the farms, those who are dedicated to animal welfare, and those who see humanity as stewards. He values the insights brought to the field by feminism, and he finds an inclusive metaphor in the Bible, with "its themes of wilderness, land, tending the garden, stewardship, generativity, compassion for the weak and suffering, and co-creativity." It is a story of a people and how they relate to the land, and within that narrative tradition are portrayals of how to engage with spirit, nature, self, and others. The scriptures offer an ecological worldview and a democratic ideal. One might also note the structure of the Ten Commandments, which have no rich descriptions or evocations, but do start with spirit and claim the presence of something holy that the individual people must notice. And then, in the fifth commandment, two things happen at the same time: each person is called to honor those who gave them life, and doing so will make "it go well in the land the Lord your God is giving you." The rest of the commandments are social laws, to define a good community. The land and the people are both mentioned for the first time in the same commandment, and together function as a prism for both the spirit and the community.

Engel was a member of the Earth Charter (2000) drafting committee, which was rooted in an understanding reminiscent of Dewey's: the integrity of ecosystems is dependent upon true democracy, where people are not living in poverty, and do not owe their existence to the whims of those granted power through unjust systems. Ecological systems and social systems are entwined; each can be addressed separately, but the effects of any attention will not be limited to one system. Engel is determined to integrate an ecological worldview with democracy, but has found that modern conservationists are so utilitarian that it is difficult to speak with ideals that are non-scientific. His comment indirectly addressed the breach formed by splitting science into professional and lay categories: He wrote "Almost everyone I meet who works on projects like the biosphere reserves personally holds such [spiritual] values: it is what keeps them going. But they do not have permission from their institutional and disciplinary cultures to admit to this."[14] Dewey was an empirical naturalist, not likely to use the Bible as a personally meaningful metaphor, but he did say what Engel repeats: Moral and spiritual development is dependent upon real democratic community and experience in nature. This is why the Ministry for the Earth can be central to the mission of the Unitarian Universalist Association (UUA): it takes advantage of the democratic community without dictating what the spiritual experience of nature must mean. Democracy is actually the most resonant spiritual narrative; every living thing is struggling to be in a community that sustains it. Such a community represents the longed-for "taste of heaven below."

---

[14] J. Ronald Engel, "Earth Spirituality is a Many Splendored Thing!" *Journal* (Chicago, IL: Meadville Lombard Theological School, 2000).

Architecture, art, and music

The current trend towards "green" church buildings among Unitarian Universalists is part of a long history of innovation and adaptation that began with secret meeting spaces and hidden chapels in sixteenth-century England, and continued in a variety of forms over the centuries. Because Unitarianism is so strongly associated with "the Word," most expositions of the faith are literary. But there is a strong visual and spatial tradition associated with Unitarianism, some of which correlates with the more elite strain for which the religion is known, and some of which provides access to a different theme within Unitarianism; one which is closely allied to the "folk" – the people who live and work on the land, and the rhythm of that life in nature, punctuated by protests against the powerful and demands for justice.

The Iowa Sisterhood, a Western group of female clergy in the late nineteenth and early twentieth centuries, was responsible for the construction of over twenty new churches in the Midwest between 1880 and 1913. These buildings had kitchens, gyms, and offices, and were intended for use seven days a week. They were practical, affordable, and communicated more than a liberal Social Gospel christology. Traditional-looking churches symbolized patriarchal power. The home, a place of power for women, became a model for these clergy.[1] Jenkin Lloyd Jones, who championed the Iowa Sisterhood, also supported the idea of church as home as it related well to the house-church tradition of his Welsh Unitarianism. The multi-purpose church buildings in the Midwest were progressive, but they actually resurrected the original Puritan ideal: democratic meeting spaces designed with practical needs in mind, not set apart as sacred space. The goal was human comfort, or uplift through service, not inspiration. Although the theological rationale differed, the early humanists revived the Puritan distrust of religious art.

---

[1] Cynthia Grant Tucker, *Prophetic Sisterhood*. (Boston, MA: Beacon Press, 1990), p. 107.

The Puritans did not believe that anything spiritual could be represented materially. The church was the gathered community, and the building was a meetinghouse, which was eminently practical and designed to foster religious practices, not symbolize a set of beliefs. Anglican churches had three liturgical centers: the altar, in the head of the church; the pulpit, in the nave; and the baptismal font, by the door, symbolizing baptism's role as entrance into the Christian life.[2] The Puritans condensed these into one location: the pulpit. The word of God was integral to all understanding. Communion was a meal commemorating Jesus, served from a table by the pulpit, not a sacrifice on an altar. Baptismal bowls could sit on the table. The pulpit was centrally located on the long wall of a rectangular room, so that everyone was close enough to see and hear. The building was used for all community meetings, not set apart from the secular world. There were no spires or belfries. In addition to the ban on graven images, Puritans did not portray people, for fear of encouraging a Catholic veneration of humans as saints.

In England, the 1689 Toleration Act initiated a period of chapel build-ing among Dissenters. These buildings, while not multi-purpose, shared the simplicity and functionality of the American Puritan meetinghouses. The English Dissenters existed within a much broader culture than did the New England Puritans, and class distinctions showed. The Pres-byterians (forebears of Unitarians in England) were prosperous and "the most intellectual of Dissenters, inclined to approve and attain to dignity of architectural design and beauty of internal fittings."[3] The Ipswich Meeting House (1699) in East Anglia demonstrated this: it had a Dutch chandelier, and richly carved walls. This chapel also had box pews built at a height enabling all to see the minister, but not each other, making an architectural association between wealth and individualism. Wealth could also drive innovation: The first octagonal church was built at Norwich in 1756. Its interior included sword rests for regalia, special seats for dignitaries, and marbling work done by a London artist.

In between the meetinghouses of seventeenth-century New England and the churches of the Midwest 250 years later, there were two basic architec-tural movements in the US: the Federalist and the Gothic Revival, which dated to the middle of the eighteenth century in England, but was most visible in the late nineteenth century. Before the War for Independence,

[2] Heather Elizabeth Peterson, "Unitarian Roots in Architecture: The Puritan Meetinghouse," *Unitarian Universalist Christian* (Boston, MA: Unitarian Universalist Christian Fellowship, 1993), p. 20.

[3] Graham Hague and Judy Hague, *The Unitarian Heritage: An Architectural Survey* (Sheffield, MA: Unitarian Heritage Society, 1986), p. 10.

the meetinghouse remained the cornerstone of a community, even dictating the size of settlements: the costs associated with becoming a parish demanded at least forty families, but more than 200 would not fit in the frame-built halls.[4] To accommodate growth, galleries and balconies were added at the beginning of the eighteenth century, altering the roof design. The galleries necessitated the elevation of the pulpit, and the addition of sounding boards, so that everyone could see and hear. The change in roof design led to a transformation of the building's exterior profile: formerly, if a church had a bell tower, it was on the lawn next to the church. Gable-ended roofs could support belfries; thus the bell moved from the lawn to a tower. Inside, bench seating gave way to boxed pews, to help keep out drafts. But pews became seating for families, which ended the opportunity to attend services alongside other community members. Box pews also ended the practice of separation by gender. Decades later, after the separation of church and state, box pews ended up functioning as real estate; valued by proximity to the pulpit, and passed down from generation to generation.

The first churches built after the war preserved very little of the original meetinghouse design, and in fact changed the role of the church completely. Prior to 1792, the meetinghouses represented stability. While houses had been incorporating architectural changes all along, the meetinghouses were not affected by trends or fashion. The only changes had been for practical purposes. But, beginning in 1784, Charles Bulfinch (1763–1844), who had grown up at King's Chapel during its transition from Anglican to Unitarian, introduced new architectural elements to Boston through church designs. The four churches he built in Boston varied widely, and included Gothic details and columns evocative of the Greek style. (Bulfinch's early interest in Greek forms would be passed on in literary form to his son, Thomas, author of *Bulfinch's Mythology*.) In 1790, a Bulfinch design ended the traditional use of space for dissenting congregations.[5] The pulpit was on the short wall, at the end of a long aisle and opposite an entry porch with triple doors. This Federalist design functioned transitionally, eroding the architectural differences between those churches that would become Unitarian and those that maintained an orthodox Christianity.

---

[4] Abbott L. Cummings, "Meeting and Dwelling House: Interrelationships in Early New England," in Peter Benes, ed., *New England Meetinghouse and Church* (Boston, MA: Boston University Press, 1979), p. 6.

[5] Harold Kirker, *The Architecture of Charles Bulfinch* (Cambridge, MA: Harvard University Press, 1969), p. 18.

In addition to celebrating American independence, the buildings erected in the boom between 1790 and 1810 reflected a huge reordering of class. With the crown officials removed, the aristocracy disappeared. Craftsmen and carpenters experienced a dramatic rise in status: they represented democracy, there was a void at the top of the hierarchy, and money was being directed towards building. Bulfinch was perfectly positioned to shape public architecture at the exact time the national identity was being formed. He designed most of Boston before moving to Washington, DC in 1814, to finish the Capitol. But if Bulfinch introduced professional architecture, Asher Benjamin democratized it. Benjamin (1773–1845), one of those sought-after craftsmen, published design handbooks that deeply influenced the appearance of the country. Adapted from the British versions and with scales changed, they were the first pattern books ever written by an American. They brought geometry, architectural history, and style directly to builders, providing full plans and details. Bulfinch's recessed porch and triple-door church plan appeared in Benjamin's 1797 *Country-Builder's Apprentice*; across the United States, there are now countless rectangular white churches entered through a set of three doors located on a recessed porch, with the pulpit located on the short wall.

Benjamin's pattern books allowed buildings to be assembled from elements, rather than envisioned as a whole. This is precisely the method used in the Midwest, by clergy who designed churches around specific functions and needs. And this approach was, financially, far safer than devotion to art: Bulfinch was once incarcerated for debt in a prison he designed. Benjamin coped with economic vicissitudes by being versatile. In the late 1820s, he functioned as a city planner and supervised the construction of canals and roads for the Nashua (NH) Manufacturing Company. This industrial venture was modeled upon the mill city of Lowell, Massachusetts: a group of Unitarian lawyers and businessmen built and owned the township. Included in the planned community was the church, designed by Benjamin, in an oak grove donated for the purpose by the company. His family worshipped there; later, Bulfinch's son Stephen served as minister. (Stephen Bulfinch also served at All Souls in Washington, DC, a church his father designed and attended.)

Soon after the Civil War, in a second building boom, Frank Furness (1839–1912) found himself shaping the city around the unfinished center of Philadelphia, just as Bulfinch had done in Washington forty years earlier. By all accounts, Furness, the son of a Unitarian minister, was a character: never indifferent, he dressed in large plaids and was able to out-curse anyone.

A loner, he spent hours drawing – flowers, animals, trees – but he also completely embraced modern technology. A heavy use of shadow and light marks his building designs, and he preferred to have his buildings emulate natural forms rather than Classical geometric shapes. Seeking color for the exterior of his buildings, Furness invented glass tiles; he also began to use abstract design in leaded glass windows toward the end of his career. Furness built two Unitarian churches: Germantown in 1866, and First Unitarian in 1883. His buildings are messy and complex, made of various materials that typically conflict with each other, such as iron with glass or brick with stone. Somehow they are both the opposite of the Puritan meetinghouse, and a perfectly logical expression of democratic engagement with the world those meetinghouses represented.

Furness was working during the period of Gothic revival, a movement based originally on the conviction that the only genuine form of religious expression was medieval. Because the dissenting congregations had achieved legitimacy and were finally free to participate in the larger culture, Unitarians in England joined in the movement, but most practiced "dissenting Gothic": rather than simply replicating old forms, they believed in meeting the current, practical needs of a congregation while building in a Gothic style. Since Dissenters, unlike Anglicans, had to pay for their church buildings, the movement at first meant that decorative details might be added, color to the windows or arches, the creation of a center aisle and shifting of the pulpit, and ornate trim which seemed Romantic. But, by the middle of the century, there were some Unitarians commissioning dissenting Gothic churches, particularly around Manchester, England where industrialization had generated wealth. The most significant work was done by Thomas Worthington (1826–1909), who designed five Unitarian churches, as well as many public buildings that served social causes: hospitals, workhouses, public baths. Worthington, a Unitarian by birth, also designed the new buildings when Manchester College relocated to Oxford University. In Ireland, the non-conforming Presbyterians built several dissenting Gothic churches, from Newry (1853) to All Souls, Belfast (1896). The church history for St. Stephen's Green of Dublin (1863) notes "the design brilliantly fulfils the requirement that in a non-conformist church the emphasis should be on the pulpit... Everyone in the St. Stephen's Green church can hear and see the preacher, emphasising the importance of the spoken word to the Unitarian congregation."[6]

---

[6] See: unitarianchurchdublin.org/history.html.

Although Gothic architecture was identified with a sense of mystery in the pre-modern church, the movement was very much related to the Industrial Revolution and rise of a new class of businessmen. In the US, the Federalist movement had established the church as a visual agent of identity and change; now, the financial status of a congregation could be reflected in the building, and its adornments. This was true in Great Britain, too. Stained-glass windows exist in many Unitarian and Universalist buildings, a sign of modernity and social status, and yet creating the impression of timelessness because of the painted glass used in Gothic churches. Thus art, never previously associated with Protestant churches, was introduced. The Unitarian involvement in art actually helped pave the way: Romantic and naturalist painting in the United States began with Washington Allston (1779–1843), whose 1839 exhibit was reviewed under the title: "The intellectual and moral made visible." Allston was a decisive influence on the Transcendentalists. His contemporary, Rembrandt Peale (1778–1860), democratized art as Asher Benjamin had architecture. In 1836, Peale published *Graphics: A Manual of Drawings and Writings*, used to teach drawing in public schools for at least two generations. Peale, who painted in the Hudson River School style, as did Christopher Cranch (1813–1892), revived ancient coloring techniques that led to new art forms, including stained glass. At first, stained glass evoked religious sentiment in the same way as the Romantic painters had, but soon, pastoral scenes were modified to signify heaven, by either faintly inscribing a celestial city in the sky, or using radiant light in a circle in the clouds.

Windows were often memorial gifts, and stained glass began to contain images that could simultaneously signify the subject of the memorial, and represent everyone. It was not long before angels appeared. Human figures were used to represent virtues, and illustrations from biblical stories became common. N. C. Wyeth (1882–1945), who painted a series of parables for the Laymen's League in 1922, illustrated classic adventure tales in a manner reminiscent of those windows, with great color and movement, always set in nature, and with a moral. Andrew Wyeth asked about the extraordinary relaxed quality of the faces N. C. drew, and his father said, "When my mother died ... they had laid her in her bed upstairs. I went up and sat there with her, with that amazing face that looked like the mother of Europe. As the sun went down, studying that face lying there on that white pillow and that waxy skin – it made such a deep impression on me. If you ever have a chance to be with someone you have loved, don't hesitate, because that's profound ... a head in death. It changed everything for me."[7] This merging of the individual with the whole of humanity, the loved one symbolizing life itself, is exactly how the memorial glass windows were designed to convey meaning.

The Gothic movement revealed an existing tension between those who were more liturgically centered and those who believed primarily in service, which might also appear to be a division between the elite and the folk, or the common people. Robert Swain Peabody (1845–1917), a son, brother and brother-in-law of Unitarian ministers, practiced architectural pluralism, incorporating some Gothic forms without adopting the movement. He designed Unitarian churches across the United States. Others, including Joseph Priestley's grandson Henry Hobson Richardson and Ralph Adams Cram, left the denomination for the Episcopal Church, and designed buildings that were elitist symbols, emphasizing a faith that measured progress through wealth rather than service. A smaller, Gothic movement representative of a more common Unitarianism – with an English design, wood and daub construction, and steeple-less churches – emerged in the 1890s. Edwin J. Lewis (1866–1937) built thirty-five churches between 1890 and 1925, all of them Unitarian or Universalist. Lewis was an incredibly active lay leader, president of both the Sunday School Union and the association for young people, and he brought his interest in religious education to the design of churches. The scale of his buildings, for between 100–200 people, was appropriate for Unitarian services, and he used settings that emphasized the role of nature in faith. In 1902, three of his plans were printed and made available to congregations at no cost.[8] Very few of these churches have stained-glass "pictures" but many have abstract designs in glass or colored tile, echoing Furness' work and presaging Frank Lloyd Wright's designs.

Edwin Lewis and Frank Lloyd Wright (1867–1959), a nephew of Jenkin Lloyd Jones, were born less than a year apart. By the time these men were working, church design had been successfully democratized, and even buildings that once symbolized wealth or status no longer represented quite the same ideal. Congregations met in buildings ranging in date from before the Revolutionary War to after the Civil War, in churches they had inherited or built, or converted from some other use. The styles were incredibly varied, and included "home-like" churches. In 1895, Wright worked with

[7] Andrew Wyeth, "N. C. Wyeth, Artist and Illustrator," in Herbert Vetter, ed., *Notable American Unitarians*, see: harvardsquarelibrary.org.
[8] James G. Smart, *The Keene Unitarian Universalist Church* (West Kennebunk, ME: Phoenix Publishing, 1995), p. 62.

William Channing Gannett to produce *The House Beautiful*, which begins, "There is a Bible verse that reads 'A building of God, a house not made with hands.' Paul meant the spiritual body in which he says the soul will live hereafter. But how well the words describe the Home – a home right here on earth! . . . Watch two birds foraging to build a nest . . . Man and woman are but two larger birds, borrowing more of the world material to make a bigger bowl a little cosier . . . " A little while later, Gannett reflects on those "world materials." "What hands took sunshine and rain and a pinecone a hundred years ago in a wild forest . . . and built up countless cells into the green tree that waited on the hillside until the axe man came?"[9] It is clear that evolution has touched theology, that nature is revered, and that what we build is our testimony to where we find meaning. It has become our job to house the infinite by participating in natural processes. Wright removed the association of timelessness from the medieval church, and placed it and faith itself in nature, saying, "Nature is the only body of God that we shall ever see . . . Buildings, too, are children of Earth and Sun." There is no room for art that is merely decorative in this understanding. Art is how we participate in nature. Wright's organic architecture had its roots in his religion, and his religion had its roots in the sense of home cultivated in the land where his grandparents farmed, and created a Unitarian community among extended family members. The first building Wright worked on was the family church in Spring Green; later, when he was a member in Oak Park, he designed Unity Temple. He also designed a building for his subsequent home church of Madison, Wisconsin – a congregation his father helped found. That building – described as a ship's prow, bird wings in flight, and hands clasped in prayer – is now part of a much larger church: in 2008, the congregation completed an extensive, "green" addition.

A near contemporary of Wright's was Beatrix Potter (1866–1943). Both visually perceptive and gifted in their abilities to communicate through drawing, Wright and Potter found imaginative ways to document the astonishing diversity of the world they observed, and each created environments that allowed others to begin to see as they did. Wright and Potter shared an interest in science and the natural world as being our primary teachers, replete with models for human interaction as well as for dwellings. Curious, willing to experiment, and determined, neither saw any possibility but intellectual independence. These are traits that mark them as having grown up in Dissenting families, simultaneously isolated and provided with a close, engaged audience. The land – its history, the life

---

[9] William Channing Gannett, *The House Beautiful* (Boston, MA: Beacon Press, 1895), pp. 9–11.

within it, the landscape itself – was precious. Potter was unable to become a professional scientist, but took her technical drawing skill and knowledge of nature to create a new form: the picture book. Later, Potter was able to purchase fifteen farms and 4,000 acres, ensuring the preservation of the English Lake District farming culture.

Preservation of a family tradition motivated Wright. As Welsh immigrants with long Unitarian roots, the Lloyd Jones family found no liberal church in 1845. They built their own, but even when Unity Chapel was complete, cousins, aunts, uncles, and assorted friends continued to assemble in a grove. They talked about current affairs, read Emerson and Thoreau, told Welsh myths, and sang hymns.[10] Civil War songs were added to the repertoire in the 1860s. The site was also home to a summer institute for Unitarian clergy. The camp-style gathering and sharing music was part of home for Wright, whose minister father alternated between teaching music and preaching. Wright was an accomplished pianist, who believed in "conversations" among instruments. A Wright-designed music stand looks like a pulpit: Accessible and lit on all sides, the stand allows a group of musicians to play while facing each other and their music. Wright liked classical music, but embodied a folk tradition of participation. This was also true of Bela Bartók (1881–1945), a concert pianist who helped found the field of ethnomusicology. Bartok documented the rhythmic patterns and themes from specific areas. Having moved home repeatedly as a child, and then being separated from his mother by divisions in the Austro–Hungarian Empire, Bartók was very interested in the borders between places, and in geography as a determinant; what can be synthesized, and what cannot be bridged. Bartók, who once said, "If I ever crossed myself, it would signify 'In the name of Nature, Art, and Science,'" overheard a folk song, and discovered the native Hungarian Unitarian tradition. Previously an atheist, Bartók appreciated the integrity and diversity he found. Criticized as unpatriotic because of his interest in people with different backgrounds, Bartók dreamed of the "brotherhood of people, brotherhood in spite of all wars and conflicts."[11]

This dream is one common to other Unitarian Universalist musicians, who frequently participate in coffee houses sponsored by their local congregations. It is a folk tradition of protest songs rooted in a vision of social

[10] Richard Lloyd Jones, "An Address to the Friends of Cedar Rock," Quasqueton, IA, October 21, 2006.
[11] Peter Hughes, "Bela Bartók," *Dictionary of Unitarian Universalist and Biography*, see: www25.uua.org/uuhs/duub.

justice. Pete Seeger (b. 1919), whose father helped create the field of eth-nomusicology along with Bartok, sings in support of civil rights, nuclear disarmament, and environmental justice. Several of the songs Seeger pop-ularized, including "God Bless the Grass" and "Little Boxes," were written by Malvina Reynolds (1900–1978), who said, "I have no religion at all except the religion of being people." Later, she added, "I care about chil-dren, and I think the world is ripping them off, taking away their natural environment and much more than that – the natural progression of their tradition – and leaving them stripped, uneasy, uncomfortable, and in deep trouble."

Reynolds gave "singing sermons" and used music to mobilize everyone to work for justice. Denied a high school diploma because her parents thought American involvement in World War I was imperialist, Reynolds traced her troubles back even further, to grammar school: "I had first come to the attention of the principal's office with a premature women's liberation movement on the school grounds. At noon, the boys could leave the grounds . . . to get hot dogs, hamburgers, and pop at the little store across the street. I circulated a petition that the girls be allowed out of the yard at noon also. The answer was no. It wasn't proper for girls to be on the street. [The girls then asked that the boys be restricted, and were told] if the school tried to restrict the boys they'd just climb the fence. Probably in the same situation now, the girls would climb the fence. Then, nothing happened except that quiet, shy me was fingered as a troublemaker."[12]

Folk music in late twentieth-century America functioned somewhat as literature did in England a century earlier. While the Romantic poets asso-ciated with Unitarianism in England expressed reverence for nature and freedom, the women had a more rational, concrete approach, rooted in both personal experience and a very particular faith. This differs from the United States, where the profoundly influential Margaret Fuller and Elizabeth Palmer Peabody were associated with the Transcendentalists, who spoke through periodicals and the lyceums. *The Atlantic Monthly* (founded 1857) promoted an understanding of Unitarianism as the liter-ature of freedom and independence. The religious life depicted became interior and psychological, as in the works of Nathaniel Hawthorne, or sentimental, with Louisa May Alcott. Unitarianism, as it was popularly conceived, shifted from a theological movement to a literary one, with a tenuous church connection and a powerful social position. After the Civil

---

[12] Nancy Schimmel, "Malvina Reynolds," in Vetter, *Notable American Unitarians*.

War, when the publishing center of the United States relocated to New York, this literary Unitarianism became the period in which New England flowered.

British Unitarian women, beginning with Mary Wollstonecraft (1759–1797), and then Anna Barbauld (1743–1825), Harriet Martineau (1802–1876), and Elizabeth Gaskell (1810–1865), examined issues of social justice, particularly the role and rights of women. Wollstonecraft and Barbauld were among the first to write for children; both wrote moral tales but their stories were radical in that the adult characters encouraged children instead of threatening them. Barbauld, daughter of a Presbyterian Dissenting minister and tutor at Warrington Academy, was encouraged to write by Joseph Priestley. Her first works were hymns and poems, and she believed that nature taught trust to those who learned to observe. When the Dissenters were attacked in the 1790s, Barbauld grew more political. She was an abolitionist, and an outspoken opponent of the war against France. She suffered both public vitriol and personal pain. Her husband became mentally ill and violent towards her, before drowning himself in 1809. She did not publish again after 1811.

Harriet Martineau, sister of James, studied in Bristol with Lant Carpenter, whose educational work with the poor clearly influenced her. The deaths of Martineau's father, brother, and fiancé between 1825 and 1826 necessitated an independent income, which she achieved through writing. Martineau was a political writer, disliked by many; but she was widely read and very effective at generating support for anti-slavery work and for women's rights. Her visit to the United States in 1835 and subsequent writing popularized the small abolitionist movement, and influential preachers and poets, especially James Russell Lowell, spoke out against slavery. This turned the tide in the American churches, and rehabilitated the career of Lydia Maria Child, whose 1833 anti-slavery tract had made her unwelcome in many Unitarian churches.

Martineau believed in evolution, and that the process led inexorably to atheism. She combined this theory with a belief in mesmerism, which she had used for healing purposes for her many, significant health problems. In its conception of an elemental unity among all life, subject to magnetic forces, mesmerism shares some background with the Romantics, but literary London did not see this. There were breaks in Martineau's relationships, including the one with her brother, James. She, however, persevered. She translated the works of Auguste Comte, whose philosophy reflected the same belief in organic unity, and learned positivism, which in many ways she had already applied to her own life.

Martineau noted that the law, in its assumption that men supported women financially, had not kept up with reality. Using census data that proved half the women in England worked outside the home, and that more than a third were entirely self-supporting, she advocated for a gender-free basis for wages, and noted the public costs of keeping women poor: asylums were full of maids and governesses, driven mad by lack of sleep, and unable to retire. Elizabeth Gaskell, too, was primarily concerned with the welfare of women. She was very critical of the way factory work determined so many lives. Her biography of Charlotte Bronte helped to legitimize women as professional writers, and to create a larger audience for them. The women in Gaskell's novels were varied, complex, and funny. Quirks of character and differences in values were accepted, and used to explore prejudice. She demonstrated a connection to the land through her language, in the form of dialect and local idioms. Her characters used expressions that tied them to a time and place, preserved in her stories.

In the United States, William Carlos Williams (1883–1963) used idiomatic language to create images of democracy. He did not like allusions to foreign places or high culture, but wrote in rhythmic units that emulated personal speech, forming images of particular people. Williams believed that religious meaning was natural, and continued to be revealed over time, and that it was the job of humanity to help one another see. In his poem *The Pink Church*, Williams invokes the pragmatists and humanists, naming John Dewey, William James, and Alfred North Whitehead, and asks us to consider where authority lies. He paints a picture of the traditional church as allied with the government in refusing to accept change or engage with new ideas. As a physician, Williams relied on science to help him heal patients. In the poem, he used an image of fellow physician Michael Servetus being burned at the stake by church fathers to question exactly what is right: love and inclusion, or the murder of those who see differently. This poem, written during an age of anxiety about communism, cost Williams a Library of Congress honor.

A contemporary of Williams, Conrad Aiken (1889–1973), was the grandson of William Potter, founder of the Free Religious Association. Aiken was musical; his poetry attempted to use language to create the rhythms of music. Aiken was also fascinated by the ordinary, and the interior response to everyday life. His second wife said he was an "undoubted Anglophile, but the history and landscape of Puritan America in his bones created his most distinguished poetry." Aiken called himself a naturalistic humanist, and believed in "the evolution of mind. Devotion to this is all the devotion we need." He always traveled with two volumes of his grandfather's sermons. "What could have been more natural, as I grew older, that in my preoccupations as to the content of the poetry I should turn to the teachings – for they were more teachings than preachings – of my Grandfather? I regard all my work, both verse and prose, as in a way a continuation of his work – the finding of the truth about man, and man's mind, and of man's place in the universe, and the telling of it as accurately and beautifully as such themes deserved."[13]

The body of liberal religionists saw formal traditions as an escape from the divine work of forming connections and being of service. Real religion fostered both, in buildings, stories, and songs; and in protests against artifice and injustice.

[13] Richard Kellaway, "Conrad Aiken," in Vetter, ibid.

CHAPTER 12

Education and social justice

Chalice used by Unitarian Universalist Service Committee

In a Unitarian Universalist setting, "education" is embodied in three distinct ways: congregationally, through religious education programs; association- ally, through theological schools and the credentialing process for clergy and religious educators; and culturally, through an understanding of the purpose and goals of secular education. The irony of a trinity of forms is furthered by the fact that it is the secular understanding of education that has the most effect within the faith, and to which the largest contributions have been made. The reasons for this are varied, being deeply connected to both rational dissent and social reform, and part of the difficulty Unitarian Universalists have had in providing a cogent explanation of exactly what is "religious" about their religious education. Unitarians and Unitarian Universalists have been criticized for believing in "salvation by education"; for practicing social work in place of religious mission; for having little or no religious content in their educational curricula; and for promoting their own religious convictions through public school curricula. It is hard to believe that all these charges could be true, especially simultaneously! However, the small truths in each of these criticisms coalesce to form a deeply engaged, unified faith. The fact that religious education can look secular is not a sign of intellectual disinterest, but an important aspect of the practice of Unitarian Universalism.

As a distinct institution, Sunday Schools were a particular innovation of the Puritans and evangelicals in eighteenth-century Wales and England. These schools promoted literacy through Bible reading, which was essential to the faith of non-conformists. However, during the industrial age, Sunday Schools began reaching out and serving the larger community. This was not a conversion attempt so much as a service rooted in the way these people understood salvation. Their religion demanded that they live out their beliefs; the colloquial expression is "deeds, not creeds." They believed in democracy and literacy. As people moved to mill cities for work, they were without supportive social structures. Urban poverty grew. Joseph Tuckerman (1778–1840), a Unitarian from Chelsea, Massachusetts, helped establish the British Domestic Mission in Liverpool in 1830, by organizing the working classes into congregations. Tuckerman had visited Birmingham and Manchester in 1816, and was deeply disturbed by both the unhealthy conditions and the "preponderance of women and children in the workforce."[1] He concluded that industrialism posed a threat to society because it undermined the family, the determinant of all social relationships. Supporting families became a prime purpose of the church, as did aid to the poor. Within a few decades of the start of the Liverpool Mission, Birmingham, Manchester, London, and Bristol all had missions established by Unitarians who believed that Christianity called them to help redeem the world. Theirs was a progressive Christianity: Darwinism was embraced, as was the historical-critical method of Bible study. Truth was inexorably related to rational education.

This is not to say that there was complete unanimity. For some, supporting those displaced by the economy meant charitable works: providing food, or clothing. Night schools or sewing classes might be offered, as a path to individual betterment. Others challenged the economic order, by preaching and by legal means. Both the American Unitarian Association and the British and Foreign Unitarian Association were founded in 1825, overcoming years of resistance to a formal institutional identity at least partially because the social issues had grown so dire, and the Unitarian understanding of faith compelled action. Character developed through action based upon theology. Religious education both offered information,

---

[1] Howard Wach, "Unitarian philanthropy and cultural hegemony in comparative perspective: Manchester and Boston, 1827–1848," *Journal of Social History*, Vol. 26, No. 3, Spring 1993 (Fairfax, VA: George Mason University Press), p. 541.

or access to it, and worked to build the Kingdom of Heaven that Jesus so fervently promoted. Neither faith nor education could be limited to the church building itself, or to an hour or two on Sundays. Back in Boston, the American Unitarian Association (AUA) authorized Tuckerman to begin a Ministry to the Poor, to combat the forces of manufacturing which left children without education and women in compromised circumstances. Tuckerman's ministry was through the Benevolent Fraternity of Unitarian Churches, in which delegates from a collection of congregations in and around Boston supported services to the poor. This mission is now called the Unitarian Universalist Urban Ministry (UUUM), and it provides after-school tutoring, summer and weekend youth-enrichment programs, a shelter for victims of domestic violence, and a food pantry specifically catering to the dietary needs of the Asian poor and elderly. The sixty member congregations of the UUUM support this ministry by volunteering as tutors, donating food and goods, hosting and attending fundraisers, and providing specialized help to the professional staff.

In England, new congregations had formed in the industrial centers, with membership reflecting the mill-working population. Slowly, a tension between sectarians and those who wanted no denominational affiliation developed, a tension that still echoes in debates about Unitarian Universalist identity, service projects, and the composition of congregations. The Dissenters' Academy at Warrington, which had begun in 1753 and served the non-conformists who were not allowed to attend British schools – with leadership from John Aiken, Joseph Priestley, and Gilbert Wakefield – was dissolved in 1786 because of conflict over the principles of education. By the late eighteenth century, Warrington had become an industrial center, manufacturing wire. The rivers were widened and canals built to support shipping. At the time the Academy was dissolved, the US had successfully revolted from British rule, and the French Revolution was under way; both causes were on the side of freedom and reason, and were supported by radical Unitarians like Priestley and Wakefield. Warrington's successor school was Manchester Academy, which, beginning in 1803, was headed by principals who refused to use the name "Unitarian." It was limiting and sectarian, according to Charles Wellbeloved and James Martineau, who promoted the use of the term "Free Christian." The academy, later a college, moved to York, then back to Manchester, and then to London in 1853. At that point, John Relly Beard (1800–1876) and William Gaskell (1805–1884) started the Unitarian Home Missionary Board. This project, like Manchester College, was dedicated to furthering liberal education in religion. But it was diametrically opposed to Manchester College's non-sectarian approach. The name "Unitarian" was claimed and advertised, as was the word "mission." The program was specifically designed to be practical for those who had little or no money or classical education, to meet the needs of ordinary people. In 1889, when Manchester College moved to Oxford, the Unitarian Home Missionary Board changed its name and, by 1925, had become the Unitarian College, Manchester. This school houses the records of the many Dissenters' Academies, and it remains explicitly committed to preparing Unitarian and non-subscribing Presbyterian ministers, whose Belfast training site closed at the end of the nineteenth century. Romanian and Hungarian Unitarians are part of the Unitarian College as well. Meanwhile, Harris Manchester College, as it is now known, has been a full college of Oxford since 1996, and is also home to the Farmington Institute for Christian Studies. This institute trains teachers of religious education in an ecumenical Christian environment, promoting relationships with other world religions.

This debate about sectarianism was also about class, and the role education played in creating and challenging a social order. The non-sectarians (Free Christians) were less interested in change, and desired acceptance, or a degree of social status that had eluded Unitarians. Non-conformist was a theological term with enormous negative social weight. Progress for the non-sectarians, then, came in the form of expansion of personal freedoms and rights, and associations with leaders of other established religions. This meant that women were able to be clergy. (In 1901, Manchester College, Oxford, became the first academic institution in Great Britain to accept a woman as a candidate for the ministry.) The increased liberties for nonconformists meant that individuals who did not subscribe to the 39 Articles of Faith could obtain a university degree, which avowed Unitarians could not. Parliament could have members with liberal theologies, who would then help press for a sympathetic agenda, especially for businesses in which Unitarians had interests. Education served individual goals within the existing social order. By contrast, those who claimed the name "Unitarian" saw the social demands of faith as preceding any personal goals. Education was both a way of living their faith and a method of changing society to be more like the one beloved community, or the kingdom of peace and justice that true Christians desired. This meant that education was not social work in which a privileged class acted upon the less advantaged. It was religious education, based on a vision of unity, or universal salvation. The debate over sectarianism obscured conflicting visions of education. Theology alone does not explain the differences. A current example of this issue exists in capitalist principles of investing. In the late twentieth century, the Unitarian Universalist Association (UUA) began promoting Socially Responsible Investing, since renamed by some as Socially Screened Investing. Member congregations were urged to put their funds in companies that practiced values affirmed by liberals. This might mean not investing in corporations involved in the manufacture of weaponry, or toxic chemicals, or those that employ children. Promoting these principles by acting on the beliefs was more important than the amount of revenue generated. Yet the UUA did not entirely invest its own funds this way. Even though the UUA was providing resources and educational material that encouraged placing social values before money, their own mission remained achieving economic, rather than theological, security.

The "Ragged School" movement in mid-nineteenth-century Britain provides a different example. In the 1830s, John Pounds (1766–1839) began taking the "destitute pupils from his Portsmouth carpenter's shop to the Unitarian Church in High Street because it was the only one which made them feel welcome. Unitarians supported, publicized, and extended his work."[2] Mary Carpenter (1807–1877), who, with Harriet and James Martineau, had attended a Bristol school run by her father, the minister Lant Carpenter (1780–1840), was inspired by Pounds and by Joseph Tuckerman. She had been working to provide education for girls both in England and in India, but, in 1846, she began a school for poor children in Bristol, England. Following the original Sunday Schools, Carpenter intended to teach pupils to read the Bible and understand its truths, but her programs were offered at night, so the working poor might attend. She also tried to change home conditions in ways that might help the students achieve. In a letter, Carpenter stated: "none have shoes or stockings, some have no shirt, and no home, sleeping in cases on the quay or on steps, and living, I suppose, by petty depredations; but all appear better fed than the children of the decent poor are. I have furnished the women of the house with towels and soap, and some sort of approach to cleanliness is insisted upon."[3] Soon a Ragged School Union was formed, to establish "Schools expressly for that destitute and depraved class, in the very localities, courts, and alleys where they abound."[4] These schools were sectarian projects

---

[2] Ruth Watts, *Gender, Power and the Unitarians in England, 1760–1860* (London, UK: Longman, 1998), p. 175.

[3] Jean S. Heywood, *Children in Care: The Development of Services for the Deprived Child* (London, UK: Routledge and Kegan Paul, 1959, 1998, 2001), p. 41.

[4] Mark K. Smith, "Mary Carpenter, Reformatory Schools and Education," *The Encyclopedia of Informal Education*, www.infed.org/thinkers/carpenter.htm. Last update: September 3, 2009.

of a variety of denominations, and they ended up countermanding the Unitarian premise of education. By the 1860s, with approximately 25,000 students enrolled, a movement began among the upper class to send these children to Australia and Canada. This forced migration was intended to provide labor in colonies where it was needed, and to reduce the economic burden that these children represented in England. Additionally, there was the hope that the move represented an opportunity for the children themselves.

Carpenter did not participate. Instead, she expanded her work, organizing industrial schools, and then reforming the penal codes so that fewer poor youth would end up imprisoned. Next, she established reformatories, providing education to those who were incarcerated. Dorothea Dix (1802–1887), an American Unitarian and teacher, had been doing similar work in the US since 1841. Recently returned from a year in Liverpool, Dix taught a Sunday School class in prison, which led her to question conditions and ultimately to a compilation of statistics related to the imprisonment of those with mental-health issues. Her work was used to lobby effectively for reform and treatment. Both Dix and Carpenter rejected the fixed social order that defined charity as removing children from a class system in which they would always lose. Both women challenged the system: they did not believe that the future would inevitably look like the present, or that progress could only be achieved by individuals. Instead of working at acceptance without threatening those in power, Carpenter promoted legal rights that would change the social order. This meant claiming the name and the rights of Unitarians, as well as those of other marginalized people.

Even though this desire to change society was heartfelt and derived from a faithful vision, it was also self-serving. Carpenter's respect for the possibilities of her students was not what multi-culturalism looks like in the current century. England's educational system relied on voluntary denominational schools that refused to admit Unitarians and Catholics. Until 1870, widespread general education had been rejected as both too expensive and likely to create dissatisfaction on the part of manual laborers, so those who were excluded from the voluntary schools had no option but to either provide their own education, or forego it altogether. Unitarians could, and did, begin Academies, such as the one at Warrington or Lant Carpenter's Bristol school, to serve their families. Mary Carpenter's schools served Catholics who were too poor to attend private Catholic schools. These were almost all Irish immigrants, and in starting this school, Carpenter was critiquing not only the British social order, but the Catholic system as well. She believed that the Catholic culture destroyed opportunities for children. Clan loyalty and tradition sacrificed the future in favor of playing and festivals. They were not working towards better lives.[5] Carpenter saw this behavior as existence, rather than a well-ordered life. Her values of conscience and self-determination seemed impossible to reconcile with loyalty to the pope or any figure that replaced the role of reason. Her objection to Catholicism was not only the rote memorization of creeds in the place of developing the mind; she also objected to the social dimension, which she perceived as a community holding back its members and thwarting progress. Carpenter did not understand the positive attributes of the culture: security, acceptance, guidance, and joy that were not predicated on status or achievement. As a teacher, Carpenter was child-centered and believed that children learned best when they were happy. But her understanding of happiness remained a Protestant one, contingent upon individual growth.

Universalists in the United States occupied a position very much like the Unitarians in England. As Christians who stood outside the prevailing definition of Christianity, and believers in science and historical critical method, Universalists too experienced rejection which was internalized by some, and defended against by others. The Unitarians in the US had issues similar to those of the British, but there was an essential difference. Unitarianism was the belief system of the ruling class in Boston and at Harvard. Therefore, the religion had historical status. Worship and social action, especially action challenging the social order and its economic basis, were as distinct from one another in Boston as they were for the British Free Christians. But throughout the nineteenth century, that separation was challenged in New England. There were many reasons for this: the growth of Unitarian congregations in other parts of the country, the disestablishment of the state church in Massachusetts, and evangelical movements. But the largest reason was the Civil War. Faith required action. Despite the fact that Unitarians and Universalists lived on both sides of the Mason–Dixon line, the Civil War was strongly supported and took on aspects of a holy war for Boston Unitarianism.[6] A decade before, many had been anti-war: In 1850, the American Peace Society, which evolved from the Unitarian Peace Society founded by Ezra Stiles Gannett in 1816, published a book by Abiel Livermore (1811–1892), which argued that education was the road to

[5] Madge Dresser, "Beyond the pale? Mary Carpenter and the Irish poor in mid-Victorian Bristol" *History in Focus*, Issue 11: Migration (Autumn, 2006), www.history.ac.uk/ihr/Focus/Migration/articles/dresser.html#1. Accessed July 10, 2010.

[6] W. Edward Harris, "Some Unitarian Universalist Responses to War," *Selected Essays*, ed., Nancy Miller (USA: Unitarian Universalist Ministers Association, 1992), p. 67.

peace.[7] Having been trained to fight by a society that cultivates war for profit, humanity needed to be willing to re-educate itself into a new way of living. Church should teach people that peace is honorable, and help challenge a culture that celebrates violence in myriad ways: music, parades, classic stories, social pressure. This belief about the power of education remained central to liberal religion, even while the Civil War became a galvanizing force within the denomination. Justice, glory, honor, and action were celebrated, and war became a means of achieving a better peace. Unitarians were "in the government, the army, and the public health activity of the Sanitary Commission; leading black regiments, starting the Freedman's Bureau, buying bonds and praying for victory. This was not merely a Just War to free the slaves . . . it would save the soul of the nation . . . (and) assure free trade, education . . . and prosperity."[8] This confluence of sacred and secular motives made action the only possible response. Families of Unitarians moved from New England to help settle Kansas as a free state. Christian duty, which had been open to different interpretations both within and without the denomination, now meant acting in order to bring about the kingdom; and Harvard College established a curriculum to do so. Even though huge theological debates and schisms defined American Unitarianism in the late nineteenth century, the direction the denomination would take was already established. The vision of unity and social salvation would come from academia rather than the church.

Understanding the role that the Civil War played in the development of non-sectarian education requires a step back to the Reformation, when universities shifted from an existence based solely on the promotion of religion to one which relied upon their capacity to become intellectual centers. As each Western nation adopted a state religion, its schools promoted that truth. The original purpose of the university was to serve society through the scholarship and unified vision of the one true church. In a post-Reformation, industrializing culture, arguments about what it meant to be socially useful changed along with the religious truth, and in some parts of Europe, particularly Germany and later Italy, the schools were secularized as education became increasingly practical. Universities needed to meet the utilitarian concerns of the society. The German idealist movement, which so deeply affected the English Romantic poets and the American Transcendentalists, was a response to both the transfer of control from ecclesiastical to civil authority, and the notion of social utility. The idealists thought that universities could improve society by creating a class of learned men. Students would simply be allowed to develop their minds,

---

[7] Harris, "Some Unitarian Universalist Responses," p. 64.   [8] Harris, ibid., pp. 66–67.

and the presence of these educated people would naturally mean progress for the whole society. In this scenario, education replaced the role of religion both socially and in the university. Instead of being instrumental in serving the external, socially defined needs of the industrial marketplace, German idealism placed more value on the arts, and self-culture, or existential needs.

In England, this vision of personal development existed without the secularization. The Romantics adopted idealism, but Christianized it and thus kept the universities closed to Unitarians and other Dissenters, and changed the cultural understanding of education. The fusion of Anglican Christianity with a civil program of progress transformed education from the static imparting of facts and doctrine into a process of growth. A better society became contingent upon access to schools, and education began to represent hope – for individuals and for a culture. Ultimately, the blending of Idealism and Christianity engendered the academic field of social ethics, and started the ecumenical movement. Universal public education grew from these developments, as did core liberal arts curricula. The relationship of information to character development, and the ultimate purpose of education, are issues arising from this period. Does a teacher transfer knowledge or encourage personal development? Does education serve the needs of the individual or of the society? Is education in and of itself religious?

Charles Eliot (1834–1926) became president of Harvard in 1869, and brought to the US the changes effected in European universities a century before. Harvard was at this point still a college; under Eliot it became a university. He promoted a non-sectarian education, with practical instruction that would serve the economic needs of the country. Eliot, a science teacher, synthesized tradition with modern disciplines of science and a very strong belief in freedom. This threatened what had been a stable, classical approach, by replacing a required curriculum with many opportunities for choice. Eliot believed that intellectual, spiritual, moral, and economic growth all relied on liberty. A uniform approach stifled both personal growth and communal development. The nurture and support of an individual's innate talents was key to social progress. Part of being non-sectarian meant that chapel requirements were abolished. There were still services, and the University Preacher was still a Unitarian, but attendance was not mandatory. Eliot was convinced that beliefs were inculcated by action. His attempts to ban football from Harvard because of its brutality have been repeated over the years; more telling was his response to baseball, when he came to understand curve balls: "Surely we do not encourage this game, comprised of an element whose sole purpose is to deceive?" Many people believed that what Eliot called non-sectarian was, in fact, Unitarian education, and some Unitarians believed Eliot had robbed students of their own heritage.[9] There was no longer one canon, one common core other than the principle of freedom. This principle, educationally, translated to a lack of requirements.

It was one thing to reform the curriculum to reflect the principles of evolution. It was another to recreate the Divinity School, which had shrunk considerably between 1840 and 1880. In order for Harvard to grow into a genuine university, Eliot believed the Divinity School needed to be strong. Among the faculty he appointed was his brother-in-law, Francis Greenwood Peabody (1847–1936), who transformed the field of ethics from a Christian tradition to a social science. Social ethics allowed for observation and factual description of conditions, a goal that represented an improvement in those conditions, and advocacy for programs that would achieve those goals. This academic field was responsible for the profoundly influential Social Gospel movement, which brought together all manner of Protestants in a way no other movement had done before or since.

Just as the Civil War had brought Unitarians and Universalists together, in support for action towards what was seen as a religious goal, the rapid growth in population and the economic disparity that developed in the decades after the Civil War required a practical response. Leaders of industrial unions publicly faulted the churches for not helping the poor off whose backs the country was becoming increasingly productive. Christianity had no defense. Settlement houses and service programs might help suffering individuals, but they did nothing to create the necessary changes to the culture at large. An ethical response based in social sciences could advance a progressive agenda[10] without directly attacking the most successful practitioners of capitalism, many of whom were funding large new church buildings. The Federal Council of Churches, formed in 1908, spread the idea that the economic system was intended to evolve past this stage of *laissez-faire* capitalism. A network of denominations rejected Social Darwinism as unethical, while embracing Darwinism and scientific method. Despite different religious doctrines, there was enormous agreement about social justice, which was predicated on economic justice.

---

[9] Stephen Shoemaker, "The Theological Roots of Charles W. Eliot's Educational Reforms," *Journal of Unitarian Universalist History*, 2006–2007, Vol. 31, p. 36.

[10] Gary Dorrien, "Social Ethics for Social Justice: Renewing an Ecumenical Tradition," A Talk before the annual General Assembly of the National Council of Churches and Church World Service, Denver, CO, November 11, 2008.

The Social Gospel was a middle-class ideal, and implicitly Christian. Peabody's principal book was titled *Jesus Christ and the Social Question*. It was a movement that captured the tension between accommodating the culture one lives in, and rejecting that culture based upon deeply held principles. In the US, as in Birmingham and Manchester in England, there were Unitarians on both sides. Generally, those with wealth, especially wealth derived from mill and factory interests, accommodated, while those without, challenged the culture they lived in. The Social Gospel movement, with its basis in ethics and academia, held the sides together until the 1930s. It re-established an essentially pacifist ethic, allowing the Christian non-resistance of Adin Ballou (1803–1890) to spread in a new generation. The identification with Gandhi on the part of Christian clergy in the 1920s can be attributed to the Social Gospel, as can Martin Luther King Jr.'s ability to reach across the color divide. But the Social Gospel movement is also the source of a paralyzing double bind for Unitarians. Establishing scientific standards with which to critique social programs sacrificed the moral status of the church. Work rooted in the academy repudiated the personal motivation of faith after the state of Tennessee put a biology teacher named John Scopes on trial for teaching evolution in 1925. In the wake of this trial, a fundamentalist Christian movement grew in the US. By the end of the 1920s, fundamentalism had divided the Protestant churches, and pushed Unitarianism closer to the academy. Much of the humanist–theist debate arose from this division in the Social Gospel movement, as one group minimized theology in favor of action, while the other made theology more central to its mission.

Education performed the critical function of promoting progress while also acting as a tool for assimilation. Charles Eliot's son, Samuel, became the executive secretary of the American Unitarian Association (AUA) in 1898, and president in 1900. He soon established a Department of Religious Education. Beginning in 1909, the Beacon series, a twelve-volume, graded curriculum[11] with a "wide range of topics and much extra-biblical material" was available. The One Topic, Three Graded Series covered seven topics in five years, and, "All except the last year are Bible lessons, and are based upon the modern viewpoint."[12] The ecumenical Religious Education Association Journal noted, in 1914, that the AUA was preparing an entirely new and

---

[11] David B. Parke, "Liberals and Liberalism Since 1900," *The Proceedings of the Unitarian Historical Society*, Vol. 15, Part 1 (1964), pp. 1–25.

[12] *Journal of Religious Education Association*, Vol. IX. February 1914 – December 1914 (Chicago, IL: Religious Educators Association, 1914), p. 200.

completely graded series, but it would be 1937 before the first of that New Beacon series saw print. This was the year that Frederick May Eliot, a distant cousin of Samuel A. Eliot, was elected president of the AUA, and growth for the denomination began again in America.

Eliot brought Ernest Kuebler (1903–1992) to the AUA as Director of the Religious Education Department, and Frances Wood (1903–1975) as the Field Secretary. Eliot brought with him the strong family commitment to non-sectarian education: his grandfather and uncle, both Unitarian ministers, founded Washington University in St. Louis, and Reed College in Oregon, respectively. The team that Kuebler and Wood assembled were progressive and diverse: Unitarian, Universalist, Congregational, and Presbyterian. They planned the New Beacon series, and professionalized the field of religious education. The Liberal Religious Educators Association (LREDA) was organized to advance the cause and encourage high standards. LREDA continues to this day, promoting both religious education and lifelong learning among the professionals. Sophia Lyon Fahs (1876–1978) was contracted to edit the curriculum. Fahs, born and raised in China to missionary parents, ended up editing, writing, or co-writing the fifteen books of the series over the next twenty years. She was 61 and a committed Methodist who believed in both the Social Gospel and in progressive education when she began her work, and she was especially interested in democracy and its capacity to transform people. The methodology in Fahs' curricula included scientific observation and the use of imagination.

The church school curricula that Fahs and Dorothy Spoerl (1906–1999) produced were the first to genuinely represent the revolution that occurred in the broader world of education a century earlier. In the late nineteenth century, church schools remained centered on rote learning, while day schools based on progressive ideals and service-oriented missions had become the primary exponents of religious values. These schools, governed early on by Unitarians such as Bronson Alcott, Elizabeth Palmer Peabody, and the Lloyd Jones family, were open to all and used liberal, creative methods, and were slowly replaced by the public school movement championed by Horace Mann (1796–1859). In England, John Relly Beard worked towards universal education as well, making the Dissenters' Academies less important. The New Beacon series brought this history together, with idealism and rigor in church school education. Teachers were to be professionally and scientifically trained to promote the religious goal of human development. Religious literacy was only part of what it meant to be fully human.

Fahs, who became a Unitarian, has been called the primary exponent of process theology in the twentieth century,[13] and is often considered to be a humanist, but understanding her faith requires the context of the Social Gospel movement. The humanism she believed in was an embrace of the social ethic of service to others, which was a way of acquainting oneself first-hand with deity. Human beings must do the work of caring for one another and for creation. Whether this work is done in God's name, or Allah's, or Buddha's, or Krishna's, or done because there is no God, is irrelevant as long as the work is done. For Fahs, it was in fact Christianity that led her to this position, and she never gave up her belief that the Bible was central to religious development. She remained frustrated that so many congregations ceased to offer religious education at the age when children were developmentally ready to study the Bible in depth. However, religious development led beyond the Bible alone. Encounters with people of other faiths or those who had different experiences of the world required that we explore fundamental human questions, and understand religion as responses to those questions. How did life begin? What happens when we die? What do we owe each other? How do the scriptures of one culture compare with those of another? Why might they differ in some ways, and be the same in others? There was no debate about the truth of Christianity, or of any particular faith. Instead, these curricula asked how to know if something is true, and what our responsibilities to truth might be. Is truth inherited or discovered? How is it embodied? Can people who do not agree on meaning still love one another and the world they share? These curricula were enormously popular after World War II. Inter-faith understanding seemed integral to world peace and global security, and human questioning in a manner which respected both science and the human role of compassion could help citizens come to terms with what had happened in our world. A global economy ended up requiring a global morality. Those who had embraced pacifism after World War I struggled profoundly when they realized that genocide was being practiced during World War II. A re-evaluation of beliefs about human nature, progress, the existence of God, and the necessity of action was required: Am I my brother's keeper? Many Unitarians and Universalists championed the formation of the United Nations, and regularly celebrated its mission in church. British Unitarians were instrumental in the growth of the "Ban

---

[13] Robert B. Tapp, "The Unitarian Universalists: Style and Substance," *Christian Century* (March 14, 1979), p. 274.

the Bomb" movement,[14] and its export to the US, where it morphed into general peace work and anti-nuclear activity.

Some degree of peace work has come under the purview of the Unitarian Universalist Service Committee, which grew in response to fascism in Europe that was threatening the Czech Unitarians. Martha and Waitstill Sharp left the US to assist in Czechoslovakia in 1938, and after providing relief aid and rescuing individuals, the Service Committee was organized in 1940 to "investigate opportunities for humanitarian service both in America and abroad."[15] Although they escorted many children to England, the Sharps and their colleagues were not able to save the Czech leader. Using his sermons as evidence of treason, the Gestapo soon arrested Norbert Capek (1870–1942), the founding minister of Unitaria in Prague, along with his daughter Zora. Capek was killed with poison gas in 1942, while Zora was sent to forced labor in Germany. The Unitarian Service Committee worked primarily in Marseilles, operating a medical clinic; and in Lisbon after the war, managing casework for refugees. The operations expanded from 1944 onwards, and by 1948 there were sixty projects in fifteen countries, providing relief and medical services of all kinds. At that point, the financial condition of the Service Committee caused divisions, and the decision was made to become independent of the American Unitarian Assocation. The Universalist Service Committee, organized in 1945, provided summer work camps for those traumatized by war. In the 1950s, the specific focus on war-related issues receded, and work focused instead on collaboration with indigenous cultures: teacher training in Cambodia, a community center in New Mexico, and the Jordan House in Virginia. The two committees – the Unitarian Service Committee and the Universalist Service Committee – merged in 1963, and, as the Unitarian Universalist Service Committee (UUSC), have had an important role in third-world development, through medical advances, fact-finding missions for congressional delegations, and the establishment of food co-operatives and job-training centers. Humanitarian aid is sometimes direct; at other times it involves empowering others to speak for themselves, defend themselves, and work for peace.

Unitarians and Universalists had long had leaders and members who were advocates for peace, including Nobel Peace Prize winners Emily

---

[14] Paul Rasor, "Beyond Just War and Pacifism: Toward a Unitarian Universalist Theology of Prophetic Nonviolence." *The Journal of Liberal Religion.* Vol. 8, No. 1 (Chicago, IL: Meadville Lombard, 2008) www.meadville.edu/journal/LL_JLR_v8_n1_Rasor.pdf. Accessed July 29, 2010.

[15] Mark Harris, *The A to Z of Unitarian Universalism* (Lanham, MD: Scarecrow Press, 2009), p. 489.

Green Balch (1867–1961) and Linus Pauling (1901–1994). A study resolution undertaken by vote of the 2006 General Assembly of the Unitarian
Universalist Association had congregations examining whether or not Unitarian Universalism should affirm a statement about the role of the church
in creating peace. A current Unitarian Universalist, Amber Amundson (b.
1973), is a co-founder of the September Eleventh Families for Peaceful
Tomorrows. She asked that President George Bush not use her husband's
death at the Pentagon as an excuse to perpetuate violence; writing that
he drove to work there in a car with the bumper sticker "Visualize World
Peace," and he was buried with an American flag draped over his coffin,
which their two small children believe represents him. She did not want
that flag used as a banner for war. But historically, the commitment to
peace, among Unitarians especially, has relied on conscience and the use of
reason more than principles of non-violence. This stance made it possible
to support individuals who differed in their perspectives, and it embraced
the principle of growth. But it has also created some disingenuous institutional revisionism. Clergy whose consciences demanded pacifism were
marginalized, only later to be lionized as heroic. This was also true of
activists for civil rights. The right of conscience and use of democratic
process can prohibit effective corporate action, yet still foster an institution
that does present as somewhat unified and not particularly interested in
dissent. This has been true since the beginning, when the founding of
the American Unitarian Association in Boston reflected a fear of Southern
power by defining Unitarianism as a New England institution; and it was
true during Samuel Eliot's presidency, which supported imperialism over
human rights. But since the late 1960s, this tendency to stifle dissent at the
Association level has grown.

This is a legacy of Vietnam. The conflict, coming at a time of distrust
and transition in leadership, financial distress, and enormous racial controversy, transformed Unitarian Universalist congregations. Their leadership
was fairly united in its opposition to US military involvement in Vietnam.
Programs to support registration as conscientious objectors were developed. Draft cards were burned in sanctuaries, draft dodgers were hidden
in parsonages, and a modern underground railroad developed. The Unitarian Universalist Association (UUA) President, Robert West, made the
decision to publish the Pentagon Papers, maintaining a belief in the power
of education to reveal the truth, and for truth to foster moral action. The
Pentagon Papers exposed the manipulation used to get Americans involved
in Vietnam, and undermined trust in the government. But this development marked a change in the church. The seemingly unilateral response

to Vietnam made Unitarian Universalism appear increasingly liberal and activist, and drove away members in the military as well as those whose politics differed. The religious nature of response and witness to political events was not always clear, and the constant discussion of current issues diminished Unitarian Universalism's stature as a church, offering sanctuary, comfort, wisdom, and beauty.

The curricula developed in that era also demonstrated this divide. The New Beacon series was used throughout the 1960s, but the centralized approach to education faltered in the 1970s. The dire financial state of the UUA, in which groups were competing for financial support, combined with cultural changes, challenged standardized approaches to education, and undermined the basic theological premise of unity contained within the New Beacon series. The new curricula were multi-media kits that focused on social issues and personal growth. Although many of these kits were excellent, they were independent of one another, and did not form a unified curriculum in which children moved steadily through a body of material. The kits were expensive, required projectors, and represented a significant purchase for congregations that were struggling; and the rapid changes in technology could quickly make the kits seem dated. Nevertheless, some, like *The Adventures of God's Folk*, in which children build the ark for the Torah scrolls and link biblical characters with big ideas and amazing achievements to folk heroes like Mike Fink, are still in use. *Haunting House*, which explores the meaning of home, has been re-invented as *Creating Home*.

During the 1970s, divorce rates in the US soared, which created the need for both supportive environments and for programs that were not contingent upon consistent attendance, as custody arrangements between parents residing at a distance from one another often intervened. It was also during this period that liberation movements – for people of color, for women, and for homosexuals – became an enormous part of Unitarian Universalist identity. This was part of what led to a time of separation in the 1980s and 1990s, in which ministers were divided into groups: Community-based, Religious Educators, and Parish. The three have since become one again. Those years represent a nadir in religious education itself: Remarkably few curricula were published by the UUA from the 1980s through the beginning of the twenty-first century. Although this led to much creativity and innovation on the part of religious educators throughout the denomination, who assembled their own curricula and made them available to others, the lack of common denominational material represents a loss as well. A whole generation will not have the benefit of the experience of older Unitarian

Universalists who grew up in the faith, often recognizing each other as kindred spirits who share an inquisitive and independent outlook developed from the approach to religious education. People from different parts of the American continent all remember the Beacon curricula stories of Martin and Judy, or science experiments resulting in live baby chicks in the classroom, or visits to the church across the street. This common experience matters because the number of Unitarian Universalists is so small, and the philosophy of education is so different from traditional religious schools.

There has often been a social cost to growing up as a Unitarian Universalist, with prejudice against members of a congregation viewed as agitators and agents of cultural change. This became particularly intense in the South during the 1960s and 1970s, when Unitarian Universalist children in public schools and sports programs were vulnerable to ostracism based on their association with the church. Children therefore experienced the limits of the freedom and self-determination being taught in church in a way adult converts might not have done. The general assumption is that Unitarian Universalism is a chosen faith; one that adults discover after a process of rejecting or being rejected by a more traditional religion. This norm simultaneously elevates and isolates multi-generational Unitarian Universalist families, who are typically not planned for in programming. Finding others who grew up in this faith and have stayed with it can be a form of homecoming; of finding the tribe one belongs to even while the larger message is against tribalism. Issues of race and diversity continue to challenge the denomination, as does youth work. Young people's groups for both Unitarians and Universalists were strong from the beginning of the twentieth century onwards. Religiously identified social groups existed under various names, and merged in 1953 to become Liberal Religious Youth (LRY). In 1981, after years of controversy over the philosophies of leadership and empowerment, LRY ceased to exist, and Young Religious Unitarian Universalists began, with a model that included more adult leadership and supervision. In 2005, the Unitarian Universalist Association (UUA) cut the budget for the youth newsletter, and in 2008 ceased all support for youth programs.

Meanwhile, identity-based movements have continued to be represented at institutional and programmatic levels: advocacy for gay, lesbian, bisexual, and transgender persons, and for their right to marry, have had high profiles. The Welcoming Congregation program, begun in 1989, provides materials to help congregations both assess themselves and to better advocate for inclusion. As of 2009, just over 61 percent of Unitarian Universalist congregations in the US had completed the Welcoming Congregation program. In Canada, 99 percent had achieved that status. A program called Living the Welcoming Congregation has been developed, to help continue the work. These programs are under the purview of the Office of Bisexual, Gay, Lesbian and Transgender Concerns (BGLT), not Religious Education. Standing on the Side of Love is a newer program, developed to help Unitarian Universalists respond to identity-based violence, and administered through the UUA Department of Social Justice. This program has been instrumental in advocacy for same-sex marriage, but came about after a tragic incident in 2008, in which a man with a shotgun and a hatred for the liberal values espoused by Unitarian Universalists, entered a service at the Tennessee Valley UU Church and proceeded to open fire, killing two parishioners.

In the US, one of the primary reasons people begin attending a Unitarian Universalist congregation is in order to give their children a religious education. This is not true in England, where the existence of a state religion means that children have some degree of religious instruction during the regular school day. The British congregations carry out special programs, but generally not whole curricula. The goals, however, are the same: to encourage growth, creativity, and a free sense of inquiry and reverence about the natural world, and to pass on stories about our religious inheritance. Other countries with a Unitarian presence have fewer specific children's programs. In Transylvania, religious education teaches a catechism and ends in confirmation. In India, as in Transylvania, the Unitarian faith is highly familial. This means the assumption is that a child simply is and will remain a Unitarian. Educational efforts tend to take the form of social service, offering non-sectarian pre-schools and opportunities for those who are underserved in the social order. As in Britain, there are more national events in Transylvania: conferences, youth programs, women's meetings, and social events. These are an important source of energy and companionship.

One of the issues involved in the 2002 separation of the Canadian Unitarian Council from the Unitarian Universalist Association was the longstanding need for education materials reflecting a Canadian heritage and audience, and there are now some specifically Canadian curricula, which include earth-based spirituality and a social justice program for young people. However, the practice and programming for religious education in the US and Canada remain very similar. A Director or Minister of Religious Education is responsible for organizing the program, while volunteers from the congregation implement it. Directors of Religious Education vary in their backgrounds and in the amount of training they have. Although Meadville Lombard, one of the two denominationally affiliated schools in the US, opened the Fahs Center for Religious Education in 1993, and later named a Professorship in Religious Education in honor of the Universalist Dean at St. Lawrence, Angus MacLean (1892–1969), there has not been a tremendous concentration of denominational energy in this field. The Fahs Center is a valuable research site for historians, and has offered a few continuing education courses, but its future is uncertain as Meadville Lombard has put its campus up for sale and is in the process of affiliating with Andover Newton Theological School, in Massachusetts. Most support for religious educators happens at the District (US) or Region (Canada) level. Consultants visit congregations which are seeking assistance with education, and the Districts and Regions provide continuing education for professional development in the form of Renaissance Modules. Congregations or Unitarian Universalist camps host these weekend courses, while the Region or District provides the co-ordination, registration, and publicity. These classes can lead to certification, granted through a committee of the Unitarian Universalist Association (UUA) Board. Canadian religious educators are allowed, for a fee, to participate in the credentialing process. Clergy, who have been trained at many different schools, are credentialed via a process overseen by the Ministerial Fellowship Committee.

Although there is enormous variety between congregations, religious education in the US and Canada is likely to be based on a spiraling curriculum, in which a few themes are repeatedly visited with increasing levels of complexity, from pre-school through age 15. These themes, broadly defined, are Unitarian Universalist identity, world religions, and Jewish and Christian heritage. Social justice, personal growth, and responsible decision-making are woven into these themes, and also form some stand-alone units. Classes are almost always concurrent with the worship services, so children start with their families, leave for a 45-minute class, and rejoin their families for social hour. The strong tradition of progressive education led to both multiculturalism and an interest in meeting special needs through multi-sensory exploration and activities. Children may be cooking, doing pottery and crafts, planting gardens, or performing in plays; or they may be in classrooms with stories and lessons. Two things determine a Religious Education program more than anything: the size and the "feel" of a congregation. Settings with many children tend to have closely graded groups in which progress through topics from year to year is reliable; smaller congregations may have more of a "one-room schoolhouse" approach, and base the programming on who is attending. The emphasis on drama, art, and advocacy or public witness in a religious education program can be associated with the institution, or with the people who happen to be running the program. Christian congregations focus on curricula in that theological tradition, while some humanist congregations may avoid teaching the Bible at all. Other humanist or theologically diverse congregations include Christianity in the same way as they do all world religions. This diversity is in style more than substance: the nuances and emphases may be strongly perceived within the denomination, but are not generally seen as significant by others. Jews, Muslims, Buddhists, and Hindus tend to categorize Unitarian Universalists as vaguely Christian, while Christians view Unitarian Universalism as secular. There was a period in the 1960s during which the stories from the Hebrew Scriptures were watered down to reflect a liberal belief in the goodness of human nature. The violence was made less physical and gory details were omitted. Most clergy and educators have since grown to believe that it is not helpful to minimize the struggles in life. There have been, and continue to be, real battles, and religious faith requires that we develop the emotional capacity to cope, the intellectual ability to understand, and the moral courage to act.

One of the most frequently used curricula today is *Our Whole Lives*, a comprehensive sexuality education program that dates from 1971, when it was created as *About Your Sexuality*, in partnership with the United Church of Christ. Originally a program for youth, it now runs from age 5 through adult. Popular both within and outside the denomination, this program has been a bellwether: though successful by all measures, it marks the beginning of noticeable concerns about identity and about religion, *per se*, in religious education. One response to this concern was a decision in 1986 that all UUA-produced curricula would explicitly support the Principles and Purposes. Not all religious professionals have found this helpful. Concerns about creedalism have developed, as has serious concern about the lack of theological content and depth that occurs when a statement of Principles and Purposes, which were simply part of the UUA bylaws, becomes a limiting factor in curriculum development.[16] A desire to inculcate Unitarian Universalist identity, and to use religious education programming to encourage children to remain in the fold, resulted in curricula that explore the heritage of Unitarians and Universalists. One of the oldest of the New Beacon series, *The Church Across the Street*, was

---

[16] Marlin Lavanhar, "Shriveled Beneath the Clods: The Use and Misuse of the Principles and Purposes Statement, 1985–2007," *The Journal of Liberal Religion*, Vol. 8, No. 1 (Winter 2008), Meadville Lombard Theological School, meadville.edu/LL_JLR_v8_n1_home.htm. Last accessed September 7, 2010.

revamped into *Neighboring Faiths*, and is a main component of Unitarian Universalist religious education. Sixth-graders often spend the year visiting temples, mosques, and churches as they learn about other belief systems. This helps young teens prepare for Coming of Age, when they write a personal credo. Currently, a program called *Tapestry of Faith* is being developed and made available online, continuing the basic premise of providing developmentally appropriate, progressive education with goals of religious literacy and respect, and a sustaining connection to Unitarian Universalism. *Tapestry of Faith*, as a free, online resource, revolutionizes religious education simply by making the material available to everyone with access to the internet, but it also recaptures some of the older approach seen in the New Beacon series, and may create a feeling of kinship with geographically disparate Unitarian Universalists. Some of the new curricula are clearly based on the successful, older ones. One such curriculum, *Moral Tales*, uses stories from diverse traditions to build character and promote ethical behavior.

The new office of Lifespan Faith Development includes worship and social action, along with curricula for children and adults. Education, carved out and professionalized during the middle of the twentieth century, is now understood as part of everything that happens in a church. This reintegration does not mean less professionalism, but less separation of spheres. The long-ago vision of one university promoting one faith as a way to build a meaningful community continues to inform the Unitarian Universalist belief in education, broadly defined and widely delivered. It is an education into awareness, not achievement; education into relationships that promote integrity and health. Sunday morning services, advocacy for social change, mentor relationships, service projects, retreats, film nights, and regular courses are all understood as part of a process of education, in which character development is fostered through different channels. Education is not just for children: adults need to learn how to examine their assumptions, and can benefit from encountering others who have had different experiences. A global theology requires the free exchange of ideas and perspectives, and enables action that promotes justice. This is the theological underpinning to all Unitarian Universalist religious education: trust in natural development and in discovery, both individually and in a group that appreciates differences. Religious learning is the result of relationships that matter, changing lives and shaping the future.

CHAPTER 13

Current issues, new directions

Unitarians and Unitarian Universalists worldwide are connected to one another, and identify with this faith, even in its various regional incarnations. This has always been the case. The burgeoning liberal movement in Eastern Europe did not appear spontaneously. The radicals read and were persuaded by Servetus, absorbed humanism, and were protected by Muslims. In Great Britain, Dissenters read and re-read continental Unitarian literature while the Church of the Strangers embraced outsiders. Even in America, where generations of students learned that Unitarianism was mostly indigenous, it is now known that the Socinianism of those earliest European heretics seeped in, despite the New Englanders' attempts to fend it off. The spirit of freedom from abroad infused those who expanded Unitarianism into the West, building new congregations. Today, the international movement seeks new avenues of expansion, and new areas of growth that may help sustain the faith in its ancient strongholds. Technology fosters bonds by making outreach, support, and connection easier. The process of sharing with one another globally also reifies the faith itself, by acting on the religious imperative to grow and learn from one another.

Yet, technology transforms the experience of church. In cyberspace, a multinational congregation of Unitarian Universalists is home to approximately 750 members. The First Unitarian Universalist Church of Second Life (FUUCSL) has two meeting times, one to accommodate the Europeans, and the other for the 30 percent of members who are North American. Second Life is a virtual world, created collaboratively. Those who participate may socialize and join in activities through an avatar, which is built using the same modeling tools that allow the design and construction of property. Second Life has existed since June 2003; three years later, one of its members built a worship space and invited those interested in Unitarian Universalism to enter. By June 2008, the church had over 600 members, only 100 of whom were Unitarian Universalists in the real (non-virtual) world.[1] Comparatively large numbers of people are first learning about, and beginning an involvement in, Unitarian Universalism through a congregation in a virtual world. This church has far fewer boundaries than any traditional one. Its members are not limited to one geographic area. They may speak a variety of languages and come from many different backgrounds. Disabilities that are barriers in one world may not be in the virtual world, where buildings that are physically inaccessible do not exist.

Although technology is sometimes seen as elitist, it has the potential to be radically democratic, and as the story of FUUCSL demonstrates, technology removes huge financial barriers that exist in the real world of church life. It can also remove social barriers of race and housing patterns. George Byrd built the Church of Second Life before he had any congregants. No capital campaign or borrowing from an endowment was necessary. After looking at empty churches,[2] Byrd built a Unitarian Universalist sanctuary, hoping that people would congregate at the services, which they did. FUUCSL is already on its second building, having outgrown its first space in 2007.[3] Yet this is not a congregation with one strong leader: It is a community that started with traditional worship services, and, inverting the traditional model of growth, evolved towards discussion groups while gaining in numbers. A volunteer co-ordinator has been proposed as the first paid staff member.[4] This congregation naturally gravitated towards the original fellowship model of discussion and shared leadership, but with much larger numbers of people.

Second Life has shown a way to use technology to promote dialogue and interchange among a diverse group of people who may never actually meet, rather than to use technology to emulate the mega-church model of big screens, amplification, and strong leaders with wireless microphones. Instead, the cyberspace church offers a connection that is personal, even among vast numbers of people. Sharing can be direct, rather than mediated through the leader. And even though this is high-tech work, there is a grass-roots feel to it. The equipment needed is quite a bit less than what would be necessary to physically build a church, and it tends to be equipment that

---

[1] Amy Beltaine, "Polity in the First Unitarian Universalist Church of Second Life." Unpublished paper written for Congregational Polity, a course at Starr King School for the Ministry, June 2008, p. 3.
[2] Kenneth Sutton, "People of the First Unitarian Universalist Church of Second Life," *UU World*, February 19, 2009. Archived at: www.uuworld.org/life/articles/16276.shtml. Accessed September 14, 2010.
[3] Beltaine, "Polity," p. 2.   [4] Beltaine, ibid., p. 6.

people own for other parts of their lives as well, such as personal computers and internet access. It is not a huge financial commitment dedicated only to faith; it makes religious dialogue and participation part of everyday life. Although it may sound odd to describe participation in something that is not quite "real" as more personal, there is a manner in which Second Life requires both a degree of intentionality and deep engagement. Avatars are fashioned by people who reveal and express themselves in their designs, and who are changed by their online activities. As one participant said, "I identify with my avatar. What I make her do has an effect on me, even if I am just moving my fingers to make her do it."[5] Byrd stated, "Your imagination is a powerful thing, and you can be just as alive and real in Second Life as you can in the real world...I built the place where the church exists, but I did not bring the people to it; they brought themselves. They come every Thursday night not because I ask them to, but because of their own free will. It is an experience they want to be part of."[6]

Can the success of this virtual church be translated into the physical world? There is a tradition of dancing after services at the FUUCSL, which is both a touching and liberating activity for participants who may be isolated by disabilities. Rather than recreate the actual dancing, the Church in Second Life can help churches in the physical world think about how to facilitate new bonds and allow limitations to be transcended, and how barriers to entry and participation might be lowered. Technology has changed the experience of time, and how information is spread. It changes who we can have relationships with, and the form those relationships take. It has changed many people's expectations of church. The "shopping" phase in which potential members might have visited different congregations now takes place over the internet, so when a visitor arrives at services, she or he is likely to have read sermons, know about the religious education program, and have made a conscious choice to be part of this group. In addition to changing the administrative tasks of running a church to include website development and maintenance as a major component of the work, this changes the role of the existing membership. What has to be offered is friendship and hospitality, not information. The facts and the philosophy are widely available in cyberspace. Visitors are assessing whether the lived experience offers more.

Thus far, technology has primarily been used as a substitute for more traditional forms. E-mails and online postings have replaced print, and meetings are set up through web-based programs. But important changes

---

[5] Christine Robinson, quoted in Sutton, "People of the First Unitarian."   [6] Sutton, ibid.

are beginning. Already, the Unitarian Universalist Association and International Council of Unitarians and Universalists websites allow people to access resources and religious education curricula. This is particularly valuable for smaller congregations and emerging groups, and removes the financial barrier of printed curricula. Online curricula are also easily translated, and can be made available in text-to-speech format, enabling greater linguistic diversity and the inclusion of those with visual impairments and reading disabilities. The seminaries offer courses online, and as Meadville Lombard prepares to close its Chicago campus, the internet courses may be the "place" where the highest concentrations of Unitarian Universalist students gather.

The Church in Second Life hints at how the meaning of the technology itself is changing, and will alter the nature of church and ministry. Web-based communication will not long be a substitution for an old way of accomplishing tasks; it is a new way of being. It is a revolution not only in how we access information, but how we engage with one another. "Twittering" and "tweeting" are the new vernacular translations, reaching new groups of people. The internet is a continuation of the radical democratic spirit at the heart of congregational polity. Everyone is included in the conversation; information is available for all, and quickly. The long history of pamphlets, newspapers, and magazines has culminated, at least for now, in web-logs, or "blogs." Blogs are participatory events; conversations among people who never actually meet, and yet who are in life-changing dialogue with one another. Instead of thinking about church websites as ways of communicating with the people in church on Sunday mornings, it must be understood that the congregation may no longer be that body of people gathered in one sanctuary. No one knows who is reading the sermons online, or watching video clips. A group of people may be talking to each other, yet there may also be a whole host of others listening to that conversation, assessing the information.[7] It is a new way of thinking about community, and will lead to a totally different form of program development and administrative needs.

In addition to churches hosting new forms of direct communication among members, through online forums and cyber-cells, professional ministry may change.

Pastoral care may evolve away from a physical presence. Adult religious education could happen without scheduling consecutive evening classes:

---

[7] Linda Hoddy, "Twittered, Tweeted and Still Lonely?" Gould Discourse of the St. Lawrence District of the Unitarian Universalist Association, delivered April 23, 2010 (unpublished manuscript).

interested people would log in to see what has been posted for content, and what others have had to say. Technology offers tremendous potential for those with disabilities to be included in the life of the church in new ways. Because they have no designated top or bottom, and they are programmed to display images in a manner that corresponds to how they are being held, ipads might become orders of service for those with physical impairments. Computers that convert text to speech could be available alongside the assisted-listening devices, so that those who cannot read easily could follow along. Churches could become multilingual through computer-based translation programs. These technical opportunities are not simply a welcoming service; when made available, they change the identity of the congregation. Assumptions about what equality looks like, what suffering means, what skills are universal – all of these are changed by befriending people with different assumptions.

Worship itself can change. Authenticity does not necessarily mean speaking and listening; and commitment might not mean one hour, once a week: People might meet less frequently, more frequently, or for longer periods at a time. Sanctuaries may become home to large screens for video-conferencing with partner churches, or for virtual tours. Visits that are prohibitively expensive for most people could become part of the regular church life. As Unitarian Universalism has been re-established in Poland, technology makes it possible both to support the growth of the Polish Unitarian Universalist congregations, and to witness this development, and have involvement among ordinary people, rather than only at the administrative or ceremonial level. Direct experience of one another's lives can become possible, even without leaving home. Free Religionists in Germany can connect with emerging groups elsewhere: their suppressed history can be uncovered, and inspiration shared.

Streamed (live) services might also provide a way of reaching those who cannot attend church in person. Prisons could offer live Unitarian Universalist church services in addition to printed matter, helping those incarcerated to identify with each other and acclimating them to services before they are released. Newly forming groups might gather to participate in a streamed service together, rather than have one person lead using prepared worship material. Nursing homes and managed care facilities could offer Unitarian Universalist services without having a UU chaplain on staff. In the military, those serving may have opportunities to "visit" their home churches.

Although technology has helped the international community of Unitarian Universalists, and although European countries that limited freedom under repressive twentieth-century regimes are now sites for a liberal religious renaissance, this religion needs to grow. This is particularly true in New England, where the rate of decline is greater than in other areas. Membership is about attracting new people, but even more fundamental is keeping the people who are currently attending. A failure to retain members over the long haul should raise questions. Instead of believing that attending a Unitarian Universalist church for a while is part of a journey towards liberation, one might ask what makes people stop feeling that church is worthwhile. For centuries, Unitarianism defined itself as in opposition to Catholicism. Universalists defined their theology as a corrective to a Christian doctrine that damned some people and saved others. True Christians, Universalists asserted, believed that all people were saved. But the antipathy towards Catholicism merits an examination. While it is true that the secular culture of New England makes it easier not to attend church there than it is in the South, and it is true that many of the New England churches, because of their endowments, do not represent a personal sacrifice on the part of the current members, these issues do not reveal why people who were committed for a time would stop. This has to do with a failure of the faith to deepen, allowing healing and personal development.

Unitarian Universalists and Catholics locate authority in very different places: the individual conscience for the former, and the Church as God's representative on earth for the latter. But both of these religions have at their heart a vision of one community, and of service to those in need as a way of serving the holy. In the US, conservative Christians speak out against universal health care or services that Unitarian Universalists and Catholics agitate for, as part of the fabric of community. Catholicism and Unitarianism, the banned faiths in England before the nineteenth century, are the religions promoting education and charity. (Although irrelevant to this particular issue, one might note, too, that Jews – banned from England in 1290, allowed back in by Cromwell, and finally emancipated in 1848 – share in this vision.) Each believes that its locus for authority is correct because it is the truest way to have God acting in this world. One church argues for structure, an external form that is recognizable and predictable; the other argues for individualism and creativity. Each has something to learn from the other.

In New England, most converts to Unitarian Universalism have Catholic backgrounds. Since Vatican II, Catholics have experienced some of the same theological belief in the importance of conscience that Unitarian Universalists embrace. But Unitarian Universalism tends not to recognize how extraordinarily deep the connections are between the two faiths, and focuses negatively on the creeds and hierarchy of the Catholic institution, rather than the lived faith of the people. It is not possible for an institution with conflicted feelings about Catholicism to help parishioners resolve their own journeys. Unitarian Universalism would benefit from a better understanding of its own argument with Catholicism; its separation issues and its floundering for structure. While resisting the Catholic system and promoting liberation, Unitarian Universalism has grown increasingly centralized and bureaucratic as it struggles to provide qualified ministers and educators, and serve congregations better, even while acknowledging that what people hunger for is greater connection and vitality. In the end, the spiritual life does not emerge out of programs for diversity or for growth. Spirit comes through engagement with depth, not breadth.

This may be an area where democratic practice seems to block progress. It is difficult to go deeply into a religious faith and establish a vision for Unitarian Universalists, because there is tremendous concern about inclusivity. But defining a core to the faith might actually allow a broader spectrum of people to find a home in a Unitarian Universalist congregation. People do not choose a church because it tries to include them; they choose a church whose mission they believe in. Engagement means getting past the superficial things that define people, to meet as human beings who care deeply about this world.

Perhaps that is the place to start. Unitarian Universalism is a this-worldly faith. It is not a church for people who are primarily concerned about a life other than the one that is unfolding this minute, here on this planet. Religious experience for Unitarian Universalists happens in nature. It can be scientific or mysterious, concrete or abstract, shared or interpersonal. But it is a faith based on love for this world, and an understanding that love makes us responsible. Care for this world is demanded, as is openness to being changed by relationships to nature. There is one living system; people grow, adapt, blossom, and die in accordance with the laws of nature and their own actions, and luck. Believing in luck is a way of confessing that humans do not have control, but that what happens to a person is not fated, or willed, or pre-ordained. Nonetheless, control is valued. It demonstrates love, and reverence.

Unitarian Universalism is often portrayed as a liberal body whose connection to faith is tenuous at best. Issues with a social or political dimension are highlighted, generally without a delineation of the theological imperative motivating action. A recent issue of the *Oxford American*, an Arkansas-based literary magazine, was dedicated to envisioning the future.

One article describes the American South as the "place where the fierce culture wars of post-Reagan America escalated into a shooting war," the name of which varied in accordance with one's bias. "The Tea Party... voted to seize its last chance and declared holy war on socialists and sinners in 2018. [They]... opened hostilities with an armed assault on a gay wedding reception in Greenville South Carolina, killing one of the brides, two bridesmaids, and a Unitarian minister."[8]

Unfortunately, this representation of the future is already a reality, including the portrayal of liberal religious values as limited to political action, rather than a lived expression of the adherents' professed beliefs. On July 27, 2008 a man fired into the congregation of the Tennessee Valley Unitarian Universalist Church, believing he was getting rid of the enemy. "I hate liberals and what they are doing to this country," he said. "We can't defeat them at the ballot box. They're like termites. The only way you can get rid of them is to kill them in the streets."[9] Yet, as the foster child of one of the murdered parishioners said, the gunman had "killed the man who would have tried hardest to help him."

Those are not the sentimental words of a grieving teen. They are a statement of theology, one that is supported by the first responders. The Knoxville Fire Chief was shocked by what he found in the church, and it was not the violence that, to him, seemed the inevitable and sad result of the current culture of negative rhetoric. The Fire Chief was surprised that no one in the church was vilifying the gunman. They were taking care of the wounded. They were calmly doing everything they could to help. The Fire Chief said, "The Unitarian Church's spiritual commitments made a big difference in how the congregation responded... Sometimes in this job you get burned out... For me it made a big difference to see people who did care."[10]

"Reverence for life affords me my fundamental principle of morality, namely that good consists in maintaining, assisting and enhancing life, and that to destroy, to harm, or hinder life is evil." So said Albert Schweitzer (1875–1965), a preacher in Germany who wrote *The Quest of the Historical Jesus* (1906) and then left the ministry to train as a physician. Schweitzer, a member of the Church of the Larger Fellowship, spent many decades as a

---

[8] Hal Crowther, "Beyond the Horizon: The furnace of democracy," *Oxford American, The Future Issue* (Fall 2010, Issue 70), p. 26.

[9] Jim Adkisson, quoted in Matt Lakin and J.J. Stambaugh, "One Year After the TVUU Church Shooting," *Knox News Sentinel*, July 26, 2009. Archived at: www.knoxnews.com/news/2009/jul/26/tvuu-church-shooting-a-year-later/. Last accessed September 16, 2010.

[10] Mike Pickett, quoted in Lakin and Stambaugh, "One Year."

medical missionary in Africa, and embodied a form of faith that is familiar to Unitarians and Unitarian Universalists. This is what the first responders witnessed in Knoxville: the love that drives out fear, the knowledge of one creation containing all of life, and a belief that worship and actions are inseparable. Behaving justly and with compassion helps members heal even as they are repairing the world. The planet is both in our hands and in a universe of its own. Good intention does not guarantee anything. Tragedies still happen and struggle continues to define many lives. Faith does not prevent people from experiencing suffering, injustice or trauma. A traveler heading out of Jerusalem and down to Jericho may still fall prey to thieves. But when our world is troubled, when neighbors are suffering, or when groups of people are unreasonably denied freedoms that others enjoy, there is both solace and the capacity for great change. Unitarian Universalists keep faith by responding as true neighbors, and asking that others go and do likewise. The religion teaches that individual salvation is a by-product of saving the whole of creation. "Faith is with respect to God, love is with respect to God **and** to our neighbor . . . Because love is more lasting; love is a natural symbol of the future kingdom . . . Faith begins; love completes."[11] Love helps preserve the capacity for awe, and allows a shared devotion to sustaining life. "Loving, not believing, is a property of divine nature . . . Therefore, one always comes to the conclusion that love is sublime and excellent, and that love is more like God."

---

[11] Miguel Servetus, *Christianismi Restitutio* (1532), trans. Christopher Hoffman and Marian Hiller (Lewiston, NY: The Edwin Mellen Press, 2008). From "Treatise on Faith and Justice in Christ's Kingdom," p. 313.

Selected bibliography

Adams, James Luther. *On Being Human Religiously*. Boston, MA: Beacon Press, 1976.

Ahlstrom, Sidney E., and Jonathan S. Carey, eds. *An American Reformation: A Documentary History of Unitarian Christianity*. Middletown, CT: Wesleyan University Press, 1985.

Andrews, Stuart. *Unitarian Radicalism: Political Rhetoric 1770–1814*. Basingstoke, UK: Palgrave Macmillan, 2003.

Ballou, Adin. *Practical Christianity*, ed. Lynn Gordon Hughes. Providence, RI: Blackstone Editions, 2002. First published in 1854 as *Practical Christian Socialism*.

Ballou, Hosea. *A Treatise on Atonement*. Edited with a new introduction by Ernest Cassara, based on 1886 edition. Boston, MA: Skinner House Books, 1986.

Bainton, Roland H. *Hunted Heretic: The Life and Death of Michael Servetus, 1511–1553*. Boston, MA: Beacon Press, 1953.

Barr, Margaret. *A Dream Come True: The Story of Kharang*. London, UK: Lindsey Press, 1974.

Bartlett, Laile. *Bright Galaxy*. Boston, MA: Beacon Press, 1960.

Bolster, Arthur S., Jr. *James Freeman Clarke: Disciple to Advancing Truth*. Boston, MA: Beacon Press, 1954.

Bowers, J.D. *Joseph Priestley and English Unitarianism in America*. University Park: Pennsylvania State University Press, 2007.

Bressler, Ann Lee. *The Universalist Movement in America, 1770–1870*. New York: Oxford University Press, 2001.

Buell, Lawrence. *The American Transcendentalists: Essential Writings*. New York: Modern Library, 2006.

Buescher, John Benedict. *The Other Side of Salvation: Spiritualism and the Nineteenth-Century Religious Experience*. Boston, MA: Skinner House Books, 2004.

   The Remarkable Life of John Murray Spear. Notre Dame, IN: University of Notre Dame Press, 2006.

Bumbaugh, David E. *Unitarian Universalism: A Narrative History*. Chicago, IL: Meadville Lombard Press, 2000.

Capper, Charles. *Margaret Fuller, An American Romantic Life. The Private Years.* New York: Oxford University Press, 1992.
Margaret Fuller, An American Romantic Life. The Public Years. Oxford University Press, 2007.
Carpenter, Victor H. *Long Challenge: The Empowerment Controversy (1967–1977).* Chicago, IL: Meadville Lombard, 2003.
Caruthers, J. Wade. *Octavius Brooks Frothingham, Gentle Radical.* University of Alabama Press, 1977.
Cassara, Ernest. *Hosea Ballou: The Challenge to Orthodoxy.* Boston, MA: Beacon Press and the Universalist Historical Society, 1961.
ed. *Universalism in America: A Documentary History.* Boston, MA: Beacon Press, 1971.
Channing, William Ellery. *The Works of William Ellery Channing, D.D.* Boston, MA: American Unitarian Association, 1875.
Channing, William Henry. *The Life of William Ellery Channing, D.D.* Boston, MA: American Unitarian Association, 1882.
Chryssides, George. *The Elements of Unitarianism.* Boston, MA: Element Books, 1998.
Church, Forrest. *The Cathedral of the World: A Universalist Theology.* Boston, MA: Beacon Press, 2009.
and John A. Buehrens. *A Chosen Faith: An Introduction to Unitarian Universalism.* Boston, MA: Beacon Press, 1989.
Cole, Phyllis. *Mary Moody Emerson and the Origins of Transcendentalism.* Oxford University Press, 1998.
Commager, Henry Steele. *Theodore Parker: An Anthology.* Boston, MA: Beacon Press, 1960.
Commission of Appraisal. *Unitarians Face a New Age.* Boston, MA: American Unitarian Association, 1936.
Commission of the General Assembly. *A Free Religious Faith: A Report Presented to the General Assembly of Unitarian and Free Christian Churches.* London, UK: The Lindsey Press, 1945.
Commissions on the Free Church in a Changing World. *The Free Church in a Changing World.* Boston, MA: Unitarian Universalist Association, 1963.
Commission on Appraisal, Unitarian Universalist Association. *Interdependence: Renewing Congregational Polity.* Boston, MA: Unitarian Universalist Association, 1997.
Commission on Appraisal, Unitarian Universalist Association, *Belonging: The Meaning of Membership.* Boston, MA: Unitarian Universalist Association, 2001.
Commission on Appraisal, Unitarian Universalist Association. *Engaging Our Theological Diversity.* Boston, MA: Unitarian Universalist Association, 2005.
Cooke, George Willis. *Unitarianism in America.* Boston, MA: American Unitarian Association, 1910.
Crompton, Arnold. *Unitarianism on the Pacific Coast.* Boston, MA: Beacon Press, 1957.

Cross, Whitney R. *The Burned-Over District: The Social and Intellectual History of Enthusiastic Religion in Western New York, 1800–1850.* New York: Harper and Row, 1965. First published in 1950.

Cummins, Robert. *Excluded: The Story of the Council of Churches and the Universalists.* Boston, MA: UUA Department of Publications, Beacon Reference Series No. 3. 1966.

Deese, Helen R., ed. *Daughter of Boston: The Extraordinary Diary of a Nineteenth Century Woman, Caroline Healey Dall.* Boston, MA: Beacon Press, 2005.

Delano, Sterling F. *Brook Farm: The Dark Side of Utopia.* Cambridge, MA: Harvard University Press, 2004.

Dorrien, Gary. *The Making of American Liberal Theology: Imagining Progressive Religion.* Louisville, KY: Westminster John Knox Press, 2001.

Douglas, Ann. *The Feminization of American Culture.* New York: Alfred A. Knopf, 1977.

Eliot, Samuel A. *Heralds of a Liberal Faith.* Boston, MA: American Unitarian Association, 1910.

Emerson, Dorothy May, ed. *Standing Before Us: Unitarian Universalist Women and Social Reform, 1776–1936.* Boston, MA: Skinner House Books, 2000.

Erdö, John. *Transylvanian Unitarian Church: Chronological History and Theological Essays.* Chico, CA: Center for Free Religion, 1990.

Field, Peter S. *The Crisis of the Standing Order: Cultural Intellectuals and Cultural Authority in Massachusetts, 1780–1833.* Amherst, MA: University of Massachusetts Press, 1998.

Floyd-Thomas, Juan. *The Origins of Black Humanism in America.* New York: Palgrave-Macmillan, 2008.

The Free Religious Association. *Freedom and Fellowship in Religion: A Collection of Essays and Addresses.* Boston, MA: Roberts Brothers, 1875.

Fritchman, Stephen H. *Together We Advance.* Boston, MA: Beacon Press, 1946.

Gausted, Edwin Scott. *The Great Awakening in New England.* Chicago: Quadrangle Paperbacks, 1957, reprinted 1968.

Gellerd, Judit. *Prisoner of Liberte: Story of a Transylvanian Martyr.* Chico, CA: Uniquest, 2003.

Gilbert, James B. *Redeeming Culture: American Religion in an Age of Science.* University of Chicago Press, 1997.

Gordon, Alexander. *Heads of English Unitarian History.* Bath: Cedric Chivers, 1895, reprinted 1970.

Greeley, Dana McLean. *25 Beacon Street.* Boston, MA: Beacon Press, 1971.

Grodzins, Dean. *American Heretic: Theodore Parker and Transcendentalism.* University of North Carolina Press, 2002.

Gura, Philip F. *Jonathan Edwards: America's Evangelical.* New York: Hill and Wang, 2005.

Hague, Graham and Judy Hague. *The Unitarian Heritage, An Architectural Survey.* Sheffield: Unitarian Heritage Society, 1986.

Harris, Mark. *Historical Dictionary of Unitarian Universalism.* Lanham, MD: Scarecrow Press, 2003.

Henry, Richard. *Norbert Fabian Capek: A Spiritual Journey*. Boston, MA: Skinner House, 1999.

Hewett, Phillip. *Racovia: An Early Liberal Religious Community*. Providence, RI: Blackstone Editions, 2004.

Unitarians in Canada. Ontario: Fitzhenry and Whiteside, 1978.

Hitchings, Catharine F. *Universalist and Unitarian Women Ministers*. Boston, MA: Unitarian Universalist Historical Society, 1975.

Holt, Raymond Vincent. *The Unitarian Contribution to Social Progress in England*. London, UK: The Lindsey Press, 1938.

Howe, Charles. *The Larger Faith: A Short History of American Universalism*. Boston, MA: Skinner House, 1993.

For Faith and Freedom. Boston, MA: Skinner House, 1997.

The Essential Clarence Skinner. Boston, MA: Skinner House Books, 2004.

Howe, Daniel Walker. *The Unitarian Conscience: Harvard Moral Philosophy, 1805–1860*. Cambridge, MA: Harvard University, Press, 1970.

Hughes, Peter, ed. *The Cambridge Platform, A Modern Reader's Edition*. Boston, MA: Skinner House Books, 2008. First published 1648.

Hunter, Edith. *Sophia Lyon Fahs: A Biography*. Boston, MA: Beacon Press, 1966.

Hutchison, William R. *The Transcendentalist Ministers: Church Reform in the New England Renaissance*. Boston, MA: Beacon Press, 1965.

Jackson, Carl T. *The Oriental Religions in American Thought*. Westport, CT: Greenwood Press, 1981.

Kaplan, Benjamin A. *Divided by Faith*. Cambridge, MA: Harvard University Press, 2007.

Karcher, Carolyn L. *The First Woman in the Republic: A Cultural Biography of Lydia Maria Child*. Durham, NC: Duke University Press, 1997.

Kot, Stanislaus. *Socinianism in Poland*. Boston, MA: Starr King Press, 1957.

Lavan, Spencer. *Unitarians and India: A Study in Encounter and Response*. Boston, MA: Beacon Press, 1972.

LeBeau, Bryan F. *Frederic Henry Hedge, Nineteenth Century American Transcendentalist*. Allison Park, PA: Pickwick Publications, 1985.

Lingwood, Stephen. *The Unitarian Life: Voices from the Past and Present*. London, UK: Lindsey Press, 2008.

Lyttle, Charles. *Freedom Moves West: A History of the Western Unitarian Conference*. Boston, MA: Beacon Press, 1952.

Macaulay, John Allen. *Unitarianism in the Antebellum South: The Other Invisible Institution*. Tuscaloosa, AL: The University of Alabama Press, 2001.

MacCulloch, Diarmaid. *The Reformation: A History*. New York: Viking Penguin, 2003.

McGiffert, Arthur Cushman, Jr. *Pilot of a Liberal Faith: Samuel Atkins Eliot, 1862–1950*. Boston, MA: Skinner House Books, 1976.

McLennan, Scotty. *Finding Your Religion*. New York; Harper San Francisco, 1999.

McLoughlin, William G. *New England Dissent, 1630–1833: The Baptists and the Separation of Church and State*. 2 Vols. Cambridge, MA: Harvard University Press, 1971.

Maffly-Kipp, Laurie; Leigh Eric Schmidt; and Mark Valeri, eds. *Practicing Protestants: Histories of Christian Life in America, 1630–1965*. Baltimore, MD: Johns Hopkins University Press, 2006.

Marini, Stephen A. *Radical Sects of Revolutionary New England*. Cambridge, MA: Harvard University Press, 1982.

Marshall, George N. *A. Powell Davies and His Times*. Boston, MA: Skinner House, 1990.

Marshall, Megan. *The Peabody Sisters of Salem, Three Women Who Ignited American Romanticism*. New York: Houghton Mifflin, 2005.

Meacham, Jon. *American Gospel: God, the Founding Fathers, and the Making of the Nation*. New York: Random House, 2006.

Mendelsohn, Jack. *Being Liberal in an Illiberal Age*. Boston, MA: Beacon Press, 1985.

Miller, Perry, ed. *The Transcendentalists: An Anthology*. Cambridge, MA: Harvard University Press, 1950.

Miller, Russell E. *The Larger Hope: The First Century of the Universalist Church in America, 1770–1870*. Boston, MA: Unitarian Universalist Association, 1979.

The Larger Hope: The Second Century of the Universalist Church in America, 1870–1970. Boston, MA: Unitarian Universalist Association, 1985.

Morrison-Reed, Mark D. *Black Pioneers in a White Denomination*. Boston, MA: Skinner House, 1980.

Muir, Frederick John. *Maglipay Universalists: A History of the Unitarian Universalist Church of the Philippines*. Annapolis, MD: UU Church of Annapolis, 2001.

Myerson, Joel, ed. *Transcendentalism: A Reader*. Oxford University Press, 2000.

Nesbitt, Paula D. *Feminization of the Clergy in America: Occupational and Organizational Perspectives*. New York: Oxford University Press, 1997.

Noll, Mark A. *America's God: From Jonathan Edwards to Abraham Lincoln*. New York: Oxford University Press, 2002.

Olds, Mason. *American Religious Humanism*. Minneapolis, MN: University Press of America, 1996.

Packer, Barbara L. *The Transcendentalists*. Athens, GA: The University of Georgia Press, 2007.

Papa, Stephan. *The Last Man Jailed for Blasphemy*. Franklin, NC: Trilium Books, 1998.

Parke, David B., ed. *The Epic of Unitarianism*. Boston, MA: Beacon Press, 1957.

Parker, Kathleen R. *Sacred Service in Civic Space*. Chicago, IL: Meadville Lombard, 2007.

Persons, Stow. *Free Religion, An American Faith*. Boston, MA: Beacon Press, 1963.

Rasor, Paul. *Faith Without Certainty: Liberal Theology for the 21st Century*. Boston, MA: Skinner House, 2005.

Reed, Cliff M., and Jill K. McAllister, eds. *The Home We Share: Globalization, Post-Modernism and Unitarian/Universalist Theology*. Proceedings of the 2nd Theological Symposium, Kolosvar/ Cluj-Napoca, Romania, 3–8 July 2006. Caerphilly, Wales; International Council of Unitarians and Universalists, 2007.

Renehan, Edward J., Jr. *The Secret Six: The True Tale of the Men Who Conspired with John Brown*. New York: Crown, 1995.

Richardson, Robert D., Jr., *Emerson: The Mind on Fire*. Berkeley, CA: University of California Press, 1995.

Robinson, David. *The Unitarians and the Universalists*. Westport, CT: Greenwood Press, 1985.

Ross, Warren. *The Premise and the Promise: The Story of the Unitarian Universalist Association*. Boston, MA: Skinner House, 2001.

Ruffin, J. Rixey. *A Paradise of Reason: William Bentley and Enlightenment Christianity in the Early Republic*. New York: Oxford University Press, 2008.

Schmidt, Leigh Eric. *Restless Souls: The Making of American Spirituality*. New York: Harper Collins, 2005.

Schulman, Frank. *James Martineau: This Conscience-Intoxicated Unitarian*. Chicago, IL: Meadville Lombard, 2002.

Schulz, William F. *Making the Manifesto: The Birth of Religious Humanism*. Boston, MA: Skinner House, 2002.

Skemp, Sheila L. *First Lady of Letters: Judith Sargent Murray and the Struggle for Female Independence*. Philadelphia, PA: University of Pennsylvania Press, 2009.

Smith, Leonard. *The Unitarians: A Short History*. Arnside, UK: Lensden Publishing, 2006.

Tomalin, Claire. *The Life and Death of Mary Wollstonecraft*. New York: Harcourt, Brace, Jovanovich, 1974.

Trigg, Joseph Wilson. *Origen: The Bible and Philosophy in the Third-Century Church*. Atlanta, GA: John Knox Press, 1983.

Tucker, Cynthia Grant. *Prophetic Sisterhood: Liberal Women Ministers of the Frontier, 1880–1930*. Boston, MA: Beacon Press, 1990.

No Silent Witness: The Eliot Parsonage Women and their Unitarian World. New York: Oxford University Press, 2010.

Uglow, Jenny. *The Lunar Men*. New York: Farrar, Straus, Giroux, 2002.

Ulbrich, Holly. *The Fellowship Movement*. Boston, MA: Skinner House, 2008.

Venet, Wendy Hamand. *A Strong-Minded Woman: The Life of Mary A. Livermore*. Amherst, MA: University of Massachusetts Press, 2005.

von Frank, Albert J. *The Trials of Anthony Burns: Freedom and Slavery in Emerson's Boston*. Cambridge, MA: Harvard University Press, 1998.

Watts, Ruth. *Gender, Power and the Unitarians in England 1760–1860*. London, UK: Longman, 1998.

Welch, Sharon. *Real Peace, Real Security: The Challenge of Global Citizenship*. Minneapolis, MN: Fortress Press, 2008.

West, Robert Nelson. *Crisis and Change: My Years as President of the Unitarian Universalist Association*. Boston, MA: Skinner House, 2007.

Wilbur, Earl Morse. *A History of Unitarianism: Socinianism and its Antecedents*. Boston, MA: Beacon Press, 1946.

  A History of Unitarianism in Transylvania, England and America. Boston, MA: Beacon Press, 1945.

Williams, George H. *The Polish Brethren: Documentation of the History and Thought of Unitarianism in the Polish-Lithuanian Commonwealth and in the Diaspora, 1601–1685*. Minneapolis, MN: Augsburg Fortress Press, 1984.

  The Radical Reformation. Philadelphia, PA: The Westminster Press, 1962.

  American Universalism. Boston, MA: Universalist Historical Society, 1971.

Williams, Rowan. *Arius: Heresy and Tradition*. Grand Rapids, MI: William B. Eerdmans Publishing, revised 2001.

Wright, Conrad. *The Liberal Christians: Essays on American Unitarian History*. Boston, MA: Beacon Press, 1970.

  The Beginnings of Unitarianism in America. Boston, MA: Beacon Press, 1955.

  A Stream of Light. Boston, MA: Skinner House, 1971.

  Walking Together: Polity and Participation in Unitarian Universalist Churches. Boston, MA: Skinner House Books, 1989.

  The Unitarian Controversy. Boston, MA: Skinner House Books, 1994.

  Congregational Polity: A Historical Survey of Unitarian and Universalist Practices. Boston, MA: Skinner House Books, 1997.

Wright, Conrad Edick, ed. *American Unitarianism, 1805–1865*. Boston, MA: Massachusetts Historical Society and Northeastern University Press, 1989.

  and Charles Capper, eds. *Transient and Permanent: The Transcendentalist Movement and Its Context*. Boston, MA: Massachusetts Historical Society and Northeastern University Press, 1999.

Yacovone, Donald. *Samuel Joseph May and the Dilemmas of the Liberal Persuasion, 1797–1871*. Philadelphia, PA: Temple University Press, 1991.

Index